The Practical Guide to Loan Processing

Copyright 2008

By Thomas A. Morgan

Mortgage Management Systems
Quality Control and Assurance
Managing the Process from Origination to Post-Closing

QuickStart
lendertraining.com

2nd Printing

ISBN 0-9718205-2-X
"The Practical Guide to Loan Processing"

© 2008 – Thomas Morgan, QuickStart Publications

ALL RIGHTS RESERVED. No part of this publication may be reproduced, stored in a retrieval system, or transmitted by any means, electronic, mechanical, photocopying, recording, or otherwise, without the prior written permission of the publisher and the copyright holder.

This publication is designed to present, as simply and accurately as possible, general information on the subject. It should be noted that the information presented is not all-inclusive. Products, programs and guidelines change due to rapid changes in the industry. This publication should not be used as a substitute for referring to appropriate experts and is sold with the understanding that the publisher is not engaged in rendering legal, accounting, or other personalized professional service. If legal or other expert assistance is required, the services of a competent professional should be sought.

Table of Contents

INTRODUCTION 1

CHAPTER 1 – THE PROCESSORS DUTIES & RESPONSIBILITIES 3
Job Description - Mortgage Loan Processor 3

CHAPTER 2 - MORTGAGE INDUSTRY OVERVIEW 7
Basic Mortgage Math 12
Loan Products 15
Understanding ARMs 16
Understanding Loan Plan Specifications and Guidelines 19

CHAPTER 3 - NEW LOAN SETUP, VENDORS AND DISCLOSURES 29
The Importance of a Thorough Loan File Setup 29
Sources of Applications and Treatment 30
Assigned Files 35
Sending Out Disclosures 39
RESPA – The Real Estate Settlement Procedures Act 39
The Truth-in-Lending Act (TILA) 43
Section 32 of Truth-in-Lending Act – HOEPA 49
The Equal Credit Opportunity Act ("ECOA") 51
Handling Missing Documentation 56
The Welcome Package - Borrower Introduction 57
Direct Verifications 59
File Order 59

CHAPTER 4 - DOCUMENTATION REVIEW – REVIEWING CREDIT AND PAYMENT HISTORY 61
Credit Bureaus vs. Credit Repositories 61
Components of the Housing and Expense Ratios 62
Credit History 70
Sub-Prime Lending 75

CHAPTER 5 - DOCUMENTATION REVIEW - INCOME DOCUMENTATION 81
Income Computation 81
Self-Employment 89
Self Employment Analysis Tools 95

CHAPTER 6 - DOCUMENTATION REVIEW - ASSETS 99
Verifying Assets 99
Seller Contributions 102
Assets for Down Payment, Closing Costs and Reserves 103
The Earnest Money Deposit 107

CHAPTER 7 – DOCUMENTATION REVIEW – PROPERTY, APPRAISALS, PROJECTS, NEW CONSTRUCTION 109
Understanding Property Types 109
Investment Property 117
Appraisals 118

CHAPTER 8 – UNDERWRITING SUBMISSION AND APPROVAL 121
Basic Underwriting Preparations 121
Detailed Credit Package Order 123
Basic Loan Submission Checklist 127

Base Processing Checklist 128
Reviewing the Application 133
Sections 1 & 2 of Application 134
Section 3 – Personal Information 134
The Approval Process 138
Understanding FHLMC Loan Prospector Results 141

CHAPTER 9 - THE CLOSING AND REQUIREMENTS 145

Brokered Transactions vs. Funded Transactions 145
Settlement Agent – Document Requirements 148
Required Closing Conditions 149

CHAPTER 10 - TIME MANAGEMENT STRATEGIES FOR PROCESSORS 155

Pipeline Management - Loan Tracking Reports 155
Processor Time Management Techniques 158
System 1 - Pipeline Review 159
Loan Status Procedure 159
System 2 - The Complete Application System 162
System 3 – Time Blocking 163
System 4 – Forms Management 163
Software Introduction 164
Status Reports 166
In Conclusion 168

MORTGAGE TERMINOLOGY .... ERROR! BOOKMARK NOT DEFINED.

Introduction

Beginning in 2006, the mortgage industry began to experience an upheaval that would ultimately bring the financial system to that point to its knees. What this is meant is that many mortgage lenders, who previously were able to casually package loan applications, must now diligently meet the most stringent guidelines and documentation requirements imposed since the late sixties. The processor is critical in meeting these requirements. Most mortgage companies and referral sources correctly believe that they live and die based on customer service and service delivery. The loan officer is a big part of this, in that he or she is responsible for taking a good application to start with. While the loan officer is the customer's representative, it is the processor who ultimately has his or her hands on the loan file and can assess what the status of a loan is.

Despite 60 years of automation improvements, the biggest problem mortgage companies report with respect to their operations is incomplete or problematic loan documentation. This is where the human factor in the application process impacts us, because we are relying on people – borrowers, real estate agents, closing agents and loan officers – to provide what we need to complete the loan.

Even if the loan application is perfect, processing is where the home loan sequence can begin to reveal its nightmarish realities. Under normal circumstances, it is the processor's duty to complete the verification process, assure regulatory compliance and prepare the case for presentation to the underwriter, loan committee or other decision maker. It seems simple enough, but here is where the effect known as "I am not sure if this is completely clear" kicks in.

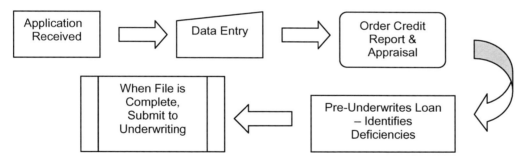

It seems like a simple process. But what seemed apparent to the loan officer isn't so apparent to the processor. If it isn't apparent to the processor, it isn't going to be apparent to the underwriter either. In an ideal situation, the processor and loan officer work together to identify "critical" items which could cause the loan to be denied and ascertain whether they can be fixed. Working together and with the borrower it is unlikely that any adverse information can't be refuted.

Then there are non-critical items - things that the loan can be approved "subject to" or as a condition of the approval - "nickel & dime" conditions. The problem comes when a processor doesn't segregate the level of importance of various documents and mails a simple list of outstanding documents to a borrower. Suddenly an inconsequential bank statement or other innocuous pieces of information are as important to the borrower as a critical document, such as proof that a delinquent account is incorrectly attributed, or the current years' tax return. The borrower receives the list and puts everything together, except for the critical document, sends it in. The mail gets reviewed a week later and suddenly - nearly 1 month into the loan process - there is a huge problem. Welcome to mortgage banking. This is why a complete application is so important.

Instead of simply acting as a checker of files and a sender of forms, the processor can be much more useful to the customer by taking their expertise and guiding the borrower through the process. This is the role of the processor.

How this position functions is different from company to company. In larger companies the processing role is often segmented into its different parts – file intake, data entry, and file review, pre-underwriting and pre-closing functions – all broken apart. In some companies the processor owns the file from "cradle to grave" and may even generate closing documentation. Whichever role the processor fills, he or she must know all the functions to anticipate issues and to be able to identify what still needs to be done.

In the past mortgage processing training has been passed down from generation to generation and person to person. This has resulted in many different approaches, emphasis on skills that may not apply to all situations, and general misinformation. There are also many "processing guides" whose pages are filled with sample forms and other industry exhibits. We believe you can find these on your own, and have tried to stay away from that in this guide. We tried to include only those things that actually affect the processors job. While it is impossible to describe all facets of a job that touches every phase of the retail mortgage business, we hope that this book will give the reader a strong foundation in understanding the processor's job.

Chapter 1 -
The Duties of the Loan Processor

Job Description - Mortgage Loan Processor

A generic description of the processor's duties might read like this; Assist Customer in obtaining approval by working with loan officer, underwriter and closing; Review Application for completeness at the time of receipt and prior to underwriting; Initiate requests for all documentation needed to support approval.

Specific Duties

- Receive loan application after registration
- Review against loan plan specifications for accuracy
- Enter into computer assisted processing program
- Generate Loan Application (1003, 2900), Transmittal Summary (1008, 2900 WS, 1802), Appraisal Request (2800)
- Generate Disclosure Documents Appropriate to Registered Loan Program
- Order and review credit report
- Order and review appraisal
- Compile case in Stack Order
- Enter Loan into Logs
- Initiate contact with customer requesting additional documentation
- Track outstanding documents and follow up with customer, loan officer, referral source
- Update Status daily as to incoming and outgoing documents
- Ascertain readiness for loan underwriting
- Pre-Underwrite case against checklist to identify problem areas prior to submission to underwriting
- Evaluate deficiencies and notify customer, loan officer and referral source of critical issues.

General Description of Duties

The loan officer, if there is one, performs the role of "field underwriter". However he or she should work with the processor to determine what information is needed prior to submitting a loan to an underwriter. The loan officer should not burden the processor with the duty of trying to qualify a borrower. Items which are generally "critical" in the determination of approval are those which materially impact the borrower's income, assets or credit history. Specifically, the file should not be submitted with critical information missing, unless it is done as a referral for judgment as to whether they missing information can be resolved. Information, which is required in order to satisfy compliance or to complete standard documentation requirements, is not critical and should not arrest the loan submission.

The Career Path of the Processor

Loan processors normally follow one of two paths as they progress in their careers. The natural graduation of credit skills, documentation review and process management leads to a career in underwriting, operations and operations management. A smaller percentage of processors extend their careers into sales and sales management. In this capacity, they use their ability to review documentation, anticipate problems and work with support staff to deliver excellent customer service. Many processors who transition into origination quickly outperform their non-processing skilled counterparts.

The Division of Duties between Processor and Loan Officer

While there is overlap between the loan officer and processor, there should be a clearly defined separation of what a processor should do and what a loan officer should do. The duties that are specifically assigned to a processor are listed in the job description. There are times that a loan officer may perform some of these functions in order to expedite the file's process. However, there are duties that the loan officer is supposed to perform that a competent processor may be able to execute. A processor should not be expected to perform these, but may concede to the loan officer and assist with guidance.

Task	Description
Interest Rate Lock-in	The loan officer will generally lock-in a borrower's interest rate when he or she gives the borrower an interest rate guarantee. When the file is in process, however, the loan officer may ask that the processor submit an interest rate lock-in request. **The risk for the processor** is that pricing mistakes can be extremely expensive. The processor may be blamed, or used as a scapegoat, for errors in pricing that the loan officer should have been aware of. If the processor can complete the lock-in request by simply making a phone call, on-line, or by faxing a request, this may be done under the loan officer's direct supervision. Confirmation should be immediately communicated back to the loan officer, particularly if there is any deviation in price at all.
Loan Registration	Program Selection and Registration should be performed by the loan officer. If the loan officer requests that the processor change the program, and this can be done easily, then the processor can accommodate that change. Again, the program change may affect pricing, and the processor needs to immediately send notification of program change to the borrower and the loan officer.

Task	Description
Qualification, Pre-and Re-Qualifying	If the borrower has not initially been qualified – that is, there is no evidence that the loan officer provided evidence that the borrower is eligible for the loan, the processor should return the loan file to the loan officer once the initial loan set up is completed. If, upon reviewing the loan file, there are substantial differences in the information that was used to qualify the borrower, the file should be returned to the loan officer to resolve the issue.

It is not the processor's responsibility to "fix-up", or otherwise repair poor quality loan submissions. This can take an inordinate amount of time and the processor is not qualified or compensated enough to perform these duties.

The processor may assist in the process by suggesting solutions to problems, or by consulting with an underwriter or other source of knowledge as to potential solutions. The loan officer is paid incentive to have qualified borrowers – the processor is not. |
| Customer Status Updates | Many referral sources and borrowers prefer to call the processor in order to obtain status updates. There are reasons for this.

- The processor is in the office and easy to reach with one phone call
- The processor has the file in his or her possession and can easily reference the answer to a question
- The processor is perceived as being more likely to give a candid answer as to problems

To the extent possible, the processor should avoid being involved with substantive conversations with outside parties. These are extremely time consuming, and often worried borrowers and referral sources will call far more frequently than necessary

Unless the processor has agreed to speak with referral sources, the real estate agent or other inquirer should speak with the loan officer. |

General Time Frames for Application Process

While the loan application process can be executed in a very short period of time, normal data collection periods, or the period of time that the processor has the loan, is the longest part of the mortgage process. In an average 45 to 60 day process, the processor is in possession of the loan file for 80 to 90% of the process.

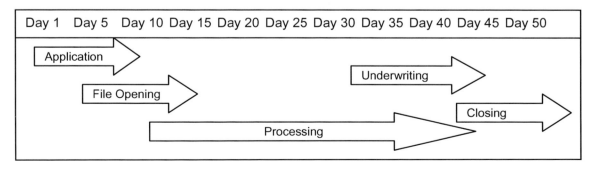

Process Flow

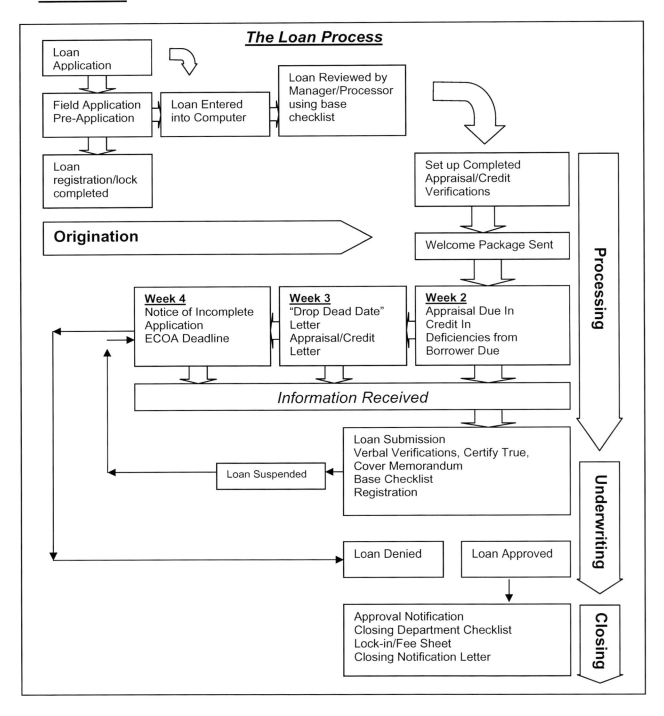

Chapter 2 – Mortgage Industry Overview

The Mortgage Business

The mortgage business today is the product of 70 years of evolution in process, technology and products. Despite this evolution, the roles personnel play in the process remain relatively unchanged. The loan originator, loan officer, or other advisor still is the primary interface between the customer and the company. This is true even though there are many business models that alter the way in which the customer deals with the loan officer. The functions of the loan process – processing, underwriting, and closing – have all been affected by automation, but still exist to support the completion of the loan process.

Types of Lenders/Primary Originators

The way different types of mortgage businesses operate is a function of the funding mechanism, or the way that loans are sold.

Entity	Description	Features
Mortgage Bankers – including banks, savings banks, credit unions	Traditional mortgage banking firms use funds borrowed on "warehouse" lines of credit to make loans. These loans are sold to investors as 1.) "whole loans" – which means that the individual loan is sold, along with the right to collect and remit payments (referred to as "servicing") or 2.) "mortgage backed securities" where a number of similar loans are "pooled" together. The securities are sold, but the mortgage banker keeps the right to collect the monthly payments ("servicing retained").	Strengths – able to control funding process and some approval issues. Can also broker loans if needed for competitive purposes. Weaknesses – on retained loans pricing is less optimal at origination.
Mortgage Brokers	Mortgage brokers do not make loans. They work with other lenders – wholesale mortgage bankers and banks (sometimes referred to as "investors") – who offer their products at "wholesale pricing". The mortgage broker fulfills the origination and processing functions and submits individual loan requests to the wholesaler. The wholesaler, who is often a mortgage banker or bank, approves and closes the loan.	Strengths – able to be price competitive with small margins, able to place many different types of loans giving borrower more choices and better chance of approval. Disadvantage – no control over approval and funding.

Mortgages are made by different types of lending entities. Referred to as primary originators they are small and mid-size traditional mortgage bankers and finance companies who fund loans by borrowing money from a temporary credit facility (warehouse line of credit) and resell the loans to secondary market "investors." They may also be large, generally bank owned national mortgage bankers performing mortgage banking functions but funding loans from their own cash. Mortgage brokers are also primary originators. They are almost exclusively small, privately owned companies who "sell" or broker individual borrower's loan packages prior to closing. This is known as wholesaling, brokering or table funding. Brokers do not lend money. Other primary originators include smaller local banks or savings banks (known as "thrifts"); and Credit Unions who originate loans either for resale or for their own portfolio.

The Mortgage Broker Business

Mortgage brokers are individuals or companies that do not underwrite, approve or fund loans. Mortgage brokers contract with wholesale lenders who approve, fund and prepare closing documentation. Mortgage brokers usually work with at least several, but often hundreds of different wholesalers. This business model allows the loan officer of a mortgage broker to seek out the best rates and terms – and can pass the most competitive rate on to the borrower. In addition, the mortgage broker has the ability to seek through the hundreds of products available to find specialty products that help borrowers with unusual circumstances or special needs. A borrower working with a broker may find a competitive advantage if the broker passes these benefits through to the consumer. The broker will select a lender and then work with the borrower to obtain all the necessary documentation to consummate the loan – referred to as processing.

Since the broker doesn't actually approve loans, prepare closing documentation, or provide funding, a potential disadvantage facing a borrower is that the wholesaler's service may not be as responsive as a direct lender's. Since the broker is the intermediary between the wholesale lender and the public, the public may never learn the identity of the final lender until closing. Since the wholesaler is insulated from the public in this way, the borrower has no recourse for service with that wholesaler. In addition, until the loan is funded, the wholesaler may continue to add loan contingencies creating delays.

Brokers earn money by adding fees to the wholesale cost of loans. The net cost to a borrower would be competitive with the price of a retail lender, depending on the margin that the broker is trying to achieve.

Broker Pricing Model Based on 1.5 Point Margin

Rate	Wholesale Cost	Broker's Margin	Net Price	Borrower Cost
6.750	102.00	1.50	100.500	-0.500
6.625	101.50	1.50	100.000	0.000
6.500	101.00	1.50	99.500	0.500
6.375	100.50	1.50	99.000	1.000
6.250	100.00	1.50	98.500	1.500
6.125	99.50	1.50	98.000	2.000
6.000	99.00	1.50	97.500	2.500

Retail Lending

In retail lending, the lender approves, closes and funds the loan, in addition to the functions that a mortgage broker conducts – taking the application, collecting borrower documentation, preparing the file for underwriting (referred to as processing). The advantage for a borrower in working with a direct retail lender is that the lender controls the entire process, so issues with service delivery, problems with contingencies, and pricing can be dealt with directly. One potential disadvantage of working with a direct retail lender is that some lenders only offer the loan products offered by the mortgage company, bank, credit union, or thrift with whom the loan officer is employed. However, many direct lenders do make selected specialty products available to meet their customer's needs on a brokered basis.

Servicing (collecting payments from borrowers and forwarding the interest to the investor) can be retained on many loans. This is a long term income source fundamental to the business plan of mortgage bankers.

The Secondary Market

Loans are packaged into "pools" or groups of loans and sold in the financial markets – known as the secondary mortgage market – in the form of mortgage backed securities. The issuers of these securities become the vehicle through which financial investors receive their money – names like FHLMC (Federal Home Loan Mortgage Corporation or "Freddie Mac"), FNMA (Federal National Mortgage Association or "Fannie Mae"), and GNMA (Government National Mortgage Association or "Ginnie Mae") are all examples institutions that bundle loans for re-sale.

A loan is referred to as "conforming" if it is eligible for sale to FNMA or FHLMC. Conventional loans are loans that are not related in any way to the government. Conventional non-conforming loans are loans that are ineligible for sale to FNMA/FHLMC. These loans may be "jumbo", or larger than the maximum conforming loan amount. They may not meet FNMA/FHLMC standard underwriting guidelines. The future of FNMA and FHLMC is

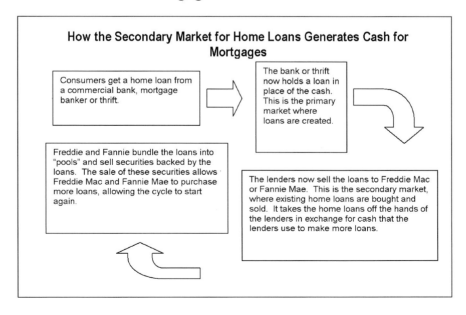

uncertain with respect to Federal oversight. Because of the government's involvement they are more readily saleable and command a better price in the secondary market. As a result, rates for non-conforming loans may be higher. FHA, FmHA, RHD and VA loans are included in GNMA securities, and also command a better price than conventional loans because of the government insurance.

Understanding Rates, Points and Lock-ins

Lock Option	Description	Protects Against
Lock-in	A lock in fixes a borrower's interest rate and point options for a specific period of time. If a lock in expires prior to the borrower's closing the borrower receives the market interest rate or the original interest rate, whichever is HIGHER. If a borrower decides to guarantee the rate and point option, the loan officer must assure there is sufficient time to process and close the loan under that lock term. The benefit of locking in is that there is certainty in the final interest rate.	Rates rising dramatically
Float	A float is a deferral of the decision to fix the interest rate. Regardless of whether interest rates increase or decrease, the borrower can lock in at those rates in the future. The benefit of floating is that the loan application can be processed and approved prior to locking in – the borrower can then execute an "immediate delivery lock" for 5, 7 or 15 days, which can be substantially better pricing than the 60 day lock-in	Rates falling or staying the same
Float Down Lock	The borrower can cap or lock in their interest rate at a current rate. If rates decline within a specific period of time prior to closing, the borrower can "re-lock" at a lower interest rate. The benefit of the Float Down Lock In is that the borrower is protected against dramatic fluctuation in rates.	Rates Rising or Falling Dramatically

Pricing for mortgages, as well of the types of loans offered, is derived from the secondary market. Rates are dynamic and lenders often change their pricing more than once a day. To protect borrowers from changing interest rates lenders offer interest rate protection. This is referred to as a "lock-in". The lock-in is set forth to the customer in a rate agreement that specifies the interest rate, fees and points and the expiration date. Rate lock-ins are offered for as few as 5 days to as long as 270 days. Borrowers may choose to defer the lock-in option which is referred to as a "float". Floating rates are not guaranteed. Customers should be informed that a loan rate is not guaranteed until the Interest Rate Lock-In Agreement is completed.

In this example, see that the price increases as the lock in period extends. This is because there is more risk to the lender for longer interest rate lock periods.

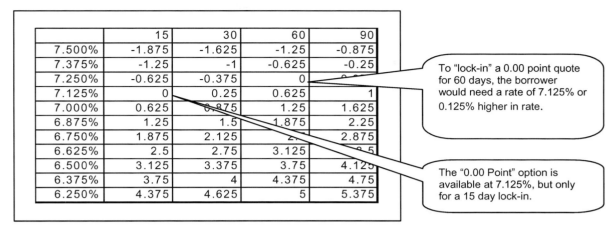

Table - Different Rate and Point Combinations vary based on Lock-in Term

Also evident in this table is the range of rate and point options.

Rates which have "0" point costs associated with them are referred to as "Par" rates. In this example, 7.250% for 60 days would be a "Par" price. In the same instance, there are lower rates available, but there is an associated point cost. Rates that have points associated with them are referred to as "discounted" rates. Paying points is also known as "permanently buying down" the rate. In this example, 6.875% with 1.875 points for 60 days is a discounted rate. When the rate is higher than "par", there may be a point credit instead of a point cost. This is called "above par" pricing. The credit is called a "yield spread premium" (YSP), "rebate" or "servicing release premium" (SRP).

A point is one percent of the loan amount. A Basis Point is $1/100^{th}$ of a point. Points are quoted to the customer as origination fees, broker fees, or discount points. A lender may charge an origination fee in addition to discount points. The lender may also cover the cost of originating the loan by using the YSP to offset the origination fee.

Price adjustments affect the final cost of a loan and offset the increased or decreased risk of a certain aspect of a loan. Higher LTV's would have higher prices, as would lower credit grades, because these represent more risk.

Interest Rate Drivers

Energy Prices	Every product or service is in some way affected by how much energy costs, because energy is used in the manufacture or delivery of every good or service. If oil prices rise, inflation will rise and interest rates will follow.
Unemployment	The cost of labor comprises roughly 2/3 of the cost of any good or service. If labor becomes scarce, prices will rise. Conversely, if there is high unemployment, labor costs should be low.
Demand/Supply	Fundamental variations in seasonal demand drive up interest rates. If the government, industry and individuals are all borrowing at the same time, there will be a scarcity of money that will tend to drive rates up. Conversely if the government doesn't borrow money (budget surplus), then demand for credit will be low reducing rates.

Currency Values	If the dollar is strong relative to world currencies, it can take more foreign currency to lend in dollars, diminishing the supply of lending capital. This can be opposed by a higher demand to invest in dollar denominated securities.
Instability	Uncertainty of any kind will generally drive interest rates higher in the interim, regardless of outcome. War, falling markets, political crises all tend to create higher interim rates.

Basic Mortgage Math

Decimals and Fractions - *Converting Decimals to Fractions*

Interest rates and points are based on fractions. These may be expressed in decimal or fraction form. Most numerical equations in mortgage lending are expressed verbally in fractions, but the written form is in decimals, which can be confusing for the uninitiated. For instance you might say that an interest rate of eight and one-half would carry two and one quarter points. Numerically, however, it looks like 8.5% with 2.25 points, which is exactly the same thing. Your high school math textbook would show you how to convert decimals to fractions like the following example:

$\frac{1}{1} = 1.0 \quad \frac{1}{2} = 0.5 \quad \frac{\text{Numerator}}{\text{Factor}}$

Example: Dividing the Numerator by the Factor Results in the Decimal Equivalent

To achieve the decimal equivalent of a fraction, you simply divide the numerator by the factor and the result is the decimal equivalent.

Converting Common Fractions to Decimals

Fraction	Decimal
1/8	0.125
1/4	0.250
3/8	0.375
1/2	0.500
5/8	0.625
3/4	0.750
7/8	0.875

While fractions in the mortgage lending business, particularly in the secondary marketing aspect of the business, can go into the 32nds (1/32 = .03125), the smallest fraction commonly found is 1/8th. (1/8 = .125) As an aid to future conversions, following is the conversion table converting fractions to decimals:

Another way of thinking about fractions and decimals is by converting fractions to fractions that you understand. For instance, if you understand that 1/8 = .125, think about 1/2 as being 4/8ths - 4 times .125 is .500.

Loan-To-Value or "LTV"

The relationship between the amount of a mortgage loan and the value of the collateral property, expressed as a percentage. Value is defined as the lesser of the contract sales price or appraised value. CLTV stands for Combined LTV – when there is more than one trust. HTLTV stands for Home Equity Total LTV, the LTV if the Home Equity Line were fully drawn.

To Determine LTV	To Determine Sales Price	To Determine Loan Amount
Divide Loan Amount By Sales Price	Divide Loan by LTV	Multiply Sales Price by LTV
$ 90,000 / $100,000 = 90% LTV	$200,000 / 90% = 222,222 Price	$150,000 X 90% $135,000 Loan

Qualifying Ratios

Qualifying Ratios are used as guidelines to set forth the percentage of income allowed to be devoted to housing expense and other debt. The "front", "top" or "housing expense" ratio is the amount that can be devoted towards expenses related to the mortgage and includes Principal, Interest, Taxes, Insurance (PITI), but may also include HOA/maintenance, ground rent or 2nd mortgages/home equity lines. The "Total Debt", "DTI" (debt to income) or "Back" ratio includes ALL OTHER debts AND the housing expense cumulatively. When Pre-qualifying the lender determines the maximum amount the borrower can afford. When Qualifying, the lender determines what the ratios are for a specific transaction.

Ratio	FNMA/ FHLMC	FHA	VA	Jumbo	ALT A - Choice
Housing Expense or "Front"	28%	31%	41%	33%	45%
Total Debt, Back or "DTI"	36%	43%	41%	38%	50%
Borrower's Income	$5,000	$5,000	$5,000	$5,000	$5,000
Maximum Housing Expense	$1,400	$1,550	$2,050	$1,650	$2,250
Total Debt (Incl. Housing)	$1,800	$2,150	$2,050	$1,900	$2,500

Different investors have different qualifying ratios. When loans are underwritten by Automated Underwriting Programs, ratios have less meaning. Please see general underwriting guidelines for the various programs.

Increasing the Ratio Increases PreQualification Amount		
Annual Income	$ 50,000.00	$ 50,000.00
Monthly Income	$ 4,166.67	$ 4,166.67
Multiply by Housing Ratio	28%	33%
Available for PITI	$ 1,166.67	$ 1,375.00
Less Tax & Insurance	$ (200.00)	$ (200.00)
Maximum P&I	$ 966.67	$ 1,175.00
Maximum Mortgage at 7.5%	$138,250.37	$168,045.71
Increase in %		21.55%

To Determine the Ratio Divide the Expense by the Income			
Monthly Income	$ 4,167		Ratio
P&I	$ 850		
Taxes	$ 290		
Insurance	$ 28		
Total Housing	$ 1,168		28%
Car Loan	$ 375		
Credit Cards	$ 190		
Total Debt	$ 1,733		42%

Pre-Qualification and Pre-Approval

A pre-qualification means that a borrower's general financial situation has been reviewed by someone who is competent at calculating ratios. A Pre-Approval means that the borrower has applied for a loan, and has been approved by an underwriter, subject to finding a property. The "Pre" in pre-qualification means "before the application". The "Pre" in pre-approval means "before the property". Brokers cannot offer a pre-approval – they must obtain one from the investor or wholesaler who can actually underwrite and fund the loan.

Calculating Payments and Interest - Simple Interest

Simple interest is the payment method for an interest only loan. It is also the method used to determine the daily interest due on a loan at closing.

Table - Calculating Interest Only

	Interest Only Payment	Per Diem (Daily) Calculation
Loan Amount	$ 100,000.00	$ 100,000.00
Times Interest Rate	7.50%	7.50%
Annual Interest	$ 7,500.00	$ 7,500.00
Divided by Months/Days	12	360
Interest Cost	$ 625.00	$ 20.83

Principal and Interest

The concept of an amortized loan adds to the complexity of financial calculations, because it is nearly impossible to calculate a correct amortized payment without the use of tables or a financial calculator. The word - **"amortization"** - comes from the Latin "a mort – to kill" and refers to payment schedule that devotes a portion of a payment towards loan principal, thereby paying the loan off over time.

Negative amortization occurs when the borrower's minimum payments do not cover the interest that is due on the loan. Interest is then added to the original loan amount – adding to the balance instead of reducing it – hence the term "negative" amortization.

Using a Principal and Interest (P&I) Factor Table to Compute a Payment

Abbreviated factors are often given on tests. Many loan officers and real estate agents use these tables as a tool on the backs of their business cards. If a factor is given, multiply the loan amount by the factor and divide by 1000.

Table - Using Factors to Compute Payments and Loan Amounts

Using Factors				
Determining the Payment			Determining the Loan Amount	
Loan Amount	150000		Payment	750
Multiplied by Factor	6.99		Divide By Factor	6.99
Result	1048500		Result	107.296137
Divided by	1000		Multiply by	1000
Approx Payment	1048.5		Maximum Loan	107296.137

The reverse can also be accomplished by taking the payment and dividing by the P&I factor to determine the loan amount.

PITI – The Components

The Housing Expense Ratio is also known as PITI and contains:

- Principal and interest payment
- 1/12 of the annual real estate tax
- 1/12 of the annual premium for Homeowner's Insurance
- 1/12 of the renewal premium for Private Mortgage Insurance/MIP
- the monthly homeowner's association fee for a condominium or a townhouse
- payment for any ground lease/land lease

Loan Products

Fixed Rate Products

Fixed rate loans are the most widely used loans, primarily because they are very easy to understand – for both borrowers and loan officers. 30 year loans suite the needs of the borrower who has a desire for security and believes that rates will rise. But loans are available from most lenders in increments of 25, 20, 15, 10 and 5 years.

Table - Pre-Payment on a Fixed Rate Loan Can Save Substantial Interest

Effect of Monthly Prepayment on Loan Term					
Loan Amount		$ 100,000.00			
Interest Rate		7.50%			
Amortized Term		30			
Principal and Interest		$ 699.21			

Extra Monthly Prepayment Amount	Total Payment with Prepayment	Loan Term in Months After Extra Payment	Loan Term In Years After Extra Payment	Total of Payments as Scheduled	Interest Savings
$0	$ 699.21	360	30.00	$ 251,717.22	$ -
$20	$ 719.21	326	27.19	$ 234,628.57	$ 17,088.66
$50	$ 769.21	269	22.39	$ 206,677.98	$ 45,039.24
$75	$ 844.21	216	18.03	$ 182,696.81	$ 69,020.41
$100	$ 944.21	174	14.51	$ 164,350.06	$ 87,367.16
$150	$ 1,094.21	136	11.33	$ 148,703.80	$ 103,013.42
$200	$ 1,294.21	106	8.82	$ 137,003.18	$ 114,714.05

Balloon Products

Payments are fixed for a certain period, and then there is one large payment - or a "balloon" payment. This feature may also be referred to as a "call," a "demand" or a "bullet." The loan is generally based on a long amortization term such as 30 years, with a balloon in 5, 7, 10 or even 15 years. There may be a feature for converting the loan to a fixed rate loan after the balloon. This is referred to as a conditional refinance.

Temporary and Permanent Buydowns

A Temporary Buydown is not a loan program. The underlying mortgage can be any fixed rate or adjustable rate program. A Buydown is exactly what it sounds like - paying fees (or buying) to reduce (down) the **payments** on a mortgage.

A Buydown may permanently or temporarily reduce the payments on a mortgage. A permanent Buydown is also known as a rate discount - paying discount points to permanently reduce the rate of the mortgage. For example, a lender may offer a rate of 10.5 % with no points, or 9.75 with 3 points. 9.75% in this example is a "discounted" rate. This is quite different from a temporary Buydown. Permanent Buydowns can be achieved by viewing a rate sheet and seeing how low the permanent rate will be by paying discount points.

Table - A Temporary Buydown Reduces the Initial Payment Rate

Buydown Cost Calculator

Use this worksheet to determine the actual buydown cost.

Loan Amount $300,000 Loan Term 30 Years
Note Rate 7.25% Loan Type 30 Year Fixed

Payment Rate Reduction	Payment Rate	Buydown Payment	# Mos	Note Payment	Monthly Cost	Annual Cost
2.000%	5.250%	$ 1,656.61	12	$ 2,046.53	$ 389.92	$ 4,679.01
1.000%	6.250%	$ 1,847.15	12	$2,046.53	$ 199.38	$ 2,392.53
0.000%	7.250%	$ 2,046.53	336	$2,046.53	$ -	

Total Cost $ 7,071.54
Point Cost 2.357%

A temporary Buydown is created when funds are placed in escrow - outside the control of the borrower or then lender - to offset the monthly payment required by the terms of the note. The funds in escrow reduce the effective payment rate but not the note rate. To illustrate this, take an example where a typical 30-Year Fixed Rate mortgage at 10% interest can carry an effective payment of 8% in the first year, 9% in the second year and revert to the note rate in the third year.

Understanding ARMs

While many people have a difficult time understanding adjustable rate mortgages, the key is that the interest rate changes. The changes are based on this simple formula:

> **INDEX + MARGIN**
> or
> **RATE + CAP**
> whichever is a smaller change

Component	Description
Frequency of Adjustments	How often the Rate Adjusts 1 Year ARM Family 1 Year, 3/1, 5/1, 7/1, 10/1 – Adjusts Annually after Fixed Period Usually tied to T-Bills 6 Month ARM Family 2/6, 3/6, 5/6, 7/6 and 2/28, 3/27, 5/27 – both are 6 Month ARMs even though they have different names Usually tied to LIBOR Index Monthly ARMs
Index	Index is the Basis for future Changes/Adjustments Should be Outside Lender's Control Treasury Bills – TCM (Treasury Constant Maturity) LIBOR – London Inter Bank Offered Rate COFI, CODI, COSI – Cost of Funds Prime
Margin	Margin is the Spread over Market – Amount over the Index that the New Rate can Be A 2% Adjustment Cap Limits the Rate Change Per Adjustment 		Loan 1	Loan 2
---	---	---
Initial Rate	5.5	5.5
Margin	2.75	3.25
Index	5.375	5.375
Year 2 Rate	7.5	7.5
Year 3 Rate	8.125	8.625	 The margin is the amount over the index the rate can change – the lower the margin, the less over market the rate will change.
Caps	Ceilings and Floors on Changes | Notation	Initial Adjustment Cap	Subsequent Adjustment Cap	Life of Loan Cap
---	---	---	---
2/6	2	2	6
5/2/6	5	2	6
3/12.75	3	3	12.75	

2nd Mortgages

The term "Second Mortgage" simply refers to the timing of the recording of security instruments such as a mortgage or deed of trust. "Second" alludes to the fact that there is another mortgage recorded prior in a first lien position, or before any other second mortgage is recorded. This means that during a forced sale the second lien holder receives proceeds after the first mortgage lender's claim has been satisfied. As a result second mortgage loans are considered riskier investments for lenders than first mortgages. The most popular reason for a first and second mortgage combination is to eliminate PMI.

Second mortgages may be fixed rate or adjustable rate term loans. The most popular form of second mortgage is the Home Equity Line of Credit (HELOC). The line of credit works like a

1st & 2nd Mortgage Comparison					
Sales Price	$	250,000.00	Loan Term in Years		30
Down Payment		10%	Interest Rate		8.75%
Standard Transaction			**1st & 2nd Mortgage**		
1st Trust Amount	$	225,000.00	1st Trust Amount	$	200,000.00
1st Trust Payment	$	1,770.08	1st Trust Payment	$	1,573.40
1st Trust PMI	$	97.50	1st Trust PMI	$	-
			2nd Trust Rate		9.50%
			2nd Trust Amount	$	25,000.00
			2nd Trust Payment	$	210.21
Standard Payment	$	1,867.58	**Combined Payment**	$	1,783.61
Monthly Savings					$83.97

credit card – charging up and paying down. The difference is that the HELOC is secured against the home. Borrowers use Home Equity Lines of Credit because, unlike a term loan, you only pay interest on the amount of money you have borrowed.

Reverse Mortgages

A reverse mortgage allows homeowners to take cash advances, based on the equity in their homes, with no repayment schedule. Borrowers must be at least 62 in order to secure a reverse mortgage. Reverse mortgages are not repaid until homeowners die or sell their homes. Advances from a reverse mortgage are not taxable. However, interest is added to the principal each month, and this interest is not tax deductible until the loan is paid off in part or in full.

Prepayment Penalties

A prepayment penalty is a charge that is added to the loan at the time it is paid off. It is also referred to as "defeasement", meaning the intent is to make it unfeasible to prepay the loan for a specified period of time. Prepayment penalties appear more frequently on sub-prime loans and loans which offer significant above par pricing. The lender wants to assure they receive their initial investment in making the loan is recaptured. Use caution to insure that any penalty does not trigger the loan to be classified as "high cost".

Traditional prepayment penalties are generally for the first years of the loan. Each lender has a specific prepayment penalty clause for their loans, but a typical prepayment penalty would add a fee that would decline as the loan matured.

Name	Description
3-2-1	First year prepayment penalty – 3%, 2nd year penalty is 2%, 3rd year penalty is 1%. Normally the borrower is allowed to prepay a portion of the loan per period – such as 10% or 20%.
Soft Prepayment Penalty	The penalty is applied only if the borrower is refinancing the loan. If the property is being disposed of, the penalty would not be applied. This may also apply when the borrower is refinancing with the same lender.
6 month	The prepayment penalty is not captured on the outstanding loan balance, but is based on the principal and interest payment. In this case the borrower would have to pay an additional 6 months of payments as a penalty.

Understanding Loan Plan Specifications and Guidelines

Loans are made based on risk – the amount of risk the lender is willing to accept comes from experience with areas of a borrower's profile that lenders have identified as having an impact on risk. The guidelines are used to limit exposure to higher risk aspects of a profile. While every program guideline has a nuance, they all address these basic elements. The loan officer must understand what these mean.

Criteria	Definition/Explanation
LTV/Occupancy	Owner occupancy (O/O) is the primary driver of risk. If the borrower lives in the property he has more incentive to make the payment than someone who rents the property. Likewise, if the borrower makes substantial cash investment, he or she is less likely to walk away from the property. Program guidelines are more restrictive as to LTV when owner occupancy is not present. 2nd Homes are vacation properties where no rent is used in qualifying the borrower – so may be treated more leniently. Investment property (NOO) is the riskiest Occupancy.
Transaction	Purchase Transaction – Risk + - when a borrower is making a cash investment in a purchase transaction, there is a positive risk aspect. In addition, when a property is being purchased, valuation is based on the truest indication of property value – what someone is willing to pay for a property – purchases are less risky.
	Rate/Term R/T (No Cash Out /NCO) Refinance – Risk = - when a borrower refinances to reduce the rate or term of a loan, the new loan is obviously more beneficial to the borrower and, hence, less risky. However, the borrower is likely extracting equity from the property to pay for the refinance, and that tempers the benefit of improved terms. In addition, valuation is based on an appraiser's estimate, so value is subjective. Rate/Term Refinances are risk neutral.
	Cash Out – or Equity Recapture – When a borrower refinances to take equity out of the property, this erodes the equity position and increases the risk. This is compounded by the valuation issue.
Eligible Properties	Property Types affect the risk of the loan. Condos and 2-4 Family (Income) properties are riskier than Single Family Detached (SFD) properties.
Multiple Properties	Many investors limit the number of properties they will finance for one borrower.
Mortgage Insurance	PMI or other mortgage insurance is required for loans with higher LTVs. Investors will specify the limits of coverage required which may be higher for riskier loans.
Assumability	Assumability is a feature that allows a buyer to take over payments on a loan with the lender's permission. Most lenders do not allow this.
Programs Offered	The type of loan programs – fixed, ARM, Balloon, and repayment plans such as Interest Only, buydowns – affect the risk of the loan.
Documentation Types	Full Documentation – Direct Verification of Income/Assets Alternative Documentation – Using Borrower's documentation i.e.; W-2's, Pay stubs, Bank Statements Reduced/Stated/NIV – Borrower States Income – Doesn't verify, Verifies Assets No Documentation – Borrower States Income/Assets Doesn't Verify No Ratio – Borrower Doesn't State Income/Assets – Doesn't Verify
Qualifying Ratios	The Debt Ratios used to qualify borrowers. Ordinarily, debt ratios will not be as important when Automated Underwriting is used.

Criteria	Definition/Explanation
Employment History	Normally, lenders want a 2 year history to verify stability as well as income.
Trailing Spouse	When a borrower is being relocated by his or her company, the non-relocating borrower is referred to as a "trailing spouse". In some cases this borrower's income can be used to help qualify.
Non-Resident Aliens	Citizenship may be required on certain loan programs, but many lenders now allow non-permanent resident aliens if they have a 2 year work and credit history.
Non-Occupant Co-Borrowers	A co-borrower is a non-occupant if they are buying a property, but will not live in the property. Even though the transaction is considered owner occupied from an occupancy perspective, the borrower who lives in the unit is perceived to be the one who will really be making the payments. They must have to have enough income to support the request individually.
Seller Contributions	The amount that the seller gives to the buyer to help pay for closing costs. Can substantially reduce borrower cash requirements. Excessive contributions can indicate value concessions so are limited by lenders
Cash Reserves	Borrowers cannot divest all their cash for closing and down payment. Lenders require that there are some post closing reserves as a contingency. Normally measured as a number of months of PITI.
Gift Letters	Bona-fide gifts that don't have to be repaid are a major source of funds. Verifying that the gift is not expected to be repaid normally means identifying the relationship between the donor and recipient, verifying the source of funds and making sure that the funds actually comes from the source listed and that those funds are deposited into the borrowers account. The risk of a gift is that it must be repaid and the repayments are not counted in the overall debt analysis.
Secondary Financing	2nd mortgages must not cause potential problems for the borrower such as a short balloon, negative amortization.
Borrowed Funds	If they are allowed, they must be counted towards borrower's debts
Credit Scores	FICO credit scores are an indication of a borrower's statistical likelihood of default on unsecured obligations. Because scores are based on statistical models, lenders use scores as another indication of a borrower's desire
Mortgage History	More than overall history, the mortgage payment history is a reflection of the borrower's commitment to maintain residence payments. A borrower who has been unable to do this is a questionable risk for the lender.
Major Derogatory Credit	Judgments, Tax Liens, Major Collection actions, Charge Offs, and Credit Counseling are all indications of current issues that could impair the borrower's ability to make future payments.

All loan programs identify these major risk criteria. The process of understanding the guidelines of each major loan program helps loan officers determine which program best suits the borrower's needs.

Major Program Guidelines - Conforming

Congressional oversight of FNMA and FHLMC extends to setting the maximum loan amounts these entities can purchase. This number is determined annually, in November, based on Median Home Prices. Because of the lower rates offered on conforming loans, many lenders anticipate the increase and start offering Conforming Loans in advance of the actual announcement as a way of capturing business.

Automated Underwriting and Qualifying Ratios

Automated underwriting – approval by a computerized grading system - has changed the way that loans are approved. Traditionally, borrowers had to meet standard income qualifying ratios of 28/36. Today, most loans are approved automatically. FHLMC uses the "Loan Prospector" or "LP" and FNMA uses "Desktop Underwriter" or "DU". The FHLMC model is a risk based system where positive or negative risk "points" are assessed for different aspects of a borrower's profile. The FNMA model is a weighted algorithm based on borrower debt patterns and post closing reserves. In addition to rendering a decision on a loan, the programs provide "Findings" that mitigate the approval including reducing or adding documentation and assessing the risk grade of the loan. In addition, the programs report the final disposition in different ways.

	Approved	Suspended	Declined
Desktop Underwriter – "D.U." – FNMA Conventional Loans, some Jumbo Loans	**Approve – Eligible**: The loan is approved and a live underwriter must simply review required conditions or exhibits.	**Approve – Ineligible**: The loan meets guidelines and receives an approval recommendation, but due to one or more characteristics, a human underwriter must approve it.	**Ineligible**: The loan does not meet A.U. parameters and must be underwritten and approved by a human underwriter.
Loan Prospector – "L.P." – FHLMC Conventional Loans, some Jumbo Loans, FHA and VA Loans	**Accept**: The loan is approved and a live underwriter must simply review required conditions or exhibits.	**Refer**: The loan meets guidelines and receives an approval recommendation, but due to one or more characteristics, a human underwriter must approve it.	**Decline**: The loan is ineligible for sale to FHLMC; must be underwritten to other guidelines by a human.

Expanded Approvals

"Flex", "Expanded Approvals (EA)", "Plus" and "A-minus" are all designations that indicate that DU or LP have approved a loan, but at a different rate or under different program guidelines than proposed.

Program	Description
Flex FNMA Alt 97/100 FHLMC	97% financing, 100% financing, Stated Income, No Income – No Asset, No Ratio, 90% Cash Out, and 90% LTV investor financing are all examples of the way Flex expands standard FNMA/FHLMC guidelines. DU/LP assigns Flex eligibility based on assets, source of down payment funds, and PMI coverage.
Expanded Approval	EA is granted to borrowers whose credit marginally misses standard guidelines. The values are assigned by DU, but generally declining credit impacts the rate. EAI + .75 points, EAII +1.5 points, EAIII + 1.5% to the rate.
A minus FHLMC	A- is similar to EA, because it deals with substandard credit. The difference is the pricing module is based upon LTV; a 90% LTV A- would have a lower rate than a 95% LTV A-.

Private Mortgage Insurance (PMI)

Since the late 1980's, the importance of Private Mortgage Insurance has declined with the advent the use of 1st and 2nd mortgage combinations to avoid PMI. However, there are occasions when

PMI is unavoidable - perhaps because the borrower doesn't qualify for a 2nd mortgage. Or the borrower may be planning to make substantial improvements to the property and the cost of PMI is lower than the cost of a 1st and 2nd mortgage.

PMI Calculation	
Loan Amount	$ 250,000.00
Multiply by Premium	0.52%
Annual Premium	$ 1,300.00
Divide by 12	12
Monthly Premium	$ 108.33

PMI insures the lender against default by insuring a portion of the riskiest part of the loan – the top part. Premiums are based on the amount of coverage the lender requires. PMI covers the top part of the loan – the riskiest part. Monthly PMI costs are calculated by multiplying the loan amount by the annual PMI premium factor and dividing it by 12.

PMI Coverage Percentage Illustration	
Sales Price	$ 200,000.00
LTV	90%
Down Payment	$ (20,000.00)
Mortgage Amount	$ 180,000.00
Coverage Requirement	22%
Lender's Exposure	$ 140,400.00
PMI Coverage	$ 39,600.00

PMI must be cancelled by the lender when the LTV reaches 78% or 77%. The borrower may petition the lender to cancel PMI once the LTV reaches 80% under certain circumstances, but it is at the lender's discretion.

Mortgage Insurance Premium Plans
survey date 10/1/08

PLAN TYPE	Standard Coverages		1st Year Rate			Renewal Rate Years 2-10		
	Coverage	LTV	30Fix	ARM	ARMI	30Fix	ARM	ARMI
Traditional/Split Plan where a lump sum premium is paid to cover year 1. Subsequent Renewals are at a lower rate	30%	95%	1.5	1.5	n/a	0.4	0.64	n/a
	25%	90%	1.25	1.25	n/a	0.18	0.33	n/a
	12%	85%	1	1	n/a	0	0.26	n/a
Monthly Plan where each month is paid as it is accrued. True pay as you go. Ensures lower escrow and closing costs.	35%	97%	n/a	n/a	n/a	n/a	n/a	n/a
	30%	95%	0.94	1.04	1.08	0.94	1.04	1.08
	25%	90%	0.62	0.73	0.78	0.62	0.73	0.78
	12%	85%	0.38	0.39	0.44	0.38	0.39	0.39
One Time Premium - may be paid in cash or financed on top of loan amount if LTV's are not exceeded.	Coverage	LTV	One Time Premiums - Cash			Financed One Time Premiums		
	30%	95%	3.05	3.4	3.6	n/a	n/a	n/a
	25%	90%	2.1	2.25	2.4	3.05	3.4	3.6
	12%	85%	1.25	1.3	1.45	2.15	2.25	2.4
Lender Paid Mortgage Insurance - Increased interest rate pays for PMI instead of borrower.	LTV		30 Year Fixed		15 Year Fixed		ARMs	
	95%		0.875%		0.625%		1.250%	
	90%		0.625%		0.375%		0.750%	
	85%		0.375%		0.250%		0.500%	

Sub Prime Loans

For many years, borrowers who did not meet investment quality guidelines for loans would have no other source for financing. With the popularity of credit-rated securities, sometimes referred to as "junk bonds", the secondary market came to accept mortgages with less than investment grade characteristics. These were made palatable to investors by "enhancing" the credit with higher rates and lower LTVs – trading higher credit risk with higher reward. This type of lending – known as Sub-prime, Choice, B/C or ALT A, helps non-traditional borrowers.

Unfortunately, statistics indicate a higher incidence of abusive or predatory lending in the sub prime market. In addition, Sub-Prime lending has been credited with the disassembly of the secondary mortgage market following the credit crisis of the 2006-2008 era.

Grade DTI	Mortgage Lates/ Credit*	Credit Score	FULL DOC LTV						
			70	75	80	85	90	95	100
AA+ 50% DTI	0 x 30 x 12 or 1 x 30 x 12 No Rolling BK = 24 Mo NOD = 36 Mo	680+	6.10	6.15	6.20	6.25	6.40	7.30	7.45
		660-679	6.25	6.30	6.35	6.40	7.60	7.60	7.65
		640-659	6.40	6.45	6.50	6.55	7.75	7.80	8.00
		620-639	6.45	6.55	6.60	6.65	7.50	8.15	8.40
		600-619	6.55	6.60	6.70	6.85	7.25	8.40	8.85
		580-599	6.70	6.75	6.95	7.05	7.60	8.90	9.15
		560-579	6.75	7.00	7.10	7.40	8.05	8.95	0.00
		540-559	7.25	7.35	7.50	8.00	8.60	0.00	0.00
		520-539	7.45	7.75	7.90	8.55	0.00	0.00	0.00
		500-519	7.90	8.30	8.70	0.00	0.00	0.00	0.00
AA 50% DTI	1 x 30 x 12 Rolling 6x30=1x30 BK = 24 Mo NOD = 36 Mo	680+	6.10	6.25	6.30	6.35	6.50	7.40	7.55
		660-679	6.35	6.40	6.45	6.50	6.70	7.70	7.75
		640-659	6.50	6.55	6.60	6.65	7.05	7.90	8.10
		620-639	6.55	6.65	6.70	6.75	7.10	8.25	8.50
		600-619	6.65	6.70	6.80	6.95	7.20	8.50	8.95
		580-599	6.80	6.85	7.05	7.15	7.75	9.00	0.00
		560-579	6.85	7.10	7.20	7.50	8.15	0.00	0.00
		540-559	7.35	7.45	7.60	8.10	8.70	0.00	0.00
		520-539	7.55	7.85	8.00	8.65	0.00	0.00	0.00
		500-519	8.00	8.40	8.80	0.00	0.00	0.00	0.00
A- 50% DTI	2 x 30 x 12 Rolling 6x30=1x30 BK = 24 Mo NOD = 36 Mo	660+	6.40	6.45	6.50	6.60	6.85	0.00	0.00
		640-659	6.55	6.60	6.70	6.75	7.10	0.00	0.00
		620-639	6.60	6.70	6.80	6.85	7.25	0.00	0.00
		600-619	6.70	6.75	6.90	7.05	7.40	0.00	0.00
		580-599	6.90	6.95	7.10	7.45	8.05	0.00	0.00
		560-579	6.95	7.20	7.35	7.65	8.35	0.00	0.00
		540-559	7.50	7.60	7.75	8.30	8.95	0.00	0.00
		520-539	7.65	8.05	8.15	8.80	0.00	0.00	0.00
		500-519	8.15	8.55	8.95	0.00	0.00	0.00	0.00
B 50% DTI	1 x 60 x 12 BK = 18 Mo NOD = 24 Mo	640+	6.70	6.85	6.95	7.45	0.00	0.00	0.00
		620-639	6.85	7.00	7.10	7.55	0.00	0.00	0.00
		600-619	7.00	7.10	7.20	7.70	0.00	0.00	0.00
		580-599	7.25	7.40	7.50	8.20	0.00	0.00	0.00
		560-579	7.45	7.60	7.90	8.40	0.00	0.00	0.00
		540-559	7.75	7.95	8.10	8.95	0.00	0.00	0.00
		520-539	7.85	8.20	8.50	9.50	0.00	0.00	0.00
		500-519	8.20	9.10	9.60	0.00	0.00	0.00	0.00
C 50% DTI	1 x 90 x 12 BK = 12 Mo NOD = 12 Mo	580+	7.60	8.00	8.65	0.00	0.00	0.00	0.00
		560-579	7.75	8.45	8.85	0.00	0.00	0.00	0.00
		540-559	8.20	8.85	9.45	0.00	0.00	0.00	0.00
		520-539	8.65	9.10	0.00	0.00	0.00	0.00	0.00
		500-519	9.25	10.30	0.00	0.00	0.00	0.00	0.00
C- 50% DTI	2 x 90 x 12 BK 7 Discharged BK 13 Paid No Open NOD	580+	9.00	0.00	0.00	0.00	0.00	0.00	0.00
		560-579	9.15	0.00	0.00	0.00	0.00	0.00	0.00
		540-559	9.65	0.00	0.00	0.00	0.00	0.00	0.00
		520-539	10.00	0.00	0.00	0.00	0.00	0.00	0.00
		500-519	10.80	0.00	0.00	0.00	0.00	0.00	0.00

As the LTV increases and the credit score decreases, the rate increases.

As the Credit Grade decreases, the LTV decreases and the rate increases.

Federal Housing Administration (FHA) Loans

FHA does not make loans, it insures loans. All FHA loans require mortgage insurance. Beginning in 2005, all mortgages require a payment of UFMIP (Up Front Mortgage Insurance Premium) and Monthly MIP. Approved lenders have the ability to approve loans for FHA insurance through the Direct Endorsement (DE) program. The general benefits of the FHA insurance program are that it offers lower down payments, more flexible income qualifying (31/43 ratios) and more lenient credit standards.

FHA Loan Amount Calculation

Effective January 1, 2009 FHA LTV's and we'll be based on a 3.5% down payment. The maximum loan amount will be 100% of the property's value, once the mortgage insurance premium has been added.

FHA Mortgage Insurance – MIP

In addition to the loan amount calculation, loan officers must understand the Mortgage Insurance Premium schedule for FHA loans. FHA requires payment of an Up Front MIP (UFMIP) and a monthly MIP for all single family lending programs. When

Financing the UFMIP	
Base Loan Amount	$ 130,000.00
Multiply by UFMIP %	1.50%
Total UFMIP	$ 1,950.00
Loan Amount with MIP Financed	$ 131,950.00

the UFMIP is in place, the borrower may – if the loan is paid off early – receive a refund of any unused MIP. UFMIP may be paid in cash, or it may be financed on top of the base loan amount. The Monthly MIP is based on the total loan amount, with or without MIP financed.

FHA MIP Premiums - Effective 10/1/08 - 9/30/09

Loan Term	Up Front MIP	Monthly MIP		
		> 95%	90%-95%	< 90%
30 Year	1.75%	0.55%	.50% -	.50% -
15 Year	1.75%	0.25%	.25% -	None
Streamline	1.50%	Same as 15 – 30	Same as 15 – 30	Same as 15 – 30
FHA Secure	3.00%	0.55%	0.50%	0.50%

Monthly MIP is a declining balance insurance policy, so the premiums decrease as the balance decreases. The Mortgage Insurance Cancellation Act requires that Mortgage Insurance Premiums be cancelled at 78% LTV (77% for High Risk Loans)

FHA Risk Based MIP Premiums - Effective 7/14/08 - 10/1/08

LTV	Scores							Monthly MIP
	> 680	679 - 640	639 - 600	599 - 560	559 - 500	> 499	No Score	
< 90%	1.25	1.25	1.25	1.50	1.75	1.75	1.50	
90.01 - 95.00	1.25	1.25	1.50	1.75	2.00	n/a	1.75	0.50
> 95.00	1.25	1.50	1.75	2.00	2.25	n/a	2.00	0.55

FHA MIP Premiums - Effective until 7/14/08

Loan Term	Up Front MIP	Monthly MIP		
		> 95%	90%-95%	< 90%
30 Year	1.50	0.50%	0.50%	0.50%
15 Year	1.50	0.25%	0.25%	None

Other advantages of the FHA program are that Gifts may be from any non-financially interested source and that non-occupant co-borrowers allowed for qualifying purposes.

Department of Veteran's Affairs (VA)

The primary benefit of the VA loan guarantee is the ability to finance up to 100% of the purchase of a home. Additional benefits include higher qualifying ratios (41/41), lenient credit qualification (no minimum credit score), and lenient asset treatment (no post-closing reserves required, gifts from any source).

The VA acts as a co-signer, guaranteeing loans from private lenders to veterans. It is not an insurance program - VA charges a fee for guaranteeing the individual loan. This is referred to as a funding fee. To receive a loan guaranty benefit, the veteran must be eligible. The veteran must have achieved a sufficient level of service. Once this eligibility is established, the veteran must have sufficient entitlement to guarantee the loan request.

A History of Loan Guaranty Entitlement	
1944 - World War II - Inception	$ 4,000
After 7/12/50 Increased to	$ 7,500
After 5/7/68 Increased to	$ 12,500
After 10/2/78 Increased to	$ 25,000
After 10/1/80 Increased to	$ 27,500
After 2/1/88 Increased to	$ 36,000
Increased 12/18/89 for veterans with full entitlement and for purchases over $144,000	$ 46,000
Increased 10/13/94 – basic remains at $36,000	$ 50,750
Increased 12/01 – basic remains at $36,000	$ 60,000
Increased 12/04 - 25% of FHLMC	$ 89,913
Increased 12/05 - 25% of FHLMC	$ 104,250

Entitlement and the Maximum VA Loan

All veterans start with basic entitlement of $36,000. In high cost areas (any area where the sales price exceeds $144,000) the veterans entitlement is expanded to 25% of the maximum FHLMC loan, which is $89,913 as of 2005. If a veteran does not use all of his BASIC loan entitlement (which is currently $36,000), he can use the remaining "partial entitlement" for another VA loan.

VA Loan Amount Calculation	Example 1: Full Entitlement	Example 2: Partial Entitlement $22,000
Sales Price X 75% + Eligibility = Base Loan Amount Plus Funding Fee = Loan Amount with Funding Fee.	Sales Price $200,000 x 75% =150,000 Eligibility + 60,000 Base Loan $200,000 = Downpayment 0 Note: Even though not all entitlement is used, the maximum LTV is still 100%	Sales Price $100,000 x 75% = 75,000 Eligibility + 22,500 Base Loan $ 97,500 = Downpayment 2,500 Note: Even though the VA Program is 100% Financing this is limited by Eligibility

There are some limitations to the use of loan guaranty eligibility: 1.) Entitlement remains tied to the property it was used to purchase, so cannot be restored until the property is sold. 2.) In high cost areas, the veteran may only use the high cost eligibility (over $36,000) with full entitlement.

The VA Funding Fee

Depending on the LTV, veteran status, and type of transaction the VA Funding Fee will vary. Disabled veterans (service related disability) receive a waiver of the funding fee.

Funding Fee Active Duty	Funding Fee National Guard/Reservist	Transaction Type
2.20%	2.40%	Purchase with less than 5% Down or Refinance
3.30%	3.30%	Purchase with less than 5% down with Restored Eligibility
1.50%	1.75%	Purchase with less than 10% Down
1.25%	1.50%	Purchase with 10% or More Down
0.50%	0.50%	Streamline Refinance

Investor	FNMA/FHLMC - "Generic" Conforming							
LTV Matrix								
LTV/Occupancy	Owner Occupied		2nd Home	Investor	Property Type	Loan Amount		(AK, HI)
Transaction	LTV	CLTV	LTV	LTV				
Purchase or Rate and Term Refinance	95%	90%	90%	70%	Single Family, Condo	$	417,000	$ 625,500
	90%	90%	N/A	70%	2 Unit	$	533,850	$ 800,775
	80%	80%	N/A	70%	3 Unit	$	645,300	$ 967,950
	80%	80%	N/A	70%	4 Unit	$	801,950	$ 1,202,925
Cash Out	75%	75%	70%	65%	Single Family, Condo	$	417,000	$ 625,500
High Cost Area* thru 1/1/09	90%	90%	n/a	n/a	Single Family, Condo	$	729,750	n/a
Refinancing	Streamline or Limited Qualifying to 95% LTV if current loan is FNMA Serviced – Over 90% cannot include Closing Costs or Prepaid Items. Existing 2nd Mortgages must be "seasoned" for 12 Months or payoff is considered "cash out". Limited Cash Out < $2,000 or 2% back to borrower.							
Eligible Properties	Single Family Detached (SFD), Single Family Attached (SFA), 2-4 Unit Residential, Planned Unit Developments (PUDs), Condominium - New PUDs, all condos have eligibility criteria - see *Chapter 8 - Property Types* for Eligibility							
Multiple Properties	Owner Occupied No Limit Investment/2nd - no more than 4 financed (FNMA)							
Mortgage Insurance	Conventional Private Mortgage Insurance required for all owner-occupied properties and second homes with loan to values greater than 80%. In some cases required for investor loans over 70% and, when allowable, 80-10-10 secondary financing.							
Assumability	Conventional loans all have a due-on-transfer clause - this precludes assumption							
Programs Offered	95%	All Occupancy Types			30, 20, 15, 10 Year Fixed			
	95%	Owner/2nd Only			7 & 5 Yr 2 Step, 2-1 Buydown, Interest Only, 3/1, 5/1, 7/1 ARM			
	90%	Owner/2nd Only			1 Year ARM, 7/23 & 5/25, 3-2-1 Buydown			
Documentation Types	Full/Alternative - Income Verification may be waived by DU/LP							
Income/Borrower Restrictions								
Qualifying Ratios	95% LTV – 28/36 or DU/LP				ARMs Qualify at 2nd Year Rate			
	75% LTV – 33/38 or DU/LP				Buydowns Qualify at Start Rate			
Employment History	Minimum 2 Years History, 2 Years in same business for Self-Employed							
Trailing Spouse	Corporate Sponsored Relocation Only. 80% LTV Max, 6 Months Reserves, 25-50% of spouse's income may be used if it can be documented that former employment is available in new location.							
Non-Resident Aliens	No restrictions - must have 24-month work, asset and credit history.							
Non-Occupant Co-Borrowers	Max LTV for using non-occupant co-borrower's income for qualifying is 90% LTV. Occupant borrower must still have 38/45 ratios and have 5% of own funds invested.							
Asset Restrictions								
Seller Contributions	95% LTV - 3% 90% LTV - 6% 75% LTV - 8%				Investor - 2%			
Cash Reserves	95% LTV - 3 Months PITI 90% or Less - 2 Months				2 months – May be waived under affordable gold, community homebuyer			
Gift Letters	80.01 - 95% LTV borrower must have 5% of own funds invested into transaction. < 80% LTV - No limit. Source, transfer and receipt must be documented. Donor must be "family" member.							
Secondary Financing	Maximum LTV for 1st Mortgage is 75% (i.e. 75-15-10 is o.k.) 2nd mortgage maturity must be at least 5 years; payments must cover minimum interest. 2nd may not be ARM if 1st is ARM. 1st Mortgage may not be a balloon.							
Borrowed Funds	Must be secured/counted for qualifying							
Credit Restrictions								
Credit Scores	Bureau Scores are applied. With two scores take the average, with three scores take the middle. Scoring regimen is not absolute but follows the following guideline.				Eligible for Enhanced Criteria Cautious Not Eligible for Max Financing			Over 700 660 - 620 below 620
Mortgage History	0 x 30 days late for last 12 Months							
Major Derogatory Credit	Must have 2 years RE-ESTABLISHED history. Time elapsed since resolution Bankruptcy - Chapter 7 - 4 Years; Chapter 13 - 2 Years; Foreclosure 4 years.							

Maximum Loan Amounts are adjusted as to high cost areas –
visit https://www.efanniemae.com/sf/refmaterials/loanlimits/jumboconf/xls/loanlimref.xls

Insurer - Guarantor	Federal Housing Administration (FHA)							9/15/2008
LTV Matrix								
Transaction	Owner Occupied LTV	Owner Occupied CLTV	2nd Home LTV	Investor LTV	Property Type	Loan Amount		High Cost (100% of FNMA)
Purchase or Rate and Term Refinance - LTVs effective 1/1/08	96.5% Base LTV, up to 100% LTV with MIP Financed	>100% only with government agency or refi	N/A	N/A	Single Family, Condo	$ 271,050	$	729,750
			N/A	N/A	2 Unit	$ 347,000	$	934,200
			N/A	N/A	3 Unit	$ 419,400	$	1,129,250
			N/A	N/A	4 Unit	$ 521,250	$	1,403,400
Cash Out	95% DU (85%)	N/A	N/A	N/A	SFD, Condo	$ 271,050	$	729,750
Programs Offered	30-, 20-, 15-, 10- Year fixed (Sections 203b & 234c). 1-Year ARM with 1/5 caps, 3/1 and 5/1 ARM (Sec 251), Rehabilitation/Construction Permanent loan (Section 203k), Reverse Mortgage (Home Equity Conversion - no high cost areas 1 family only), FHA Secure, Energy Efficient, Disaster Recovery							

Assumability	Mortgage Origination Date	Assumability Feature
	prior to 12/1/1986	Fully Assumable for $125
	12/1/86 - 12/14/89	Fully Assumable for $125 for owner occupants, Investors must put 25% down
	12/15/89 - present	Assumable by approved Owner Occupants only for $500

Mortgage Insurance (10/1/08)	Loan Term	Upfront MP	Monthly Premiums Based LTV		
			90% or Less	90.01 - 95%	over 95%
	30-Year	1.75	.50 to 78% LTV	.50 to 78% LTV	.55 to 78% LTV
	15-Year	1.75	None	.25 to 78%	.25 to 78%

Automated Approval	Yes - "Total Scorecard" / DU/LP or other AUS
Refinancing	Streamline Refinance FHA to FHA only (No FHA Secure) - With 12-month mortgage payment history and payment reduction, borrowers do not requalify. No income/asset documentation is required. Loan amount can only be increased for closing costs with new appraisal. UFMIP is 1.5%. May subordinate existing debt regardless of LTV.
Eligible Properties	SFD, 2-4, Condo, PUD - Condo Units must be approved https://entp.hud.gov/idapp/html/condlook.cfm
Income Restrictions	
Qualifying Ratios	31/43 ARMs and buydowns qualify at 2nd Year rate if LTV is greater than 95%. Or TOTAL Scorecard, DU or LP. May exceed with documented factors
Documentation Types	FULL and alternative documentation
Non-Occupant Co-Borrowers	No Restrictions - May not be used for qualifying on 2-4 family properties, Cash-out Refinance over 417,000
Self-Employment	Minimum 2 years, recommend 5 Years
Trailing Spouse	Not considered. CAUTION - may only have one FHA insured loan.
Secondary Financing	1.) must still make required down payment 2.) cannot exceed statutory sales price/mortgage amount, 3.) No Prepay Penalty 4.) regular payments 5.) Min term > 10 yrs. Refinancing existing debt or FHA Secure may subordinate excess payoff into 2nd lien. Count monthly payments unless no repayments required for >36 mos. May exceed with state agency assistance programs/financing
Asset Restrictions	
Cash Reserves	15-days interest - borrowers with alternative credit files need 2 months
Gift Letters	Acceptable from any source. FHA "prefers" buyer has 25% of own cash. Donor may borrow (secured) funds for downpayment. Must still verify gift, transfer and receipt of funds. Non-Profits funded by sellers are closely watched - may be eliminated.
Seller Contributions	6% of Sales Price, including discount, buydowns and prepaid items.
Required Contribution	Borrower MUST invest 3.5% downpayment, excluding closing costs or downpayment.
Borrowed Funds	Must be secured/counted for qualifying.
Credit/Borrower Restrictions	
Credit Scores	Scores affect LTV and Risk-based Mortgage Insurance Premiums
Multiple Properties	ONLY ONE PROPERTY WITH minimum down payment
Non-Resident Aliens	No restrictions
Major Derogatory Credit	Significant derogatory credit may be tolerated with documented extenuating circumstances. Refer by TOTAL on Bankruptcy, Chapter 7 - 2 Years from discharge; Chapter 13 - 1 Year from discharge. Foreclosure - 3 Years from discharge.

Insurer/Guarantor Department of Veterans Affairs

Transaction	Owner Occupied LTV	Owner Occupied CLTV	2nd Home LTV	Investor LTV	Property Type	Loan Amount at 100%	High Cost Areas*
Purchase or Rate and Term Refinance	100%	100%	N/A	N/A	Single Family, Condo, 2-4 Family	$ 417,000	$ 625,500
Cash Out	90%	90%	N/A	N/A	Single Family, Condo	$ 417,000	$ 625,500
High Cost Areas		up to the FHLMC High Cost limit. Guarantee will still be 25% of that amount (Up to $182,437)					
Refinancing	Streamline Refinance - With 12-month mortgage payment history and payment reduction, borrowers do not requalify. Loan amount can only be increased for closing costs with new appraisal.						
Programs Offered	10 - 30-Year Fixed Rate.						
Mortgage Insurance	VA Funding Fee is in lieu of Insurance. See "Risk-Based" Premium Charts						
Eligible Properties	SFD, 2-4, Condo, PUD - Condo & PUD Units must be approved						
Eligible Borrowers	Servicemen with documented eligibility have at least the following active duty: **90 Days** WWII 9/16/40-7/25/47 Korea 6/27/50-1/31/55 Vietnam 8/05/64-5/7/75 **181 Days** Pre-Korea 7/26/47-6/26/50 Post-Korea 2/1/55-8/4/64 Post-Vietnam 5/8/75 to for Enlisted 9/7/1980 for Officers 10/16/1981 **24 Months** Current Active Duty after 9/7/80 for Enlisted after 10/16/81 for Officers 6 Years Reservists/National Guard Members (Expires 10/99) Also Eligible NOAA Officers; Commissioned Public Health Officers; ESSA Officers; C&G Survey Officers; Veterans discharged prior to eligibility due to service-related disability; surviving spouse of veteran who died as a result of service related injury or disease. **Veterans and their Spouses.** Eligible Veterans have served continuous active duty for at least the time frames listed and have an honorable release or discharge.						
Secondary Financing	Allowed. Note must be at least 5 years in length. Since VA is no money down formula, 2nd mortgage would only be used to exceed the maximum financing of $240,000/$359,650						
Automated Approval	Loan Prospector						
Assumability	$500 Fee and the Borrower must Qualify. No Release of Liability.						

Income Restrictions

Qualifying Ratios	41/41
Documentation Types	Full, Alternative Documentation
Trailing Spouse	Not Considered - Veterans regularly relocate
Non-Occupant Co-Borrowers	Veterans and their Spouses ONLY. Eligible Veterans have served continuous active duty for at least the time frames listed and have an honorable release or discharge.
Self-Employment	Minimum 2 Years - Recommend 5 Years

Asset Restrictions

Seller Contributions	4% of sales price, not including points. Transaction may be structured so that borrower pays no money at closing, but borrower may not receive cash back at closing.
Cash Reserves	None Required
Gift Letters	May come from any source not involved in transaction. Must verify donor, transfer and receipt of gift funds.
Borrowed Funds	Funds may be borrowed - must be counted for qualifying.

Credit Restrictions

Multiple Properties	Number of VA Loans is limited by entitlement.
Credit Scores	Not considered.

Chapter 3 – New Loan Setup, Vendors and Disclosures

The Importance of a Thorough Loan File Setup

File opening, or loan file setup, is the first quality control step in the mortgage process. Almost all problems encountered in the loan process can be caught at file setup. Knowing this, you would think that mortgage companies would have their most skilled employees performing this function. Unfortunately, file opening is considered to be the most mundane of all tasks in the mortgage industry. We would encourage you to be diligent at this step. It is a repetitive and clerical task, and if you rely only on your own instincts, you are sure to miss something important. Having a system by which you can review file documentation at the beginning of the process will allow you to alleviate many problems at the end of the process.

Materials Needed
- 2 Hole Punch
- 2 Hole Fasteners
- Legal File Folders
- Tacky Finger
- Certified True Copy Stamp
- Highlighter

File Handling Technique – "Riffling"

Correct Method	Incorrect Method
Riffling is the location of a specific document in a loan file by handling the most consistent area of document texture – the upper left or right hand corner of the stack. Using a finger moistener you can review 100's of pages a minute.	Paging through a file requires the handling of the loose side of the file stack and reviewing each page individually. This method is acceptable for page at a time review, but is extremely awkward for locating an individual page.

Sources of Applications and Treatment

The processor will receive applications from numerous sources. While the manner in which the information is transmitted may vary, the information contained therein is the same, and should be treated exactly the same in terms of the set up process.

New Retail Application

This file will have been taken and assembled by a retail loan officer. It is the retail loan officer's job to complete all of the initial application, and all of the disclosures except for the Truth-in-Lending Disclosures. The Loan Officer is also responsible for reviewing the file documentation for completeness, and whether the borrower qualifies for the loan program.

In theory a complete retail loan application should only need to have the disclosures prepared within 72 hours of the time the application is signed, the documentation and file exhibits reviewed for completeness, and submitted for final underwriting review. However, because of the lack of training endemic to our business, it is worthwhile to consider a quality control check at the time of the loan file set up.

This process consists of preparing the formal typed loan application (entering data) re-checking the loan officer's field underwriting against the pre-underwriting submission checklist, and compiling the missing data into the computer to communicate it to the borrower.

Internet Loan Application/Lead

Your company must make the distinction between what is considered a loan application and what is a lead. Generally, if the borrower has selected a property, locked in an interest rate, or signed an application form, the borrower can be considered to have applied. This distinction is important because it is the beginning of the application starts the clock for disclosure purposes.

An internet lead is usually a form response generated by an internet service providers scripting. Essentially, it is a list of data. If the form is called an application, it is imported into the Loan Origination System (LOS) application via an Electronic Data Interface. If the Data does not contain a property address, if the client does not have a credit report in file, or if the interest rate is not locked in, then the application can be processed as a pre-approval. Disclosures do not have to be sent until the application is completed.

To process an internet submission is to rely almost entirely on the borrower's representations of income and assets. If is this is case, the forms required should be generated and, based upon the information provided, the file pre-underwritten. This will generate a lengthy list of documentation requirements.

It is critical that the borrower understands that additional information may be requested depending on what the initial response reveals. To assure this insert this line at the beginning or end of the documentation request.

"PLEASE BE ADVISED THAT WE BELIEVE THE DOCUMENTATION BEING REQUESTED IS SUFFICIENT TO BASE AN UNDERWRITING DECISION ON. HOWEVER THE DOCUMENTS YOU PROVIDE MAY RAISE QUESTIONS WHICH REQUIRE FURTHER CLARIFICATION, SO WE RESERVE THE RIGHT TO REQUEST ADDITIONAL DOCUMENTATION TO COMPLETE THE APPLICATION.

This should allow the processor to request additional information from the borrower, if necessary, without leading the borrower to believe that he or she is being subjected to unreasonable and repeated requests.

Assigned/Transferred Applications

There are two instances in which a processor would receive an assigned file; in the case of a brokered/wholesale loan or in the case of a transfer from another lender.

Brokered/Wholesale

In the course of regular business, there are lenders who accept wholesale applications from other lenders. These are brokered loans and there is usually an established business relationship and flow for this type of application.

The important thing to consider regarding this type of application is that the borrower normally expects to deal with the originating lender, not with your company. In this case, forms which are required to be signed by the borrower, additional information requests and coordinating activities must be directed through a contact at the originating lender's office.

There is a credit report and appraisal already provided on this type of case. There will not be application deposits/fees.

Transferred Files

In some circumstances a case may be transferred from one lender to another because 1.) a disagreement between borrower and loan officer; 2.) the lender could not approve the application; 3.) the lender did not have a program that the borrower wanted. There may be other reasons. In this case the borrower is your customer. All correspondence may be directed to them.

There may or may not be an appraisal or credit report in the file. Keep in mind that you may or may not be able to obtain or utilize either of these.

Loan File Set-Up Procedures - Set Up Checklist

	Perform Data Entry from application or pre-application
	Enter loan into branch loan log
	Copy Application Fee Check – 2 Copies; 1 file, 1 Bookkeeping
	Order the credit report
	Order appraisal, include all property information available - contract, listing, deed
	Is borrower currently renting? Request a landlord reference – print VOR from Verifications
	Print Employment Verification and Deposit Verification. Attach credit authorization and mail.
	Condominium or PUD (Townhouse) Letter/Questionnaire to agent if sale - borrower if refinance
	Print the application (1003 - all pages) and the Transmittal Summary (1008)
	Assemble File in Stack Order on right side of folder
	Complete Application Checklist – Enter all missing documentation in "Tracking"
	Print the Borrower Introduction (Welcome) letter
	Prepare Truth-in-Lending all other Disclosures
	Prepare Welcome Package using the checklist to assure all supporting documents are included
	Fasten copies of all borrower correspondence on left side of file

Entering the Loan in the Loan Log

All loans taken in by the branch, processor, loan officer or other source must be registered in the company loan log. Sometimes this is done on the company's processing system, but because electronic records can be modified or lost the processor should assure there is a manual record of all files received and the date received.

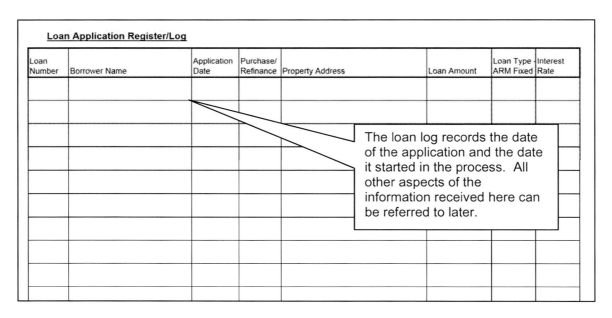

The loan log records the date of the application and the date it started in the process. All other aspects of the information received here can be referred to later.

The loan log records the date of the application and the date it started in the process. All other aspects of the information received here can be referred to later.

File Handling Technique – The "Windstorm"

One frequent source of confusion and lost efficiency is the piece of misplaced paper in a loan file. To alleviate this issue follow these rules:

1.) Always close and replace one file before opening another.
2.) Always punch and file and loose documents – even if you only place the document on the left side of the file awaiting review.

If you pretend there is going to be a windstorm in your office, you're file will be safe.

Ordering the Credit Report

Loan Officer/Originator/AE May Order Report

In today's world many loan officers utilize credit reports as part of the pre-qualification process. In fact, they may have a credit report in file at the time the application is submitted for set up. This does not mean the processor should not order or address the credit report issue. The correct application date must be reflected on the credit report. This affects compliance in all facets of the post-closing audit.

Depending on the circumstances the processor may utilize the initial credit report, or may modify, update re-order or correct the report to reflect the correct dates.

Types of Credit Reports

Name	Data Collected	Description	Cost
In-File	One repository	Usually used to "peek" at what the borrower's credit history is like. This preview allows the loan officer to see how the overall credit is without expending substantial cost and affecting the borrower's credit scores with multiple inquiries	$5 - $8 - can be converted to full tri-merge at no cost.
Tri-Merge	three repositories	Data is sorted and merged eliminating duplicate, old and paid accounts. May also include scores.	$15 - $25
RMCR	three repositories direct references	Residential Mortgage Credit Report is used to verify additional data, such as employment, rental history and unverified debts. The RMCR allows the credit bureau to provide third party verification.	$50 - $60

The processor must understand the varieties of credit reports. Reading, understanding and adjusting credit reports for underwriting are additional duties of the processor.

In-File, Pre-Qual or Tri-Merge vs. Full RMCR

There are two kinds of reports ordered at the time of loan setup. While they are called different things they refer to the same thing. An "In-File" is the preliminary data contained in the repositories. This initial credit information allows us to screen for adverse information as part of the borrower introductory package. Most programs allow an in-file with at least 3 repositories (Tri-Merge) provided.

The loan officer and processor can determine during initial review of the case whether a full Mortgage Credit Report is required.

RMCR

RMCR stands for Residential Mortgage Credit Report. Although the RMCR is in very limited use today, certain loan programs require that the credit bureau verify income, employment and rental or mortgage histories, conduct their own interviews and check public records directly.

Credit Report Order Methodology

There are 3 procedures for ordering credit reports; download from Bulletin Board System via Modem Dial-up, Order on-line via the internet, or Faxing the request to the local credit bureau.

Download Via Internet

Dependent upon the provider, utilize the proprietary interface built into your LOS to request credit reports, download files and receive reports.

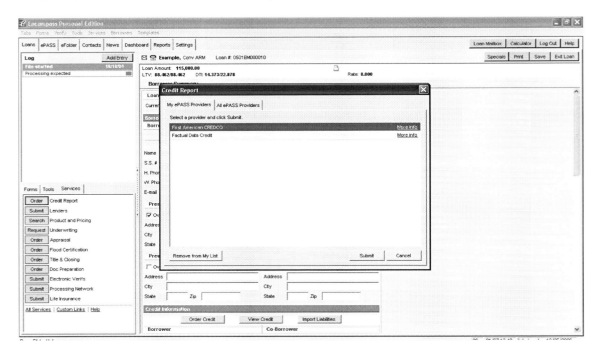

Fax Order

For many full RMCR requests a copy of the application must be faxed or mailed to the credit bureau. You may use a custom letter (Credit Report Request) as a cover letter for this request.

Full Mortgage Credit Report

If there is a significant (more than 3) number of delinquent accounts, a full Residential Mortgage Credit Report (referred to as an RMCR) should be ordered from the provider of the In-File.

Alternative Credit Report

If the borrower has no credit history, an Alternative Credit Report must be requested. Follow the procedures for ordering a full RMCR. This also requires the borrower to provide 12 months cancelled checks for utilities, cable, regular savings deposits.

Business Credit Report

If one of the borrowers owns a Corporation, a Business Credit Report must be requested
This is only applicable if the borrower owns more than 25% of the corporation.

Adverse Summary

When a borrower has negative credit references, the credit bureau will usually provide a summary of derogatory information. This summary should be provided to the borrower in the welcome package. The processor must also indicate in "Loan Tracking – Conditions" a request for an explanation or proof regarding circumstances. The condition should read "Pursuant to Adverse Summary attached – explanation and documentation for Negative Credit References."

Assigned Files

The borrower's file may already have a credit report if the file is assigned. The key concept with an assigned file is to take the extra time to determine what you can do to save the customer money and not damage their credit history with excessive inquiries - which is what you would do if you just order another credit report.

1. Is the credit bureau one of your approved providers? If so, contact them and request a "reprint" of the report with your firm's name on the mast head.
2. Is the credit report a full Residential Mortgage Credit Report? If so make sure that the new report doesn't have omissions or show things that have been corrected on the new report.

Appraisal Order

The Appraisal Request document is generated by the Data Export/Mail Merge. This procedure is for conventional loans only. FHA and VA loans have separate appraiser assignment and request procedures.

Appraisal Checklist

	Choose Approved Vendor – Ensure on Investor's Approved List
	Copy of Vital Portions of Sales Contract if Purchase
	Copy of Survey if Refinance
	If Property Value is over $650,000 require 5 Comparables and Interior Photos
	If Rental/Investment Property include lease Require: • Operating Income Statement • Rental Comparable Schedule
	If 1st & 2nd Mortgage Combination – request 3 copies of appraisal
	Condominiums – Include Condo Questionnaire

Approved Vendors – Appraisers

Mortgage lenders normally maintain an approved list of service providers. Among these, appraisers are the most important, because the appraiser substantiates the value on behalf of the lender. As a lender, the appraiser's relationship is one of client to vendor.

As a broker, the situation is more difficult. Appraisers now have two clients – the broker and the investor. These client's interests are divergent. The broker wants the highest possible value for the sake of the transaction. The investor wants the most accurate value from a portfolio perspective. If the investor refuses the appraisal, it is now the broker's responsibility to pay for an acceptable appraisal, and the valuation concern may again be a concern.

Brokers should actively seek relationships with appraisers who are accepted at the widest number of secondary market outlets, investors and wholesale lenders. In this way they can standardize the process.

Always check the investor's approved list before ordering appraisals.

Appraisal Order Issues

Appraisals for properties worth over $500,000 - $750,000 will often have special requirements. The investor may require additional comparables. Depending on the vendor, the cost for higher value appraisals can be an additional $150 - $350 dollars. Some investors require two appraisals for loans over $1,000,000.

Investment property appraisals for properties which utilize rental income to qualify for the loan will require an operating income/expense statement and a schedule of rental comparables to support to cash flow of the subject. These add additional costs to the appraisal.

For new construction, attached PUDs and condominiums, the appraiser will have to address the project's overall marketability. These will add to the cost.

If the property is a condominium, immediately request the Condominium Pre-Sale Questionnaire be completed by the management company. The processor must verify the percentage of investor owned and multiple unit owners.

Condominium/PUD Questionnaire

When processing a loan in a Condominium (Condo) or Planned Unit Development (PUD) special processing guidelines apply. Just like verifying an applicant's creditworthiness, the project must be evaluated. A property is generally a Condo or PUD if there are monthly assessments for common area maintenance. The borrower or realtor needs to provide a contact for a property manager who can provide the following information.

Condominium/PUD Checklist

	Request Check from Borrower in Amount Required to Complete Pre-Sale Letter
	Print Condo Questionnaire (Data Export - Condo.doc)
	Request Name of Insurance Carrier from Management Agent
	Print and Mail Insurance Request
	Assure Project Meets Guidelines

If possible, obtain verbal information to preliminarily complete the questionnaire pending receipt of the original letter.

Ordering FHA Case Numbers and Appraisals

FHA has joined the 20th Century and created an interface for lenders to order appraisals, case numbers and transmit and receive other information, such as CAVIRs clearance.

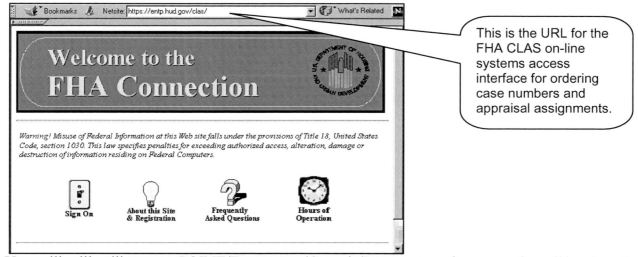

You will still utilize your POINT/Encompass/Genesis/Byte system for generating all copies of the appraisal request forms (9-2800). You must be signed up for this system or call in to your local FHA field office to request FHA Case numbers and appraiser assignments.

VA Online Ordering

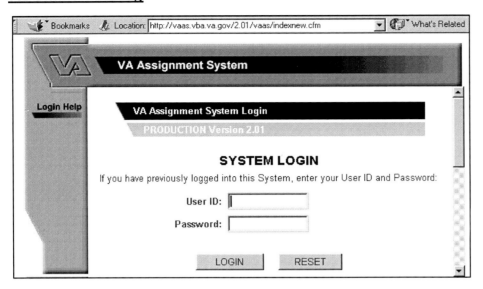

You must be approved to utilize this system or call in to your VA local field office for appraiser assignment.

Condominiums and Government Insured Loans

In order to assure that the loan you are contemplating is in an FHA or VA approved subdivision or condominium you must check the FHA Lenders website and print the page showing the project appears on the approved list. This must be included in your submission.

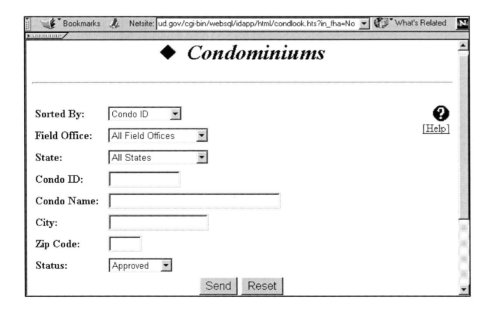

Sending Out Disclosures

One of the pivotal responsibilities of the loan set up process is the initiation of federal and state mandated disclosures. These "early disclosures" are required to be given when any federally related mortgage loan – this means nearly every loan – is initiated to any residential borrower.

These disclosures are mandated by different departments and agencies of the Federal Government. To understand the significance of these disclosures, you must understand the scope of the regulation.

Real Estate Settlement Procedures Act ("RESPA")
Also known as Regulation "X"

Governs Real Estate Transaction Practices

Regulation Title	Practical Application	Disclosure	Highlights/Features of the Law
Real Estate Settlement Procedures Act **RESPA - Regulation X** Department of Housing and Urban Development – HUD (also supervises FHA, GNMA, Housing Programs)	Application	• Good Faith Estimate of Closing Costs • Special Information Booklet - HUD Guide to Closing Costs	Residential Only, < 25 Acres, Lot Loans, Commercial Exempt Deliver to customer within 72 Hours Customer uses special information booklet to shop for services
	Business Practices	Section 8 - Anti-Kickback Provision	No "thing of value" in exchange for referrals. Payment for referral when no service is rendered is considered Kickback. Gifts must be given to all. Penalty – up to $10,000 per
	Business Practices	Controlled/Affiliated Business Arrangement Disclosure	Interested parties must disclose nature of business relationship at time of sale
	Closing	HUD-1 Settlement Statement	24 hours prior to closing borrower may inspect HUD-1
	Application/ Servicing	Transfer of Servicing/Servicing Practices	Signed disclosure within 3 days. Borrower has right to 1.) Annual analysis, 2.) 15 day notice of loan sale from selling and buying lender 3.) Max "cushion" 3 months (2+1) 4.) 60 day Late Charge and Late Payment waiver

Purpose of the Law

The purpose of the law is to protect consumers from excessive settlement costs and unearned fees. RESPA

- Establishes prohibited practices to protect consumers from unearned fees (Kickbacks and Controlled Business Arrangements)
- Allows consumers to obtain information on the costs of closing so that they can shop for settlement services. (Good Faith Estimate and Closing Cost Booklet)
- Gives consumers a complete and accurate accounting of all funds collected and disbursed in conjunction with the transaction. (HUD-1 Settlement Statement)
- To protect customers from financial loss when their loan or the servicing of their loan is sold. (Servicing Practices Act)

Exempt Transactions

- Loans for 25 acres or more
- Loans for business, commercial, or agricultural purposes
- Temporary financing, such as bridge loans
- Loans secured by vacant land

- Loan assumptions which are permissible without lender approval
- Loans sold in the secondary market
- Loan conversions, when a new note is not required and the provisions are consistent with those of the original mortgage

Transactions which ARE subject to RESPA are loans secured by a first or subordinate lien on residential property which are made with funds insured by the federal government, from a lender regulated by the federal government, intended for sale to Fannie Mae or Freddie Mac, or any creditor regulated under the Truth in Lending Act.

RESPA is regulated by HUD

The Department of Housing and Urban Development ("HUD") is the department responsible for issuing implementing regulations (Regulation X) for RESPA and for enforcement of the law. HUD is a large department that also regulates or administers the Government National Mortgage Association (GNMA), Federal Housing Administration (FHA) and many other agencies relating to housing and cities.

Kickbacks and Referral Fees and Fee Splitting

Section 8(a) of RESPA prohibits anyone from giving or receiving a fee, kickback, or "anything of value" pursuant to an "agreement or understanding" for the referral of settlement business. The purpose of the prohibition is to protect consumers from the payment of fees when no additional work is actually performed. Kickbacks tend to increase the cost of the transaction, since the borrower will have to be charged more in order to cover the cost of the referral fee. Penalties for violations of the anti-kickback provision include fines of up to $10,000 and up to one year in prison.

A "Thing of Value"
• Money
• Discounts
• Commissions
• Salaries
• Stock
• Opportunities to participate in a money-making program
• Special or unusual banking terms
• Tickets to theater or sporting events
• Services of all types at special rates
• Trips and payments of another's expenses

The "Agreement or Understanding" does not have to be a formal agreement, but can be a verbal agreement or even an agreement established through a practice, pattern, or course of conduct.

Fee Splitting

Fess splitting is when a service provider inflates charges and splits the excess funds with another service provider in exchange for the referral of business. This is tantamount to a kickback and is a prohibited practice. Service providers may attempt to circumvent this prohibition by establishing joint ventures or entering into business arrangements that allow referrals between organizations and conceal the fee splitting arrangement.

Affiliated and Controlled Business Arrangements

In some cases, there can be fee splitting or referral fees paid under what is known as an "affiliated business arrangement". An affiliated business arrangement is where a person who refers settlement services has an "affiliate relationship" or "an ownership interest of more than one percent in a provider of settlement services."

The payment of fees is acceptable as long as the relationship is disclosed to the borrower and the referrer actually performs a service – or somehow adds value. The referral service provider may NOT be a REQUIRED provider of services, such as an appraiser or credit bureau that the lender must select. In addition, an affiliate relationship structured simply to legitimize a kickback or referral fee is referred to as a "sham". They must be a "Bona Fide Provider of Services" to receive a referral fee legally.

Disclosures - At Application

The Good Faith Estimate of Closing Costs and Special Information Booklet.

The Good Faith Estimate ("GFE") is required to be given at the time of application, or mailed within three business days after completion of loan application. Business days do not include federal holidays, Sundays, or Saturdays.

The GFE is a reasonable estimate of all charges which are due at the time of settlement.

The idea of the Good Faith Estimate of closing costs is to give the borrower advance notice of the costs of the transaction. A properly explained GFE will help borrowers understand their cash requirements better and will result in a borrower who shops less. The reality is that a relatively small portion of the costs reflected on the GFE are paid to the lender whereas the borrower's perception is that they are ALL paid to the lender. The Settlement Costs Booklet, sometimes referred to as the "Special Information Booklet", will help the borrower understand how to shop for settlement services.

The Special Information Booklet

The Special Information Booklet is what HUD calls the Settlement Cost Booklet. The borrower acknowledges receipt of the document at the time that the Good Faith Estimate is signed, so it must be provided at application, or mailed within three business days after completion of loan application.

Loan originators can use their own booklet, or use the HUD booklet entitled, "Buying Your Home", "Understanding Settlement Costs", or any other name that contains prescribed content explaining the settlement process.

Most importantly, this booklet tells borrowers that they have the right to negotiate the terms of a loan and shop for providers of settlement services.

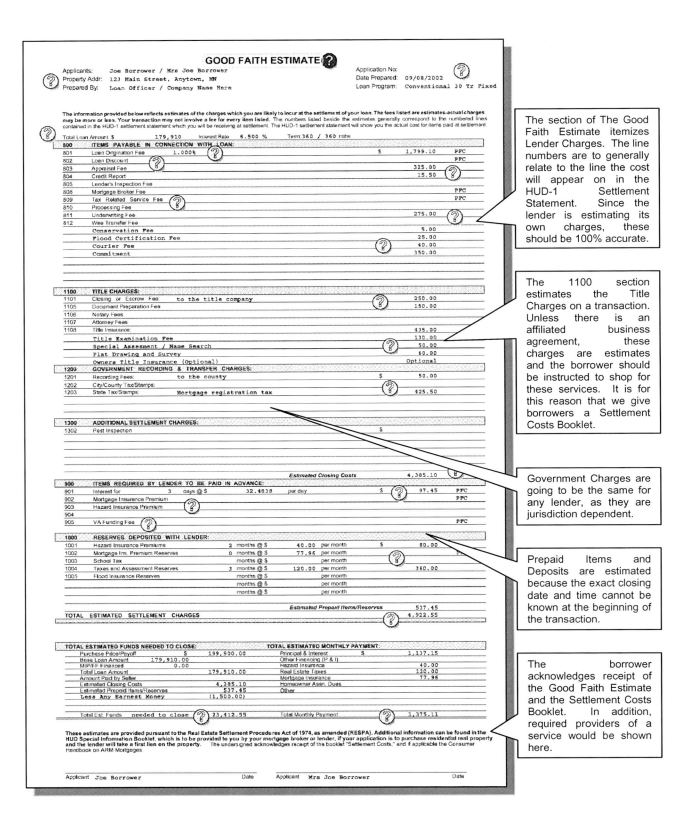

Disclosures - At Application –
Notice of Transfer of Servicing - Mortgage Servicing Disclosure Statement

As with the Good Faith Estimate, the lender must deliver at application, or within 3 business days of application, a statement from the lender telling them that their loan servicing may be transferred to another lender. The Transfer of Servicing disclosure describes the percentage of loans the lender currently intends to sell – from 0-25%, 25-50%, 50-75%, or 75-100%.

In addition, the Transfer of Servicing Act protects the borrower in that

1.) The borrower must be notified 15 days prior to a loan sale by both the selling and purchasing lender
2.) Late payment charges may not be levied within 60 days of the transfer
3.) The borrower's escrow accounts can never include more than a 2 month cushion (plus one current month) for real estate taxes and insurance.

Servicing transfer practices mandates that the borrower receive an escrow analysis at the time of closing, at least annually thereafter, and at the time the loan is sold.

Section 6 of RESPA, the Transfer of Servicing Act, allows consumers to file individual or class actions against loan Servicers for RESPA violations. In individual actions loan Servicers may be liable for damages up to $10,000. In class actions damages may not exceed $1000 for each member of the class and total damages may not exceed $500,000 or 1 percent of the net worth of the Servicer.

Section 10 of RESPA provides special protections for escrow accounts. Failure to submit initial or annual escrow statement can result if a civil penalty of $55 with a $1,000,000 limitation on the penalty for any one loan servicer.

The Truth-in-Lending Act ("TILA")
Also known as Regulation "Z"

Governs the Disclosure Loan Terms and Costs, Regulates Lending Practices

- Applies to Loan Terms

Truth-in-Lending Act TILA Regulation Z Federal Reserve Board	Application/ Closing	APR Disclosure	Truth in Lending delivered to borrower within 3 days of application and again at closing. Owner Occupied Only. Discloses cost of credit, prepayment, late charges and other loan terms.
	Application	ARM Disclosure "Consumer Handbook on Adjustable Rate Mortgages" (CHARM Booklet) "When your Home is on the Line"	If loan is an ARM, borrower receives ARM disclosure (terms, index, history and CHARM (Consumer Handbook on ARMs) Booklet) HELOCs – Borrower receives "When Your Home is on the Line" booklet
	Business Practices	Advertising	Advertised interest rates must give APR at same size. Quoting rates – must quote APR before contract rate.
	Closing	Right of Rescission Final APR Disclosure	Owner Occupied Refinance only. Borrower has 3 day right to cancel transaction. Each borrower must receive 2 copies. Final APR Disclosure must be correct +/- .125% Fixed +/- .25% ARM
	Application/ Closing	Home Ownership Equity Protection Act (Section 32 – High Cost Loans) Disclosure and Truth in Lending.	Loans with rate > 8% (10% for 2nds) over Treasury, > 8 points are considered "High Cost". NO 1.) Negative Amortization, 2.) Balloons < 5 years 3.) Prepayment Penalties 4.) Demand/Call provision 5.) 50% DTI, 6.) Lending without regard to repayment, 7.) HOEPA to HOEPA refi within 12 months, 8.) HELOCs exempt, but may not structure loan as HELOC to avoid. Borrower has 3 days PRIOR to closing + 3 days after Closing to Cancel.

The Board of Governors for the Federal Reserve is the federal agency responsible for issuing implementing regulation (Regulation Z) for TILA and the Federal Trade Commission ("FTC") is responsible for enforcing the law and the regulations.

Purposes of Truth-in-Lending Act

- To protect consumers by disclosing the costs and terms of credit;
- To create uniform standards for stating the cost of credit, thereby encouraging consumers to compare the costs of loans offered by different creditors; and
- To ensure that advertising for credit is truthful and not misleading.

Understanding Truth-in-Lending

Loan officers receive more calls with regard to the Truth In Lending Disclosure than any other form. The Federal Reserve Regulation Z was authorized by the "Truth-in-Lending" Act of 1969. It is such a complex and causes more confusion among borrowers than it resolves. The intent of the Law was to create a uniform method of calculating the cost of credit by developing an APR - Annual Percentage Rate. The APR weighs the monthly payments against the non-interest finance charges on a loan. Another significant aspect of Regulation Z is that it gives borrowers the right to cancel a transaction which results in a lien against their primary residence - a Right of Rescission.

One impetus of the Law was to provide for "early disclosure" of the APR. This means the disclosure must be delivered to the applicant within 3 business days. The purpose of early disclosure of the APR was to allow a consumer to comparison shop and avoid "hidden" finance charges. If this is the reason for the disclosure, it seems contradictory that it would be delivered after a borrower has submitted an application. Every borrower receives the form, though, so it is important to alert them ahead of time. Without the warning the loan officer can expect an angry or panicked call from a customer within the first week of the application process. It is an unfortunate way to start the process, too, because even after a thorough explanation there may be the foundation for mistrust between customer and lender.

The confusion stems from words. Annual Percentage Rate and interest rate mean the same thing to a borrower, though they refer to two different concepts. When the APR appears on a form and is higher than the interest rate discussed during the application there is understandable concern. From the consumer's perspective the APR is the Rate, because most consumer loans, credit cards and car loans carry a simple rate with no fees. Likewise, the phrase "Amount Financed" sounds like lender jargon for the loan amount, but is invariably lower than the amount applied for. "Why was my loan reduced?" is the question. There are 4 boxes on the form. The APR, Finance Charge, Amount Financed, and Total of Payments. Then there is a Payment Schedule, followed by a number of other disclosures describing the loan terms.

To understand the Truth-in-Lending Disclosure (TIL) start with the concept that it is only a theoretical measure of the cost of credit. For example: If you borrow $100, but there is a $1 charge for the loan, then you really have only received $99 in usable cash. However, you will still make payments on the loan based upon the $100 principal balance. The TIL determines what the theoretical rate on the loan is considering the fact that there was a fee due to make the loan - that is the APR. The $1 in this example is a finance charge.

The first step in determining APR is to subtract the prepaid finance charges from the loan amount. The result is the Amount Financed. Then the full principal and interest payment (including PMI) is applied against the Amount Financed as if it were the loan amount. The resulting interest rate is the APR. There are some nuances.

Determining the Amount Financed - What are Finance Charges?

Everything paid for in exchange for obtaining a loan is considered a prepaid finance charge. Loan Fees include discount points, origination fees, Private Mortgage Insurance, miscellaneous fees such as Tax Service, Underwriting, Document Preparation, and Lender Review Fees. In addition, prepaid items such as per diem interest and escrows for PMI or prepaid PMI, FHA One Time MIP, and the VA Funding Fee are considered finance charges. Interestingly, appraisal fees, credit reports, termite reports and other inspections such as completion inspections (except for construction loan draw inspections), well and septic inspections which are required by lenders are not considered finance charges. Neither are fees for recording a deed of trust. These are excluded from the amount financed calculation because - theoretically, anyway - would be incurred by a buyer or borrower regardless of whether a loan was involved or, in the case of the appraisal and credit report, are required to determine if a loan will be made and are "passed through" to service providers.

There is a catch. Any item that the borrower does not pay for is not included in the calculation. This would be the case when a property seller is contractually obligated to pay the fees, or in a Lender Funded closing cost situation.

Payment Schedule

The Payment Schedule is the second half of the APR equation. If you borrow $100 and you have $99 to use, how are you repaying the $100? On a fixed rate loan, the payment schedule is quite simple - the monthly payment is the same through the life of the loan. There are variations which impact the payment schedule.

PMI is considered a finance charge. The initial PMI premium, MIP or Funding Fee must be considered in the amount financed. If there is money placed in escrow for PMI or MIP, this is considered in the amount financed as well. Generally Private Mortgage Insurance premium plans call for a significant reduction in premium rates after the 10th year. This must be factored into the payment schedule. With the FHA Monthly MIP, the premium is based upon the loan balance so that, while it never goes away, the premium declines until the loan is paid off.

Variable payments are also a factor when there are changing payments on the loan as in an ARM, Buydown, GEM, or GPM. The payment schedule varies in these situations. *To determine the payment amount to apply against the Amount Financed the **number of payments from the payment schedule to derive an average payment divides the Total Payments**. **The Total of Payments** are the cumulative amount of all of the scheduled payments.*

It is important to note that buydowns, GPMs and GEMs have fixed payment schedules, and so the APR on these loans will not change. ARMs have a payment schedule which may vary depending on interest rate changes.

The payment schedules for the initial TIL disclosure of an ARM is based upon current the current index information. The disclosure states that the APR can change. The payment schedule should be based upon the initial rate, and show the changes that would occur as if the rate were changing today.

Finance Charge

The APR, Amount Financed and Total of Payments have been calculated as explained above. What is the total finance charge? The difference between the Total of Payments and the Amount Financed represents the cumulative total of all interest and prepaid finance charges accrued on the loan. Subtracting the Amount Financed from the Total of Payments reveals this number.

Other Considerations

Program Disclosures - work in tandem with the Truth-in-Lending Statement and should be given in conjunction with the TIL. They explain more fully the historical performance of the ARM, when the consumer has applied for one. All programs should have disclosure describing fully how the payment schedule works, whether there is any prepayment penalty, late charges, tax and insurance escrow treatments, due on sale clauses and any other nuances of the program.

The "Refund of the Prepaid Finance Charge" - Again terminology can cause confusion between the intended meaning of a phrase and how the consumer interprets it. In the context of the TIL, this applies to Prepayment and Mortgage Insurance. In the event that there is prepaid Mortgage Insurance, such as the Up Front FHA MIP, Monthly FHA MIP or traditional prepaid or financed PMI, if the loan is paid off early the consumer may receive the cancellation value of that insurance. Consumers sometimes equate the Finance Charge box from the TIL with this statement and assume they will still be obligated for the interest under the loan, even though the loan is paid off.

Recording Fees/Security Interest - Even though they are not included in the finance charge, fees to record a deed of trust in the jurisdiction are shown. All mortgages loans are secured by a property, the address of which should be shown.

Late Charge - Stating the what the late payment percentage (Normally 4% for Government 5% for Conventional) is, when the payment is considered late, and that it is based on the Principal and Interest portion of the payment only.

Assumption - Stating whether the loan is assumable. There are no new unconditionally assumable loans being made institutionally. Some loans are assumable with the new borrower's approval by the existing lender. However, even if assumption is allowed, many lenders will change the terms to reflect the current market or disallow the assumption.

Insurance - States what insurance is required for the loan.

APR (Annual Percentage Rate) The cost of your credit as a yearly rate.	FINANCE CHARGE The dollar amount the credit will cost you.	AMOUNT FINANCED The amount of credit provided to you on your behalf.	TOTAL OF PAYMENTS The amount you will have paid after you have made all payments as scheduled.
① %	$ ②	$ ③	$ ④

1.) Compute **total of payments** by multiplying payment schedule, including PMI by amount of payments
2.) **Amount Financed** is the loan amount, less points, prepaid interest, PMI, and lender fees.
3.) **Finance Charge** is the **Total of Payments** less the **Amount Financed**
4.) Compute the **APR** by dividing the **Total of Payments** by the number of payments and apply that against the **Amount Financed**, as if it were the loan amount.

APR Tolerance

At the time of application the borrower receives an Annual Percentage Rate disclosure, also referred to as a "T-I-L", or APR disclosure. During the process of the loan, if the terms of the loan change, the lender must re-disclose the APR. If the terms do not change, the APR must still be re-disclosed at closing. That FINAL Truth-in-Lending statement must be correct as to the actual loan terms. The margin of error for the final disclosure is referred to as "tolerance".

Loan Type	Tolerance
Fixed	0.125% up or down, for a total of .25%
ARM	0.250% up or down, for a total of .50%

Determining the Amount Financed - What are Prepaid Finance Charges?

Everything that one must pay for in exchange for obtaining a loan (charges you wouldn't incur if you were paying cash for the property) is considered a prepaid finance charge. This includes loan fees such as discount points, origination fees, private mortgage insurance; miscellaneous fees such as tax service, underwriting, document preparation, and lender review fees. In addition, prepaid items such as per diem interest and escrows for PMI or prepaid PMI, FHA upfront MIP, and the VA funding fee are considered finance charges. So are credit life insurance premiums. Interestingly, appraisal fees, credit reports, termite reports and other inspections such as completion inspections (except for construction loan draw inspections), well and septic inspections that are required by lenders are not considered finance charges. Neither are fees for recording a deed of trust. These are excluded from the amount-financed calculation because a buyer or borrower would incur them regardless of whether a loan was involved. Appraisal and credit report fees are "passed through" to service providers.

The APR disclosure is given again at the time of closing in final form. The initial APR disclosure may be incorrect, but the final APR disclosure must be accurate to within .125% in rate.

At Application – ARM Disclosure

If the loan is an Adjustable Rate Mortgage (a Variable Rate Transaction) the borrower must also receive an ARM disclosure at the time of application.

The ARM disclosure gives the specific details of how the ARM interest rate can change – how often the rate changes, what the initial and periodic changes are based on (the margin and index) and how much the interest rate can change at the adjustment (caps). The ARM disclosure must provide a specific example of how the interest rate would have changed based on historical examples.

In addition to the ARM disclosure, the borrower must receive The Consumer Handbook on Adjustable Rate Mortgages ("CHARM" Booklet), which explains how ARMs, in general, work.

Home Equity Lines and Open-Ended Credit

Closed-end credit is credit that is advanced for a specific time with a fixed schedule of payments. Purchase money mortgages are an example of closed-end credit. Open-end credit is consumer credit that is used repeatedly - the consumer pays a finance charge on the outstanding balance. A home equity line of credit is an example of open-end credit. Open-ended lines of credit, such as home equity lines of credit, require additional disclosures.

When Your Home is on the Line

The Booklet "When Your Home is on the Line - What You Should Know About Home Equity Lines of Credit" is provided by the Federal Reserve and describes how failure to repay the loan could result in the loss of the consumer's dwelling. In addition, negative amortization may occur, resulting in an increase in the principal balance and a reduction in equity in the home. The consumer should consult with a tax advisor regarding the deductibility of interest and charges.

Notice of Right to Cancel (Right to Rescind)

Rescission is a legal remedy that voids a contract between two parties, restoring each to the position held prior to the transaction. No right to rescind exists for purchase money mortgages. Home equity credit lines or refinancing of credit already secured by the borrower's principal dwelling are transactions which are subject to a right of rescission.

Creditors must provide two copies of the notice of right to rescind on a document that is separate from other disclosures. They must provide each party who has a right to rescind with a copy of the notice.

The notice states that there is a security interest in the borrower's principal dwelling, instructions on how to exercise the right to rescind, including a form with the borrower can use, and stating the creditor's business address, the date the right of rescission expires.

For a fixed term loan, the closing date establishes the timing for rescission. With a line of credit or open-end transaction, such as a home equity credit line, the rescission period starts when a.) the credit plan is opened and loan documents are signed, b.) credit extensions are made above previously established limits, or c.) a security interest is added or increased to secure an existing plan

Waiver of Right to Rescind

A consumer can waive the right to rescind in situations in which credit is needed "…to meet a bona fide financial emergency." The waiver must include a description of the emergency and signatures of all parties that have a right to rescind a particular transaction.

Three Day Right to Cancel

In calculating the time limitations for the right to rescind, note that "business days" include Saturdays.

Regulations - Advertising

TILA governs the advertising of consumer credit. An advertisement – which is "any offer to extend credit" that states in interest rate must also state an "annual percentage rate", using the term "APR". The APR must have the same prominence as the contract interest rate advertised.

The act does not require the disclosure of lending terms in an advertisement, but an advertisement may not mislead consumers by promoting the most advantageous terms of a loan while failing to mention other terms that are less attractive. For example, an advertisement cannot offer consumers a loan with "low monthly payments" without also stating the number of payments, the interest rate (expressed as an APR), down payment, monthly payments, and other terms related to the cost of the loan

Section 32 of Truth-in-Lending Act – HOEPA

This act is also known as the Home Ownership and Equity Protection Act ("HOEPA"). It is the Federal high cost loan law. Congress amended TILA in 1994 to protect consumers from a number of "predatory" lending practices associated with high cost loans. HOEPA is enforced by the Federal Trade Commission.

Loans Subject to Section 32

HOEPA covers closed-end home equity loans and refinance mortgages that meet certain interest rate and points/fee triggers.

Interest Rate Trigger

For 1st lien mortgages the rate trigger is **8 percentage points** above the rate of Treasury securities with a comparable maturity.

For 2nd or subordinate liens, the rate trigger is **10 percentage points**.

Points and Fees Trigger

A loan is classified as high cost if 8% or more of the loan amount (or $510 - adjusted annually for 2005) is charged for loan related fees. Points and fees include loan points, mortgage broker fees, loan service fees, fees of a required closing agent, premiums for mortgage insurance, and debt protection fees.

Section 32 Disclosures

Three days prior to closing, the borrower must receive a disclosure stating the amount borrowed, whether credit debt-cancellation insurance is included, or whether there is a balloon. The APR disclosure must be given with large, 32 point bold type across the top stating the borrower is not required to complete the transaction and that loss of the home could result from the loan if payments are not met.

Section 32 Prohibitions

On high cost loans lenders are prohibited from "loan flipping" which is defined as the repeated refinancing of a loan with no true benefit to the borrower. No HOEPA loan can be refinanced within twelve months of the initial extension of credit unless the refinancing is in the borrower's interest. Lender must assure the borrower can qualify for the loan – no lending without regard to the borrower's ability to repay. There may be no direct payments to home improvement contractors. Negative Amortization and interest rate acceleration features are prohibited.

- Due on Demand Clauses are only allowed to protect the creditor from misrepresentation or from any action by the borrower that adversely affects the lender's security for the loan.
- Balloon Payments are not allowed for loans with terms of less than five years, except for bridge loans.
- Advance payments are restricted, and do not allow from more than two periodic payments to be paid from the proceeds of the loan.
- Prepayment penalties can only be assessed within the first five years of the loan.
- Single Premium Credit Life insurance premiums may be financed, but the cost must be included as part of the APR calculation.

Penalties for HOEPA Violations

Creditors who violate HOEPA may be liable for all the finance charges and fees paid by the borrower. In class action suits, damages are limited to $500,000 or 1% of the creditor's net worth.

Equal Credit Opportunity Act ("ECOA") and Fair Housing Act
Also known as Regulation "B"

Regulates how decisions are made and prohibits discrimination in lending

Equal Credit Opportunity Act ECOA and Fair Housing Act Regulation B Federal Trade Commission	Application	Non-Discrimination Disclosure "Decisioning" Guidelines	No discrimination on Race/Ethnicity, Gender, Childbearing, Age. Cannot discourage applicant from applying. Must give written notice of status within 30 days. Credit report, app, pre-qualification starts timing. Borrower has right to appraisal copy.
	Processing	Fair Credit Reporting	State ALL reasons and provide all sources for adverse information. Borrower may receive copy of credit report.

Purpose

The purpose Equal Credit Opportunity Act is to discriminatory treatment against credit applicants. The Federal Reserve is authorized to promulgate regulations for implementation of ECOA known as Regulation B.

The enforcement of ECOA is left to the regulatory institutions that supervise the lending activities of particular institutions. Banks are regulated by The Office of the Comptroller of the Currency, the Office of Thrift Supervision, Federal Deposit Insurance Corporation, The Board of Governors of the Federal Reserve, National Credit Union Administration. Mortgage Bankers and Brokers are regulated by The Federal Trade Commission ("FTC"). The FTC has enforcement responsibility that is not specifically delegated to another agency.

Unlawful Inquiries

Lenders may not base decisions on questions regarding marital status, gender, child bearing, race, color, religion, or national origin, or age. Lenders may not make oral or written statement that would discourage prospective applicants from applying for a loan.

Prohibitions

Lenders may not refuse to consider public assistance as income, assume a woman of childbearing age will stop work to raise children, refuse to consider income from a pension, annuity, or retirement benefit or refuse to consider regular alimony or child support. Borrowers don't have to disclose alimony and child support unless they want to use it as qualifying income.

Notification Requirements

Timing requirements are the most critical elements as to mortgage applications and ECOA regulations. Lenders MUST notify consumers of action taken on an application within 30 days of its receipt.

Lenders must provide notification of ALL reasons for adverse action. In addition, notification is required when loan terms are changed for any reason, if an application is withdrawn, whether additional information is required, or even if the customer withdraws the loan.

Lenders must disclose all bases for making decisions. As a consequence, the borrower may receive a copy of all documents used in making the loan decision. This includes the appraisal, credit report or any other 3rd party verification.

Penalties

Violations of ECOA are subject to civil penalties of up to $10,000 in individual actions or $500,000 or 1% of the creditor's net worth in class actions.

Fair Housing Act

The Fair Housing Act is enforced in conjunction with ECOA by the Federal Trade Commission and the department of Housing and Urban Development, and is designed to prevent housing discrimination. Since discrimination in Housing is more pervasive and more difficult to document, Department of Housing and Urban Development and the Federal Trade Commission each have "shoppers" who will pose as buyers or renters to determine if discrimination is present.

The Fair Housing Act prohibits Discrimination on the basis of race, color, religion, gender, handicap, familial status or national origin in residential real-estate related transactions.

The Fair Housing Act prohibits "redlining" which is the practice of denying applicants loans in certain neighborhoods, even though they would otherwise be eligible for credit. Racial redlining has been held to be illegal, and lenders and appraisers cannot use this as a basis for credit or value determination.

HUD is the agency responsible for issuing regulations and for enforcement pursuant to the Fair Housing Act. Violations of the law are reported to HUD. If an administrative law judge finds that a discriminatory housing practice has occurred, financial penalties may be imposed. Penalties are more severe if there is a finding of a "pattern or practice" of discrimination.

Fair Credit Reporting Act ("FCRA")

The purpose of FCRA is to ensure accuracy and privacy of information used by credit reporting agencies. The Federal Trade Commission enforces FCRA. Under this act, consumers have the right to correct errors on their credit reports, and may require a written request prior to release of his or her credit report.

Chapter 7 Bankruptcies over ten years old and other negative information that is more than seven years old unless must be removed.

Many of the provisions of the FCRA allow consumers to repair incorrect items or have them deleted if the creditor cannot substantiate them.

The Fair and Accurate Credit Transactions Act ("FACTA")

Effective December 1, 2004, a phase in of FACTA began, allowing consumers to obtain free copies of their credit reports. The phase in was completed in September, 2005. This provision of the Fair Credit Reporting Act allows the consumer to block the accounts that may have been opened as a result of identity theft and allows consumers to place a fraud alert on their credit report to keep new accounts from being opened.

Home Mortgage Disclosure Act ("HMDA")
Also known as Regulation "C"

Governs the Disclosure of Lender Data to the Public

Home Mortgage Disclosure Act **HMDA Regulation C** Federal Reserve Board	Application	1003 Data Collection	Lenders must reporting data. Federal Reserve compiles to identify discriminatory practices. Request Borrower Data – Must guess if borrower refuses. State "Lender Designation".

HMDA is a reporting law that allows the Federal Reserve to determine if depository institutions are meeting the housing needs of their communities to identify discriminatory lending practices. This data adds in the determination of how to distribute public-sector investments.

Depository Institutions Subject to the Act

Banks that have a branch office in a metropolitan area, have originated at least one home purchase or refinance during the preceding year and are federally-insured or regulated, or originate loans that are federally-insured, or intended to be sold to Freddie Mac or Fannie Mae.

HMDA also applies to not-for-profit institutions which originated home purchase or refinance loans that equaled 10% of its loan-origination volume, were at least $25 million or more than 100 home purchase loans. State-chartered or state-licensed financial institutions are exempt.

Reportable Events and Transactions

Institutions must report data on loan originations, purchases and applications. They must also report pre-approval requests.

- The purpose and amount to the loan;

- The action taken on the loan;
- The location of the property related to the loan;
- The owner/occupant status of the property;
- Ethnicity, race, sex, and income of the applicant;
- The difference between the loan's APR and the yield on Treasury securities with comparable periods of maturity.
- If the difference is greater than 3 percentage points for first liens on a principal dwelling,
- or greater than 5 percentage points for loans secured by subordinate liens;
- Identification of a loan that is subject to HOEPA

This data helps to show if different or more onerous lending terms are offered to different loan applicants on the basis of personal characteristics such as ethnicity, race, or sex.

Data Collection

Lenders collect HMDA data on the Real Estate Loan Application Form 1003. The form requests that loan applicants disclose information on their national origin, race, and sex, but allows them to opt out of providing the information. Lenders must attempt to collect this data, and must designate the data if the borrower refuses.

Community Reinvestment Act (CRA)

Enacted in 1977, the CRA is intended to encourage depository institutions to meet the credit needs of the communities where they are located. The Federal Reserve System, the Federal Deposit Insurance Corporation, the Office of the Comptroller of the Currency, and the Office of Thrift Supervision conduct periodic examinations of the depository institutions which they supervise in order to determine if the institutions are meeting the credit needs of their communities, particularly those communities characterized by low incomes.

Home Owner's Protection Act

Congress passed the Homeowners Protection Act in 1997 to protect consumers from excessive payments on private mortgage insurance (PMI). PMI protects the lender if a borrower defaults on a loan. The risk of default decreases over time, thereby reducing the need for PMI.

PMI Cancellation

When the LTV reaches 78% PMI cancellation is automatic, and does not require a borrower's request. Although the law does not apply to FHA loans, FHA made a change to its MIP premium structure to drop the Monthly MIP portion of the borrower's monthly payment, based upon projected amortization (for example – after 12 years on a 30 year fixed rate mortgage).

If the LTV reaches 80% based on the value of the home at the time of the loan origination, and the borrower requests termination, lenders are forced to honor the request.

These provisions apply to mortgages closed on or after July 29, 1999. PMI for loans closed before that date can be cancelled at the borrower's request after he/she has paid 20% of the principal on the loan. The provisions of the Homeowners Protection Act do NOT apply to FHA-insured or VA guaranteed loans.

Gramm-Leach-Bliley Act

Informational privacy is an issue of increasing concern to Americans, and both state and federal legislators have responded by offering statutory solutions. In response to this need Congress created the Gramm-Leach-Bliley Act (GLB Act) of 1999. Under this law, financial institutions, including mortgage brokers, are required to provide notice to consumers about their information practices, and to give consumers an opportunity to direct that their personal information not be shared with non-affiliated third parties. This is referred to as "opting out" of information sharing.

The anti-Pretexting provision of GLB provides that financial institutions may not contact a consumer who has opted out, and ask them to allow the release of financial information under the pretext of maintaining their accounts.

USA Patriot Act

The USA Patriot Act of 2001, enacted because of terrorist attacks, impacts mortgage lending by requiring Borrower Identification and by requiring that private financial information be released to the government. The Act requires increased due diligence by banks, trust companies, savings associations and credit unions in establishing the identity of consumers who apply for loans. Proof of identity will be required, even in lending institutions where the consumer has a long-standing account. In addition the act overrides the FCRA is a consumer-protection statute. The Patriot Act requires consumer reporting agencies to furnish all information regarding a consumer to a government agency if the government certifies that the records are relevant to intelligence action in response to terrorist threats or activities.

The Nature of "Disclosures"

The critical issue with disclosures is that they must be sent to the borrower. Under most circumstances – again dependent on the underwriter and investor - the borrower does not have to sign and initial disclosures because the documents will be signed again at closing. The processor must be able to prove that the documents were delivered. For this reason, it is important to document what was sent and on what date.

Handling Missing Documentation

Dependent on the manner of the application, the supporting documentation may be complete, partially complete or there may be no information at all.

To ascertain the missing documentation in a loan file, utilize the complete application checklist to review file documents. REMEMBER THE SETUP POSITION IS NOT A PRE-UNDERWRITING FUNCTION. THE PURPOSE IS TO REQUEST OR FOLLOW UP STANDARD BORROWER PROVIDED DOCUMENTATION.

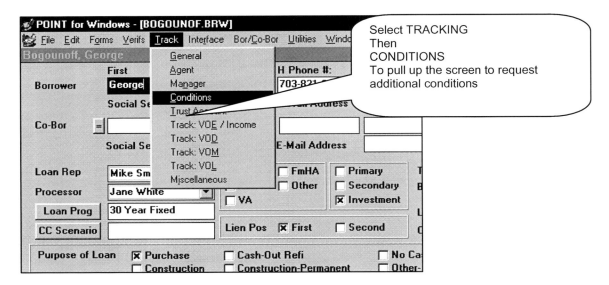

Then going through each item in the file, identify the missing documentation and enter it in the CONDITIONS fields. These documents are logged in as required prior to submission.

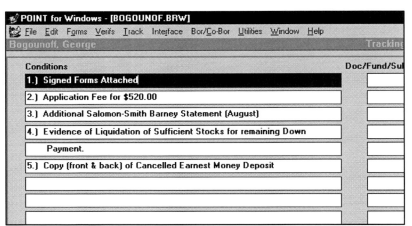

One manner of checking the documentation requirements against the provided material is by assembling the file in the required stack order. As the file is assembled and entered into the computer, deficiencies are to be listed under "TRACKING – CONDITIONS" in numerical order.

A file with no documentation contingencies should be passed immediately to the processor to expedite submission to underwriting.

There are two methods of reporting the outstanding items required of the borrower within the welcome kit. Include these as part of the (Welcome Letter.doc) by including merge codes for these fields in your merge letter, or print the "Conditions" list. Or you may use a handwritten complete application checklist to communicate missing items.

```
                         C O N D I T I O N S
                         ===================
  File No      - BOGOUNOF                    Date/Time - 09/02/1999 4:44PM
  Borrower     - George Bogounoff             Days in process -

  Property     - 3815 S Street, NW
                 Washington, DC 20007
  Loan Agent   - tmortgan
  Processor    - Jane White

  Condition                                                       Doc/Fund/Sub
  1.)  Signed Forms Attached
  2.)  Application Fee for $520.00
  3.)  Additional Salomon-Smith Barney Statement (August)
  4.)  Evidence of Liquidation of Sufficient Stocks for remaining Down
         Payment.
  5.)  Copy (front & back) of Cancelled Earnest Money Deposit
```

The "Conditions" list should be attached to the Welcome Letter as an attachment.

The Welcome Package - Borrower Introduction

The "Welcome Package" is really the preliminary disclosure kit and Equal Credit Opportunity act compliance. However, it is used to squarely place upon the borrower the requirements to complete their loan application and outline the schedule to complete their closing.

Welcome Package Checklist

	Welcome Letter (welcome.doc)
	Conditions (printed from point)
	Closing Requirement Checklist
	Preliminary Application (1003) Stamped "Preliminary Application"
	Borrower's Authorization & Certification
	Truth-in-Lending/Regulation Z Disclosure
	Questions and Answers regarding Truth-in-Lending Disclosure
	Product Disclosure(ARM/ Balloon/Buydown)
	Consumer Handbook on ARMs
	Good Faith Estimate of Closing Costs - Copy of Loan Officer's Good Faith Estimate, highlighting items included in "Finance Charge"
	HUD Booklet – Closing Costs
	Lock-in Agreement
	Transfer of Servicing Disclosure
	Request for Copy of Tax Return (IRS) - 4506
	Credit Report Adverse Information Summary

Sample Complete Application Checklist

The following information is needed to complete your loan application. Your cooperation in providing these items quickly will expedite the processing of your loan.

COMPLETE APPLICATION CHECKLIST
Personal/Financial Information

Complete Address for:
___ Landlord: _____
___ Phone Number: _____
                             Current Lender: _____
___ Account Number:
                             Current Lender: _____
___ Account Number:
     Other _____

Financial Documentation
Copies of ___ Most Recent Paystubs Covering 30 Day Period ___ W-2 Forms For 2006, 2007, 2008 (circle) ___ Federal Tax Form 1040 (with all Schedules Attached) for 2006, 2007, 2008 (circle) if you are a commissioned sales person, have any bonus income, rental income, or income from other sources, these forms are required even if you do not consider yourself self-employed) Please sign these forms in original prior to submitting them to us. ___ Federal Corporate Tax Returns Form 1120 or 1120S (with all Schedules attached) for 2006, 2007, 2008 (circle) or applicable 2 year fiscal years. Please sign in original before submitting to us. ___ 2 (or 3) Most Recent Months Bank Statements - all pages. Please include Savings, Checking, Investment, Stock, Mutual Fund, 401(k), IRA and Keogh Accounts. ___ Year to Date Income and Expense Statement (Profit & Loss) and Balance Sheet. Must be signed by preparer.
Ancillary Documentation
___ Copy of Green Card (Alien Registration – if less than 2 years in country) ___ Divorce Decree/Separation Agreement ___ Transcripts/Diploma ___ Proof of Loans Paid Off in Last 3 Months ___ Copies of Note(s) Held ___ Proof of Social Security, Pension, or Disability Income. Please provide copies of award letters and checks. ___ Child Support - 12 Months Cancelled Checks ___ Trust Agreement - Copy of Trust, Documentation verifying underlying value.
Real Estate Information
___ Copy of Sales Contract - Subject Property ___ Copy of Sales Contract - Current Home ___ Copy of Deed/Deed of Trust - Subject Property ___ Settlement Statement for any Property Sold in last 12 months ___ 12 Month Payment History for Current Mortgage(s) ___ Current Leases for all Rental Property. Expired leases must be accompanied by signed extensions. ___ Pre-Sale Questionnaire Completed by Management Company.. Condominium Documents as requested on Closing Requirement Checklist attached.
Letters of Explanation
___ Gift(s), with Donor Verification. Form & Instructions attached ___ Credit Problems/Inquiries - Credit Report attached ___ Reason for Refinance ___ Gap in Employment/Job History ___ Increase in Account Balance/Large Deposits
Other Information
___ Check in the amount of $_____ ___ 5 Days Prior to closing - all documents required on Closing Requirement Checklist ___ _____ ___ _____

Direct Verifications

When certain documentation is not available from the borrower, we request the information directly from the source by sending a request for verification. We print the form directly from the loan processing software, and attach a copy of the Borrower's Signed Certification and Authorization.

Many banks require payment for Deposit Verification. (VOD) In most cases the borrower provides adequate bank statements. We do not request bank verifications unless the borrower is unable to provide statements, or does/will not have sufficient funds until just prior to closing.

Employment Verification (VOE) is required if the borrower has been on the current job for less than 2 years. All investment property loans and FHA loans require direct verification of all listed accounts. If a borrower has been renting the current residence, require landlord verification. (VOM-VOR) If a mortgage or other account is listed on the application, but does not appear on the credit report, request a Verification of Liability (VOL)

Direct Verification Checklist

Circumstance	Yes/No	If No Must Verify
3 Months Bank Statements?		VOD
Sufficient Funds for Closing per 1003?		VOD
2 Years Employment, Same Employer?		VOE
Owner Occupied?		VOE, VOD, VOL, VOR
Mortgage on Credit Report, Cancelled Checks in File?		VOM
Currently Renting, Cancelled Checks in File?		VOR
All Loans listed on application on Credit Report?		VOL
Conventional Loan?		VOE, VOD, VOL, VOR

File Order

Since the mortgage process is basically one of substantiating all facets of a borrower's creditworthiness, a file is established to assemble all of the supporting documentation accumulated in support of the decision. Depending on the loan type there is different documentation required, but it falls into the same basic categories.

The left side of the file is basically a correspondence and chronological order file. Closing requirements are stored here for use by the closing department. All conversations are recorded on the conversation log.

The right side of the file is the "Credit Package". All of the verified information is accumulated in this order for eventual underwriting review. While there is a detailed stack order following this section which will guide the uninitiated, there is logic to the order. It follows the application order. The application is the information which the borrower has provided. Substantiation of each section follows the section of the application to which it belongs.

<u>Left Side (top to bottom)</u>
Loan Status Report
Conversation Log
Items Required to Complete
Lock-in/Registration
Closing Requirements
- Hazard Insurance
- Title Binder
- Survey
- Termite Report
- Well/Septic
- Final Inspection
Pre-Application Kit
Copy of Application Fee
Correspondence and all
Other Miscellaneous Information

<u>Right Side (Top to Bottom)</u>

Application Documents
Credit Information
Income Information
Asset Information
Property Information
Disclosures

See Following Section for Detailed Order of Credit Package

Section III is the borrower's general information, including social security number. It simply makes sense to have the credit report verifying all of the borrower's personal identity first in the file order. In addition, it tells the most important part of the story to the underwriter – how is this borrower at paying bills? Section IV is the employment section, so it makes sense to verify the income information next. Section VI is assets and liabilities, so this is where we start with Deposit Verifications. Then the real estate schedule – and items such as leases would go here. "Details of transaction" follows so there is the sales contract. Last are all the regulatory compliance issues – such as disclosures.

Within each section we go from most recent to old; most important to least; most liquid to least – so the most critical items are addressed first in each section.

Chapter 4 – Documentation Review
Reviewing Credit and Payment History Related Items

The credit card application process is a "raw" credit experience. You are analyzed on the data that is contained in the repositories. One of the benefits of the mortgage process is that the borrower has the opportunity to address and correct items that arise during the process.

Credit Bureaus vs. Credit Repositories

The credit repositories do provide direct reports to the public. It is this direct report that a car dealer or bank will examine when deciding to grant credit. These reports are referred to in the mortgage business as an "in-file" report. This report is the "raw" data contained in the database. There are now companies that will merge 2, 3, 4 or 5 repository reports into one "in-file" report that can give a wider review of an applicant's history. The credit repositories do not make changes to data. Only a creditor or reporting subscriber can change the data recorded among the repository. Repositories are not very customer friendly.

Credit Bureaus are service providers to the mortgage industry. They assemble data and present it in a "decoded" format merging data from multiple repositories. In addition, they may verify employment and check accounts like landlords or mortgages which are listed but not reported. This "decoded" format is referred to as a "Standard Factual Data Credit Report". This format allows huge flexibility for mortgage lenders because, regardless of what data the repositories report, the customer may refute that information. With compelling documentation a bureau can:

1. confirm and eliminate duplicate accounts
2. delete accounts that appear to belong to someone else
3. verify that late accounts are misreported
4. update balances on accounts that have been paid

The old adage regarding first impressions is true in this respect. An underwriter may be jaundiced in the loan review process if a borrower's credit history appears immediately negative. To present an applicant's credit history in the best possible light some bureaus go so far as to present all of the accounts which were paid timely on the first page. Then, at the end of the report, show all negative accounts.

It is important to remember that, no matter how much a borrower accomplishes with an individual credit bureau, the information in the repositories is not updated when a standard factual data report is modified. Only the creditor or subscriber can modify information with the repository directly. This can present a problem if significant modifications have been made and a loan is submitted to a reviewer who compares "in-file" data to the factual reports.

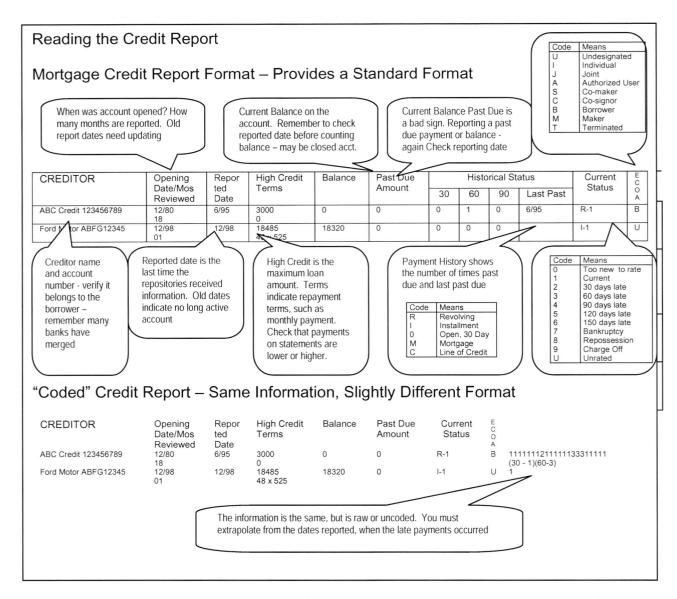

An individual's largest debt or obligation is normally the housing expense. Because having a roof over your head takes precedence over anything else, the percentage of your income devoted to housing expenses is called the first ratio, housing expense ratio or front ratio.

Then there are the other debts that must be repaid, such as credit cards, car loans, other loans for education and debt consolidation. Any other obligation, such as alimony, child support, or regular payments for maintenance of negative cash flows on rental properties or mortgages must also be considered. The total debt is then added to the housing expense in total. The sum of these two obligations, when compared to income is referred to as the second, back, or total expense ratio.

The Housing Expense Ratio

Following are the components of the Housing Expense Ratio, also known as PITI:

- Principal and interest payment
- 1/12 of the annual real estate tax
- 1/12 of the annual premium for Homeowner's Insurance
- 1/12 of the renewal premium for Private Mortgage Insurance
- the monthly homeowner's association fee for a condominium or a townhouse
- payment for any ground lease/land lease

Assume, as a starting point, that the maximum housing expense one can afford is 28% of gross monthly income. The question being answered is, "how much can I really afford to pay monthly for my home?" Numbers are only as good as the information you apply against them. For the loan officer, it is important to understand how to manipulate them.

Playing with Principal

Reducing interest rate/payment is the simplest way to achieve additional qualifying power. The example utilizes 28% as the maximum housing expense. A 2% reduction in interest rate can dramatically increase the maximum loan amount. How do you achieve interest rate or payment reduction?

Illustration of Changing Interest Rate Impacting Loan Size		
Based on Income of		$ 4,166.00
Qualifying Ratio %	28%	$ 1,166.48
Less Tax & Insurance		$ (250.00)
Maximum Principal & Interest		$ 916.48
At rate of	9%	7%
Results in Maximum Loan of	$ 113,902	$ 137,754

- Changing program to a lower rate programs: a 7-year or 5-year program may carry a lower than 30 year fixed rate. An adjustable rate mortgage with start rate qualification might achieve the objective. Keep in mind that many ARMs have minimum qualifying rates.
- Subsidizing the monthly payment for a fixed period of time with a temporary buydown.
- Extending the amortization period of the loan from 30 to 40 years.

Playing With Other Components of the Front Ratio

We have shown how reducing the interest rate increases the maximum loan amount. There are other factors that can be considered to achieve the same effect.

HOA/Condo Fees

If financing of a condominium is contemplated, there will be a homeowner's association fee. This fee is for the maintenance of the common elements and for the operation the project. When **unit** utilities are included in the fee, one can deduct the portion of fees devoted to unit utilities from the condominium fee used to calculate ratios. The argument can even be made that the utility payment for the common elements can be excluded from the condo fee. To determine the amount to be deducted, analyze the project's current year operating budget. Add <u>all</u> utilities that are shown as line items in the budget. Divide the annual figure for utilities by the annual assessments to be collected from unit owners - do not include amounts from other sources, such as parking, laundry, vending etc. - to arrive at the percentage of condo fees attributed to unit utilities. The unit's fee may be reduced by this percentage for qualifying purposes.

Another tactic in reducing the fee for qualifying purposes would be to have the seller participate in condo fee abatement by pre-paying a portion of the condo fee for a set period of time. If reflected correctly by the association or management company, this can reduce the assessment for qualifying purposes.

A ground lease, where the land on which the property sits is not owned, is another component of the housing/front ratio. This may be the same of a cooperative apartment where there may be an underlying mortgage included in the maintenance fee.

Real Estate Taxes

Can the real estate taxes be adjusted for qualifying purposes? If the current tax rate is incorrect or inappropriate for the subject property purchaser, they may be. Often the posted real estate taxes for a property are for a rental unit - thus the property might be taxed at a higher commercial rate.

If qualification is a challenge, it is worth checking to make sure the current assessment is correct. Also, read the tax laws for your jurisdiction - do they offer tax break for primary residences or homestead exemptions? Are there breaks for owner-occupied properties, first-time buyers, senior citizens or low-income borrowers?

Private Mortgage Insurance

Private Mortgage Insurance, or PMI, is generally required whenever the loan to value ratio is greater than 80% (less than 20% down payment). PMI premiums may be reduced or eliminated dependent on circumstances.

1. Can changing from an ARM to a fixed rate reduce the coverage requirement?
2. Premium financing, while increasing the loan amount, can eliminate PMI from the ratio entirely. This will increase the loan amount, but the dollar for dollar savings to the

customer will be magnified, because monthly PMI premiums are not tax deductible, while the interest on financed premiums may be.

3. Can PMI be eliminated to the customer's benefit by utilizing a first and second mortgage combination? (See Chapter 2 - Loan Programs)

The Total Debt Ratio

The total debt, back or bottom ratio is the measure of all other obligations a borrower is responsible for in addition to the total housing payment. As an example, if we use qualifying ratios of 28/36 this allows 8% of total income to be devoted to debts. A borrower has accumulated a large amount of consumer debt this can present a qualifying problem. In pre-qualification the loan officer works backward through the ratio analysis to see whether the housing expense will be limited by total debts. To determine this:

1.) <u>Multiply Total Monthly Income by 28%</u>. Enter Result as Total Housing Payment
2.) <u>Multiply Gross Monthly Income by 36%.</u> Enter Result as Total Monthly Obligations. Deduct all debts. Enter Result as Total Housing Payment.
3.) The <u>smaller</u> of these two numbers is the maximum PITI. Subtract all components (taxes, insurance, etc.) from the smaller number. The result is the Maximum Principal and Interest payment.

In the following <u>Example 1</u> the debts **do not limit** the qualification. In <u>example 2</u> the maximum housing expense **is limited - lower** because of higher debts. Some guidelines do not mandate that you compute a front, or housing expense ratio. In any situation a detailed analysis of debts is important. There are many details involved in correct treatment and computation of debts.

Example 1				Example 2		
Step 1	Monthly Income	$	4,000.00	Step 1	Monthly Income	$ 4,000.00
	x Housing Ratio		28%		x Housing Ratio	28%
	Available for PITI	$	1,120.00		Available for PITI	$ 1,120.00
Step 2	Monthly Income	$	4,000.00	Step 2	Monthly Income	$ 4,000.00
	x Total Debt Ratio		36%		x Total Debt Ratio	36%
	Available For Debts	$	1,440.00		Available For Debts	$ 1,440.00
	Less Actual Debts	$	100.00		Less Actual Debts	$ 400.00
	Maximum PITI	$	1,340.00		Maximum PITI	$ 1,040.00
Step 3	Smaller of 1 & 2	$	1,120.00	Step 3	Smaller of 1 & 2	$ 1,040.00

What is a Debt?

Basically, any monthly payment that can be collected from an individual - that must be paid - is considered in the debt ratio. The payments for credit cards, student loans, car loans, signature loans, rental negative on rental properties, alimony and child support or other support obligations, payments for other mortgages. Items that are elective in nature, such as automobile insurance, health insurance, life insurance, library fees, membership dues, savings plans and others are not considered debts, because you can choose not to pay these, and your privileges will simply lapse. You won't suffer a collection action if you don't pay your parking fees, you just don't park in the lot.

Understanding the nature of each obligation - how it can be repaid in minimum, and how it impacts other aspects of a personal financial situation is - allows the loan officer to develop the maximum qualification potential of a borrower. We will discuss these in depth here - what the obligation is and how the repayments can be minimized for qualifying purposes.

Credit Card Obligations - Credit cards are the single most abused forms of credit available to consumers. This is because many people receive offers to lend money at times when they are inclined to spend it in an ill-advised manner. For example, college students may receive a check from a credit card company saying just endorse this check. Often a college student could not possibly hope to make a payment beyond a minimum. In some circumstances, they may not even be able to meet that. What may ensue is a growing spiral of debt in which the borrower continues to borrow money to pay obligations, and supporting a lifestyle deficit - enhancing living expenses - with credit card purchases. In some situations, people in this situation earn their way out of difficulty - their income increases to keep pace with the expenditures. In some cases people discipline themselves to curtail the escalating expenditures. Unfortunately, there is often the sad conclusion where borrowers give up and their credit is destroyed.

Why is this description important? Maximizing a borrower's qualification is appropriate for individuals who have shown that they can manage their credit, despite complications - it is a measure of character. In other words, someone who has managed his or her debts impeccably is an individual for whom qualification maximization is appropriate. Alternatively, someone who has periodically bailed out, or is in the credit spiral, is not necessarily a good person to whom the maximum amount of money should be loaned.

Tactics for Handling High Card Payments

Credit cards are revolving credit lines. Their minimum payments are based upon current balance, interest due and the previous payments. For a thumbnail qualification one would calculate the minimum payment at 5% of the outstanding balance. Actual minimum payments vary from 1 to 10% depending on the cardholder. But think about it. If the credit card company is earning 18% interest on the credit card balance, do they really want you to pay the balance down? Not really, so they encourage you not to make a payment for a month, or allow you to make a smaller than normal minimum payment.

> 1.) A copy of all credit card statements should be brought to loan application. Occasionally, because of fluctuating balances, the correct minimum payment will not be reported to the credit bureaus. Having the statements at application will allow the loan officer to review that the correct minimum payments are reported.
> 2.) Another strategy involves planning. You may recommend that the borrower make a payment that is slightly higher - approximately 1.5 times the required minimum. Then when the next statement comes, the cardholder may require a smaller than normal minimum payment.

Alternatively, if debts must be paid off for qualifying purposes, it must be determined that the borrowers are not simply going to re-extend themselves with new credit. For this reason, an underwriter may not allow revolving debt to be paid for qualifying purposes. If there is a possibility of paying off revolving debt, the balances should be compared against the monthly payments to get the biggest bang for the buck - so to speak. Payoff the lowest balances with the highest minimum payment.

Student Loans: Recent college graduates almost always have incurred some student loan debt to complete their education. Generally, the repayment terms are fairly favorable. However, student loans also have deferments that can allow a borrower to graduate from college, and wait for **a period of 12 or more months** before beginning repayment. From a qualification standpoint the question is, if the borrower is in a deferment period, can they afford to make the payment after the deferment is over? However loans that begin maturing more than 12 months into the future can be eliminated if the borrower has the assets to offset the payments once they take effect. If excessive student loans are a qualifying issue, Sallie Mae - the major student loan lender - does offer consolidation loans, which may reduce the overall debt service for a borrower.

Installment Loans May Be Excluded

Car loans/Installment loans: When there are scheduled payments on a loan, unlike a credit card or long-term obligation like a student loan, the loan served a purpose. If it was a car loan, the purpose is obvious. However, if it was a consolidation loan, or a signature loan, watch for the credit spiral. On the other hand, if the debt was established some time ago, there is a likelihood that the debt will be repaid soon. As with any loan, the balance may be refinanced. Car loans may be structured initially with 24- or 36- month payment schedules. This can make the payments troublesomely high. If a short-term car/installment loan is a problem, investigate the terms being offered by banks for similar loans - and the borrower's own bank too. You can refinance home loans - why not refinance all the borrower's loans to get a lower payment?

> If an installment debt has less than ten months remaining at the time of application, it may be excluded from qualifying ratios. For example, a borrower considering a home purchase might consider paying the balance on a car loan with 15 or 20 months remaining down to less than 10 months prior to application. This strategy should not be executed at the expense of post closing reserves - a borrower with no reserves might not be granted the leniency of excluding a low balance installment loan.

Rental Properties: Income properties often create problems for potential homebuyers. Aside from the difficulties of managing rental real estate, lenders may have a disparaging view of the impact rental real estate has on the prospective borrower. Restrictions on rental income include:

- Exclusion of 25% of the gross rental income as a vacancy/loss factor. Although a property may carry a positive cash flow, lenders adjust this income significantly to take into account the potential for the property being vacant with no rental income for an extended period of time. This is known as a vacancy/expense factor. While most rental properties experience a 5 - 10% vacancy factor, an additional expense must generally be considered to determine the wear and tear on the property. The exception to this is FHA/VA loans, in which the borrower can demonstrate a lower vacancy factor, or previous experience as a landlord. Then the vacancy expense factor can be as low as 7%. If this is a factor, then examine the actual cash flow of the property. Has it been rented for more than two years? If so, can you examine the borrower's Schedule E, Rental and

Royalty income, from their tax returns? Adding the actual income, less actual expenses (depreciation and depletion added in) may result in a more favorable net rental income than a 25% vacancy factor.
- In many lease situations, properties are rented on a month-to-month basis. If this is the case, the tenant must be contacted to provide a letter attesting to the fact that they intend to continue residing in the property.
- How many properties are financed? If a purchaser owns more than four 1-4 family properties that are financed, and the subject property is an investment property, they are generally ineligible for financing on conforming loans.
- Each property's mortgage must be verified. Also, the taxes and insurance must be obtained separately, either by proving that they are held in escrow, or by providing copies of the paid bills for the obligation.

Alimony/Child Support/Separate Maintenance: Ironically, in this case, what is a debt to one person is income to another. Since half of all marriages end in divorce, understanding the financial obligations and legal documentation of marital dissolution is requisite for lenders.

- If there is a support obligation, is it either child support or alimony. If it is alimony, it is taxable to the recipient. This means that it is tax deductible for the payer. If this is the case it will appear as a deduction on the front page of the tax returns. This can be viewed **not as a debt, but as a deduction from gross income,** which can drastically reduce the qualifying impact of the obligation. Remember the example

> 1.) While a divorce can work against a borrower who must pay support, the opposite is true of the recipient. This can work to the benefit of the creative loan officer who can add income and remove debts of one borrower by implementing advantageously a divorce situation. 2.) Be sure to examine tax returns, bank statements and credit histories for evidence of these liabilities. There are many instances in which these debts can easily be concealed by a borrower, which could circumvent the intent of maximizing qualification.

of how it takes $3.00 of income for every $1.00 of debts. This is another example of how it is more efficient for a borrower to reduce debt load to qualify for a mortgage than to increase their income. Nothing in the following examples changed except for the treatment of the alimony as a reduction in income instead of a debt. This results in an additional $220 monthly of qualification power.

Treating Alimony as an Income Deduction Increases Qualifying Power							
Alimony as a debt				**Alimony deducted from income**			
Step 1	Monthly Income	$	4,000	Step 1	Monthly Income	$	4,000
	x Housing Ratio		28%		Less Alimony	$	(750)
	Maximum PITI	$	1,120		"Net" Income	$	3,250
Step 2	Monthly Income	$	4,000		x Housing Ratio		28%
	x Debt Ratio		36%		Maximum PITI	$	910
	Max Total Debt	$	1,440	Step 2	Monthly Income	$	3,250
	Less Alimony	$	(750)		x Debt Ratio		36%
Step 3	Result	$	**690**		Max Total Debt	$	**1,170**

- If it is child support, how long will it continue? Are the children going to be old enough so that the obligation disappears soon? If so then an argument can be made for excluding the obligation. Can the balance be paid off or down to reduce the amount owed? To the recipient, child support is non-taxable income and may be "grossed up".
- Depending on the circumstances a legal separation agreement, post-nuptial agreement, divorce decree, court order, and/or property settlement agreement must be reviewed to determine the extent of obligations.

Regular Business Expenses/Self Employed Borrowers

Self-employment presents a separate challenge from an income point of view. These borrowers may be able to deduct many of their normal living expenses from their income, they achieve a higher standard of living by reducing their tax burden. Unfortunately, as lenders we believe that you cannot tell the federal government that you earn a certain amount of income and expect your lender to count a higher amount. It is important to get all income documentation and to attribute debts owed by or paid by a business to the business. *If an expense is actually paid by the business, providing 12 months canceled checks will allow the debt to be deleted from the borrower's personal qualification calculation.*

In many situations borrowers extend their personal credit to establish a new business. While this new business may not have been established long enough to have income that can be utilized for qualifying, it may present an excellent compensating factor for someone who looks as if they are caught in the credit escalation spiral, and may compensate for higher qualifying ratios.

When someone is commissioned, they may write off or deduct their business expenses. Do these debts or expenditures reduce gross income or are they simply allowable deductions? This is a delicate question. For instance, you can argue that union dues must be paid to ensure continued employment. This might be construed as a debt. On the other hand, a commissioned sales person might deduct un-reimbursed employee business expenses, such as mileage.

Because these expenses are generally the result of additional efforts to achieve additional income, these are deducted from gross income to determine what the actual net income is or was. However, the actual amount of the expenditure must be evaluated to determine what income was actually earned.

Contingent (Recourse) Liabilities

A contingent liability is an obligation that may come due if another event does not occur. For instance, a borrower obligated on a commercial loan would not necessarily have the commercial loan counted against him, because a business entity is paying it. It is contingent because it has no impact unless there is a problem with the entity and they seek repayment from the guarantor. This liability is not unlike a co-signed loan.

Credit History

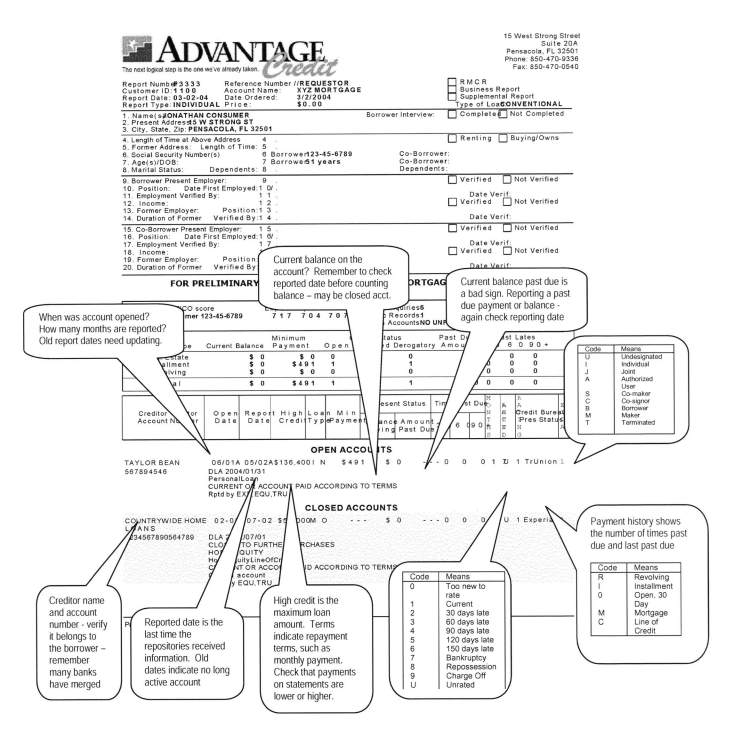

More and more, the most critical aspect of the loan approval process is the review of the credit history. In 1987 the mortgage industry - in a revolt against the massive, time-consuming paper monster created by verifying all aspects of an applicant's personal history - began to trend towards reducing documentation. Dependent on the relative amount of down payment, many loans were approved entirely upon the strength of credit reports. While some lenders made poor decisions by not verifying more information, time has proven that a perfect credit history is the most reliable indicator of future willingness and ability to repay an obligation. A large emphasis on credit is appropriate and, in fact, a credit report is the first thing a loan reviewer sees.

"Coded" or "Raw" Credit Report – Same Information, Slightly Different Format

CREDITOR	Opening Date/Mos Reviewed	Reported Date	High Credit Terms	Balance	Past Due Amount	Current Status	ECOA	
ABC Credit 123456789	12/80 18	6/95	3000 0	0	0	R-1	B	1111111211111133311111 (30 - 1)(60-3)
Ford Motor ABFG12345	12/98 01	12/98	18485 48 x 525	18320	0		U	1

The information is the same, but is raw or uncoded. You must extrapolate from the dates reported, when the late payments occurred.

A credit history is like an opinion - almost everyone has one. An immense amount of data is accumulated as you interact with creditors. You report employers and residence addresses when you apply for a loan; lenders report applications, balances, payment amounts and payment histories as you transact business; the courts report any legal actions against you. Credit data is stored among 3 major private companies referred to as "repositories": TRW, Trans Union (TU), and Equifax (CBI). Depending on geography - the South, or East or West of the Mississippi - all consumer credit providers, most mortgage lenders and even some major landlords will report to at least one and perhaps all three of these repositories. They assemble what amounts to a massive, interactive, and open database. This is "raw" credit data.

The credit card application process is a "raw" credit experience. You are analyzed on the data that is contained in the repositories. Period. If you have missed a payment in the past due to extenuating circumstances, or if there are erroneous data in the system, you may be declined. Then your experience can become Orwellian. You don't generally get to talk to a human being and review a negative credit decision. Most consumer credit decisions are based on scoring systems. The scoring is based on the repository information. You are considered guilty if there is a problem and there is very little you can do to prove your innocence.

One of the benefits of the mortgage process is that, as a borrower, you have the opportunity to address and correct items that arise during the process. A negative credit history is like an illness - people don't like to talk about it or admit an error. It is this pain or fear that causes an aversion to dealing with credit issues. Unlike credit card transactions a mortgage application, because of its human element, can be a healing experience. Like jumping into a swimming pool, once you're in the water it doesn't seem that cold. Understanding the process can allay the fear.

Co-signed Loans

It seemed like a good idea to help your friend or daughter buy that car. The bank just needed a co-signer to make the loan. Surely the original borrower would be responsible for the debt? This is significant. If a borrower has co-signed for someone it must be substantiated that the primary borrower is making the payments in a timely manner. Without this the co-signer is called upon to make the payments. Unfortunately, many of these obligations do not get paid in a timely manner. And the co-signer is adversely impacted.

Credit Verification – Liability, Mortgage or Rental Verifications

A credit report is used to verify most obligations. There are circumstances when a direct verification is need, such as an unverified obligation, or a creditor who does not report to credit bureaus. Direct verifications may not pass through the hands of any financially interested person or the borrower.

The disadvantage of direct verification is that it is time consuming and can be costly as institutions may charge a fee to provide verification.

Understanding the Ratings - What is "Bad"

We expect that applicants should have "perfect" credit. Perfect credit means **no negative ratings/incidents ever.** Perfect credit is the **basis** for obtaining a loan to be sold into the secondary market and, at least theoretically, the most competitive rates offered. Anything less than perfect credit is considered adverse and is a basis for loan declination.

Beyond perfect is where the credit evaluation process becomes almost purely subjective. We have obtained a consensus definition of acceptable negative ratings to eliminate some subjectivity. A survey of underwriters for major lenders indicates that there can be some lenience in allowing less than 100% perfect credit. (Nobody readily commits to lenience in this regard. To achieve lenience no other negative factors may be present.)

Generally Acceptable Adverse Credit History	
Mortgage Payments	NO Late Payments in last 12 months
Credit Card/Consumer Loans	TWO (2) 30 day late payments in last 12 months
Legal Actions	NO Open Liens, Judgments or Collection Actions
Inquiries	THREE (3) Inquiries in previous 3-6 months prior to application

While the loan reviewer places most emphasis on the preceding 12-24 months, **all** negative instances must be clearly explained. Again, this is because the basis or standard for obtaining a marketable loan is "perfect" credit.

No Credit is **not** perfect credit. Standard guidelines require 3 - 5 pieces of credit maintained for at least 2 years to qualify as "established" credit. There are alternatives to having no commercial credit history. Payment

What is the Problem with Inquiries?
It's not the inquiry itself - too many inquiries indicate:
- A borrower with latent credit problems that cause him/her to repeatedly attempt, unsuccessfully, to obtain new loans to conceal delinquent accounts
- Someone who is trying to borrow for the down payment
- Someone who is trying to obtain multiple owner-occupied loans simultaneously
- Someone who cannot obtain credit or is desperate for credit

records to landlords for rent, utility companies, and installment purchases, merchandise redeemed from a pawnbroker all can be compiled to develop a repayment history.

Credit Explanations

As discussed, all adverse credit notations must be addressed in writing by the borrower. While it would be naive to think that a credit explanation could change a loan reviewer's opinion to approve or decline an application, there are scenarios that can be effective in addressing serious or recent adverse incidents which could compromise loan approval.

- A logical explanation that compellingly indicates an applicant's efforts to properly handle an account.
- Someone else's fault - documentation that the responsibility of an incident was out of the applicant's control.
- Extreme Contrition - an earnest admission of responsibility and recognition of how to avert future incidents.
- The Big Bang - The event or circumstance that caused the delinquency is no longer a factor.

From Bad to Worse

Unfortunately many Americans fall prey to the lure of easy credit, becoming victims to a tempest of red ink. An understanding of credit status is important because in certain situations a borrower is not eligible for traditional financing any more. If an applicant falls out of the generally acceptable range, or displays any of the following characteristics, they need more help than what a traditional loan officer can offer. We will discuss this later.

Credit Issue	Description	Resolution
Late Mortgage	Over 30 days past due on rent or mortgage in last 12 months; currently past due	**Get direct mortgage verification** or canceled check to refute exact timing; 12 months time elapsed since incident
30 – 60 Days Past Due	If an account has been handled well historically, some creditors are loath to report minor late payments. Current 30- or 60-day late references are emblematic of a serious situation arising. Reported as an I-2, R-2, I-3 or R-3.	**Pay Off Account** prior to application; pay account current; depending on circumstances may require 12-24 months time elapsed since incident.
Over 60 Day Past Due	This indicates a serious unwillingness on the part of the borrower to repay a debt: I-4, R-4 to I-6/R-6	Pay Account Current/**Pay Off**; 12-24 mos. time elapsed
Collection Action	Anyone who can report to credit repositories (collection agencies, doctor's offices, parking enforcement, etc.) can file a collection action against you. All that is required is an unpaid invoice. Normally these are nuisance actions too small to go to the expense of obtaining a ruling via a judge. No action can result from a collection, but it will impede your ability to obtain credit.	Pay off collection.

Charge Off	Means that the creditor gave up trying to get payment from you and wrote the account off as a loss.	Evidence of payment/dispute
Judgment	A judgment is a collection action that has been reviewed for merit by a small claim, circuit or district court depending on the amount or size of the claim. A judgment is serious because the party to whom the ruling inures may seize your property, wages and assets to satisfy the obligation.	An attorney may appeal the judgment and, if successful, the ruling may be vacated, or thrown out.
Tax Lien	Federal or state tax liens are more serious than judgments because the government is very good at seizing assets and collecting for money owed. Even though tax liens can come about as the result of legitimate disputes over tax practices, they are viewed primarily as a credit problem.	Release of lien
Consumer Credit Counseling	A borrower enters into a credit repair agreement with a non-profit counseling agency. The account will show up on the credit report as "CCCS account." The account will be CCCS until it is a "0" balance.	Borrower may not have open CCCS accounts. Pay off and close.
Bankruptcy Chapter 7 - Liquidation	A filing under any chapter of the bankruptcy code creates an estate. The Courts act as trustee over the estate. Under Chapter 7 all of a debtor's assets (with some exceptions) and liabilities are liquidated. Unless a creditor objects, all debts included in the bankruptcy are discharged within a few months of filing.	Some lenders will never consider a borrower after bankruptcy is declared. FNMA/FHLMC allow financing 4 years after discharge Chapter 7 and 2 years after Chapter 13 with re-established credit. Chapter 7 is the most negative form, philosophically, because the debtor has walked away from assets and liabilities and let the court force creditors to take less money than owed in what is known as a "Cram-Down." Because all debts are discharged this may disguise a previous pattern of debt mismanagement. "Dismissal" means that the court did not approve the filing.
Bankruptcy Chapter 13 - Adjustment of Debts by Wage Earner	This chapter allows debtors to pay back creditors in full or in part, based upon income, over a period of up to 5 years. The payments are made to a trustee who begins paying creditors as soon as the plan is approved. You must have less than $350,000 in secured debt and $100,000 in unsecured debt to file	
Bankruptcy Chapter 11 - Reorganization	This plan is available to all individuals and entities, but is intended to allow an ongoing business to restructure its debt. The filing must be accepted by the court as well as creditors	

Relief From the Tide of Red Ink

Depending on the seriousness of the situation there are ways to avoid being subjected to intense pressure from creditors.

<u>Non-Standard Credit Mortgages</u> - If you are fortunate to have a large down payment or have built up equity in your home, or in other improved property (not land), you may be eligible for a higher risk mortgage. These are referred to as "Sub-Prime," "Credit-Rated Paper," "B, C & D Paper" (as in, not "A"), and "Equity Based" loans. They are offered under the same terms as the "junk bonds" of the 80's, giving investors a higher rate of return, or yield, than standard

investments in exchange for accepting higher default risk. Theoretically, the interest rate premium and the fact that a larger equity position is required offset the investor's risk of default. A standard grading apparatus would show an increasing interest rate and equity requirement as the credit quality deteriorates.

Credit Counselors/Agencies - There are credit counseling agencies which can help borrowers who have over-extended themselves work out repayment plans with creditors, re-arrange financial plans, and arrange consolidation loans. For a local agency, call the National Foundation for Consumer Credit (301) 589-5600, a non-profit organization. As seductive as it may sound, there is no bona-fide way of obtaining a new, completely repaired credit history without dancing around ethical barriers and breaking laws. If a company offers to repair credit and charges a large up-front fee, you are dealing with a "credit doctor." See – Strategies for Improving Credit History for ways to work that may or may not improve the ability to obtain credit.

Ways to Improve Credit

Problem	Tactic	Result
No Credit	Obtain secured credit card or work with loan officer to obtain credit cards/loans.	Positive Outcome - establish credit. Could have been achieved without credit doctor.
Credit Problems (Minor)	Utilize multiple correspondence addressing each incident and follow up systems to test creditors responsiveness. Creditors only have 30 days to respond to written request in writing. If they do not, they must remove the notation under ECOA.	Positive Outcome - there is a chance that the creditor will not be able to respond to some or all of the requests in a timely manner and will have to remove negative references. On the other hand, there is no guarantee - you might do this yourself.
Credit Problems (Major)	New Social Security Number or Tax I.D. number.	Negative - this is highly illegal.

Credit Counseling is perceived as a negative. This is counter-intuitive to many borrowers' instincts. Their thought is "I'm getting my credit cleaned up!" Our perception is that they gave up on doing it themselves – couldn't handle it – so why are they trying to borrow money again?

There is one positive thing to be said about adverse credit history - it eventually does go away. The statute of limitations for delinquent credit reporting is 7 years. Judgments and liens are removed after 10 years. Often a lender who reported negative ratings will delete them if the account has been reestablished in a positive way. For instance delinquent student loans may have their negative ratings removed once paid. Even though lenders have an obligation to report delinquencies, guaranteed student loans were made available to help the students, not destroy financial futures.

Sub-Prime Lending

The fact remains that, despite some options, there is very little a mortgage lender can do to help a borrower who has poor credit. Some first time homebuyer programs are more liberal in determining creditworthiness, such as FHA, VA and Community Homebuyer programs. If a borrower fails eligibility for any other program, they can avail themselves of what is known as "Credit Rated," "B, C & D," "Choice," or "Graded" paper mortgages. Lenders, conduits and even some mortgage companies are offering Credit Rated loans to borrowers who cannot find financing elsewhere on the basis of a larger equity position and a higher interest rate.

There are scoring systems which underwriters use to determine how large of an equity position and how high an interest rate they will require to offset credit risk posed by a borrower. It is interesting to note that these programs also offer higher qualifying ratios in addition to more liberal standards. The reason for this is that in order for a borrower to afford a higher interest rate there needs to be more leniencies. Humorously, we refer to this as "if you can't afford it, we charge you more." Here is a consensus of the ratings, indicative rate premiums and required equity positions.

Rating	Description/Allowable Derogatory	Ratios	Equity (LTV)	Rate Premium
FHLMC A- FNMA EA1, 2, 3	Mortgage - Current; 2x30, 0x60; Consumer Credit - Generally excellent, no more than 20% of all other accounts report delinquencies; No bankruptcy; No judgments over $100	42/42	80-90	0.00 - 2.50%
B	Mortgage - Current; 4x30, or 2x30 & 1x60; Consumer Credit - Reasonably good, no more than 40% of all other accounts report past delinquencies. No bankruptcy in 24-36 months; No judgments over $250	45/50	75-90	1.50 - 3.00%
C	Mortgage - Slow; 6x30, 1x60, 1x90 - Can be currently past due; Consumer Credit - Significant past problems; Many accounts late; Open judgments; No bankruptcy within last 18-24 months;	50/60	70	2.00 - 6.00%
D	Mortgage - Currently Past Due/Foreclosure; Consumer Credit - Serious problems, collections, judgments, delinquencies; Recent but inactive Bankruptcy	60/60	50-60	4.00 - 12.00%

High-Rate, High-Fee Loans (HOEPA/Section 32 Mortgages)

The Home Ownership and Equity Protection Act of 1994 (HOEPA) addresses certain deceptive and unfair practices in home equity lending. It amends the Truth in Lending Act (TILA) and establishes requirements for certain loans with high rates and/or high fees.

> **Section 32 Loans**
> - A first-lien loan where the annual percentage rate (APR) exceeds the rates on Treasury securities of comparable maturity by more than eight percentage points;
> - A second-lien loan where the APR exceeds the rates in Treasury securities of comparable maturity by more than 10 percentage points; or
> - The total fees and points payable by the consumer at or before closing exceed eight percent of the total loan amount. The Federal Reserve Board, based on changes in the Consumer Price Index, adjusts this dollar amount annually.) Credit insurance premiums for insurance written in connection with the credit transaction are counted as fees.

The rules primarily affect refinancing and home equity installment loans that also meet the definition of a high-rate or high-fee loan. The rules do not cover loans to buy or build your home, reverse mortgages or home equity lines of credit (similar to revolving credit accounts).

The following features are banned from Section 32 high-rate, high-fee loans:

- All balloon payments for loans with less than five-year terms.
- Negative amortization.
- Default interest rates higher than pre-default rates.
- A repayment schedule that consolidates more than two periodic payments that will be paid in advance from the proceeds of the loan.
- Most prepayment penalties, including refunds of unearned interest calculated by any method less favorable than the actuarial method. Unless
    - The lender verifies that your total monthly debt (including the mortgage) is 50 percent or less of your monthly gross income;
    - you get the money to prepay the loan from a source other than the lender or an affiliate lender; and
    - the lender exercises the penalty clause during the first five years following execution of the mortgage.
- A due-on-demand clause unless
    - there is fraud or material misrepresentation by the consumer in connection with the loan;
    - the consumer fails to meet the repayment terms of the agreement; or there is any action by the consumer that adversely affects the creditor's security.
- Creditors may not:
    - make loans based on the collateral value of your property without regard to ability to repay the loan.
    - refinance a HOEPA loan into another HOEPA loan within the first 12 months of origination, unless the new loan is in the borrower's best interest. The prohibition also applies to assignees holding or servicing the loan.
    - document a closed-end, high-cost loan as an open-end loan. For example, a high-cost mortgage may not be structured as a home equity line of credit if there is no reasonable expectation that repeat transactions will occur.

Understanding Credit Scoring

The development of credit scoring has been touted by the banking industry as a panacea to the problem of maintaining consistency in underwriting and assuring quality loans. Credit scoring is the process of numerically grading the overall profile of a borrower to ascertain how the profile has historically performed and making a credit decision on that basis. The Fair-Isaacs Company (FICO) developed a predictive model for Experian/TRW that has become the basis for many credit models that now exist. In fact these models have taken on a life of their own. They can be

How Good Is My Score?	
700 & Above	Excellent
680 - 700	Very Good
640 - 680	Generally Acceptable
620 - 660	Marginal
below 620	Caution

Credit Scoring Models
CBI/Equifax – **Beacon** – Most Conservative Model
TransUnion- **Empirica**
TRW – **Experian** – Most Active in Consumer and Business Reporting

adjusted or enhanced by the ordering party to reflect their particular underwriting preferences.

The scores are designed to predict, based upon past experience, how a customer will repay the loan. These scores, combined with specific risk grading criteria, are how banks have traditionally approved credit cards, auto loans, home equity loans and other minor consumer loans for the past 10 years. "Risk-based" underwriters like PMI companies have utilized the methodology for years. It is the contribution of mainstream commercial banking to the evolution of mortgage banking evolution. However, it is a negative for the mortgage business because in this industry lenders have given traditionally given borrowers a closer look. In the interests of speed, many borrowers may fall between the cracks. The risk score is not supposed to make the decision to approve a loan. But one can't help but think that an adverse credit score is sure to impede the approval, while a positive score is a confirmation.

The basic theory of risk scoring is that there are historical factors that impact a borrower's ability - or willingness - to meet obligations. The factors are, not surprisingly, credit history, source of income, down payment, debt to income ratios, and loan type.

Credit Score Reason Code/Description	CBI	TU	TRW
Amount owed on accounts is too high	1	1	1
Delinquency on accounts	2	2	2
Too few bank revolving accounts	3	n/a	3
Too many bank or national revolving accounts	4	n/a	4
Too many accounts with balances	5	5	5
Consumer finance accounts	6	6	6
Account payment history too new to rate	7	7	7
Too many recent inquiries last 12 months	8	8	8
Too many accounts opened in last 12 months	9	9	9
Proportion of balances to credit limit is too high on revolving accts	10	10	10
Amount owed on revolving accounts is too high	11	11	11
Length of revolving credit history is too short	12	12	12
Time since delinquency too recent or unknown	13	13	13
Length of credit history is too short	14	14	14
Lack of recent bank revolving information	15	15	15
Lack of recent revolving account information	16	16	16
No recent non-mortgage balance information	17	17	17
Number of accounts with delinquency	18	18	18
Too few accounts currently paid as agreed	19	19	19
Time since derogatory public record or collection	20	20	20
Amount past due on accounts	21	21	21
Serious delinquency, derogatory public record or collection filed	22	22	22
Too many bank or national revolving accounts with balances	23	n/a	n/a
No recent revolving balances	24	24	24
Proportion of loan balances to loan amounts is too high	33	3	33
Lack of recent installment loan information	32	4	32
Date of last inquiry too recent	n/a	19	n/a
Time since most recent account opening too short	30	30	30
Number of revolving accounts	26	n/a	26
Number of bank revolving or other revolving accour	n/a	26	n/a
Number of established accounts	28	28	28
No recent bankcard balances	n/a	29	n/a
Too few accounts with recent payment information	31	n/a	31

Risk Grading

There are numerous risk scoring devices. As the consumer credit business seeks ways to automate and streamline credit approval we add new tools constantly. In mortgage lending, none of these are designed to be exclusive; they are used in tandem with each other. Unfortunately, most of these tools currently take the form of what we refer to as automated underwriting protocols. These "proprietary underwriting models" include FHLMC and FNMA models as well as privately developed models.

There are 3 possible outcomes from Automated Underwriting: Approve, Deny or Refer. *It is loans in the "deny" and "refer" categories where loan officers to earn their money.* Obviously, mortgage companies don't need loan officers if a machine can approve a loan; so knowing the ins and outs of the guidelines is how the lender adds value.

The developers of these programs – not surprisingly - don't give much insight as to how to work within the models. These organizations are purposely secretive about the specific guidelines they set for rendering Automated Underwriting Decisions. If they told us what the guidelines were and how it worked, we could simply tailor every application to meet the system's requirements and it would be relatively easy to manipulate the model's outcome.

However FHLMC has published a manual scoring worksheet – "The Gold Measure Worksheet." The Automated Underwriting that is becoming more prevalent through computer approval programs is merely a risk scoring mechanism where the machine finds enough positive criteria present to eliminate the need for a subjective positive decision. The FHLMC Gold Measure is simply one of many scoring systems. Although it is extremely simple, it has been statistically more accurate than many more complicated models. It is represented by a self-explanatory one-page worksheet. From this one can see where the weight is placed. Each attribute is a positive or a negative. How strong or weak the attribute is in the overall consideration is indicated by how dramatically the overall score can be impacted by the measure. Attributes are ranked in "Risk Units," with the objective of obtaining the lowest possible score. (A minus is a good thing!)

Scoring Positives	Scoring Negatives
- Perfect credit file with 11 or more open accounts - Revolving balances below $500 - Percent of all trade lines with derogatory rankings; 0-10% - 2 years on job - **Good** - 30% down payment - **Best** - down payment of 40% or more - Previous housing expense that is <120% of the proposed payment - Loan term < 25 years	- Percent of all trade lines with derogatory rankings; 16-40% >60% - Worst delinquency ever is >30 days - Judgments or collections - More than 3 delinquent public records - **Bad** - 2-3 inquiries - **Worse** - more than 5 inquiries - Less than 2 years work history - Self-employed/commissioned borrowers - Less than 2 months reserves - Over 40% total debt - ARMs - **Bad** - Condominiums and 2 units - **Worse** – 3-4 unit properties

Hopefully there will always be the lender that makes an individual decision on each loan. For years the loan officer has been able to present a case that challenges established guidelines. The loan officer's job in that situation is to argue the case, its merits, support compensating factors, dig for details that can give the underwriter a visceral sense that the case is solid. This process has also helped many individuals gain respect for creditworthiness. By understanding the challenges they present to lenders, borrowers can improve or modify their behavior to make financing easier for them in the future.

Fraud Alerts

When dealing with borrower's credit reports, care should be taken to look for issues that might indicate a borrower is misrepresenting or concealing information. These "Red Flags" can cause problems in the loan process.

CREDIT / CREDIT REPORTS

- No credit (possible use of alias)
- High income borrower with little or no cash (undisclosed liabilities)
- Variance in employment or residence data from other sources
- Recent inquiries from other mortgage lenders
- Invalid social security number
- AKA or DBA indicated
- Round dollar amounts (especially on interest-bearing accounts)
- Borrower cannot be reached at place of business
- High income borrower with no "prestige" credit cards

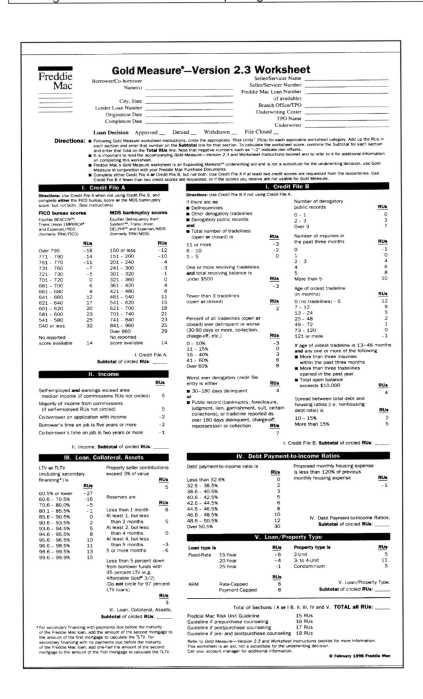

Chapter 5 – Documentation Review
Income Documentation

Income Computation

The greatest discrepancy between underwriting and processing comes from the income computation process. This is so true that at some companies the processors are required to place an income computation form on top of the income documentation in the file order. This shouldn't be necessary in cases when the borrower has a base salary and no other income is used to qualify the borrower. However, most cases aren't like this, so provide the computation, even if you simply attach a piece of adding machine tape to the verbal employment verification form.

Calculating Base Income

Hourly	Weekly	Bi-Weekly	Semi-Monthly	Monthly
Rate x hours/week X 52 weeks divided by 12	Rate x 52 divided by 12	Rate x 26 divided by 12	Rate x 2	Rate
$8/hr x 40 = $320 x 52 = $16,640 /12 = $1,386.66	$800/wk x 52 = 41,600/12 = 3,466.66	$2,000 x 26 = 52,000 /12 =$4,333.33	$1500 x 2 = $3000	$3000

In the mortgage industry we are trying to compare monthly income to monthly expenses. Income is always calculated on a monthly basis despite how the borrower is paid. One of the biggest "rookie" errors made by loan officers is calculating salary based on 4 weeks in a month. There are actually 52 weeks in a year. The income treatment is designed to convert all incomes to monthly income.

Documentation Review – Paystubs

Reviewing the income documentation once it is in the file is part of the job of the processor. Understanding that the underwriter will question any item that is out of the ordinary, the processor should look at each document and ask if it raises any questions. Aside from verifying the way the loan officer calculated the income, the authenticity and consistency of the document relative to the information given on the loan application must be questioned.

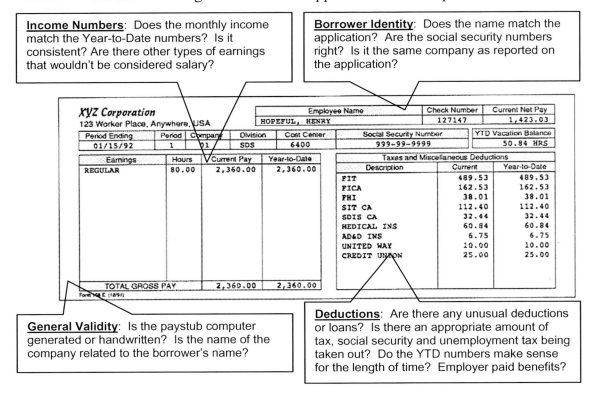

Questionable Paystubs

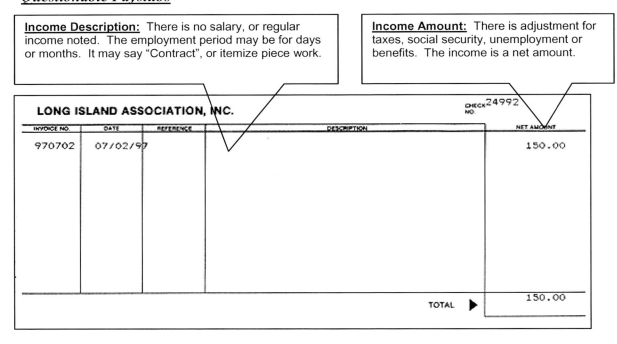

Reviewing Documentation – W-2's

Annual income statements are utilized to assure that the income is consistent and stable. These documents reveal a great deal about the borrower's profile.

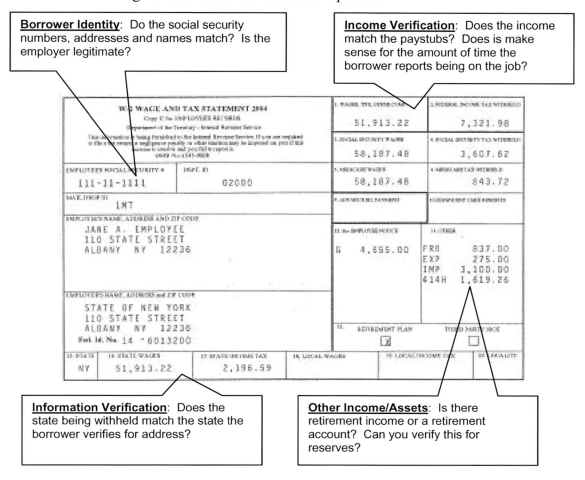

Borrower Identity: Do the social security numbers, addresses and names match? Is the employer legitimate?

Income Verification: Does the income match the paystubs? Does is make sense for the amount of time the borrower reports being on the job?

Information Verification: Does the state being withheld match the state the borrower verifies for address?

Other Income/Assets: Is there retirement income or a retirement account? Can you verify this for reserves?

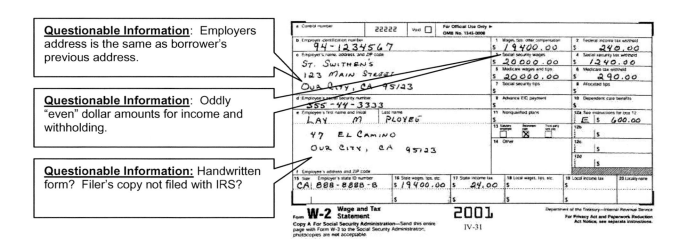

Questionable Information: Employers address is the same as borrower's previous address.

Questionable Information: Oddly "even" dollar amounts for income and withholding.

Questionable Information: Handwritten form? Filer's copy not filed with IRS?

IV-31

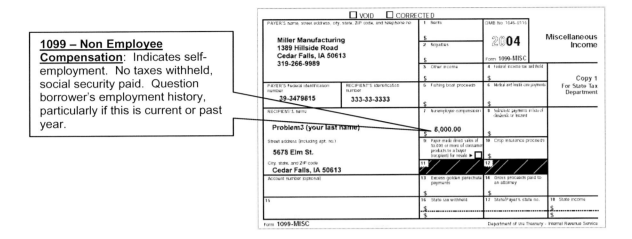

1099 – Non Employee Compensation: Indicates self-employment. No taxes withheld, social security paid. Question borrower's employment history, particularly if this is current or past year.

Income Computation

There are basic methods for arriving at stable qualifying income. You should select the easiest to comprehend, which still arrives at income sufficient to qualify the borrower.

"Stable" Income

With individuals who work for a company and are paid a regular salary, there is no ambiguity over the amount of income available for debt service. However, the temptation to utilize a higher level of income exists for borrowers who have variable income or who are self-employed. It is for these borrowers that we must address income. Each category of income has different attributes that affect the manner of treatment. Within each category there are different ways of increasing the amount of income that can be used for qualifying. To determine the manner of treatment we must ask the same basic question again; "How much income is needed for qualification?" because there are conservative, less conservative and aggressive approaches for each category.

Base Income with Enhancements

If the income needed for qualification is higher than what is available from the base alone, the treatment of additional sources becomes important. The biggest question from a qualifying perspective is at what point does the borrower stop being a salaried employee and become technically self-employed. The standard definition is that where 25% or more of the income required for qualifying is of a variable nature, the borrower is considered self-employed and is subject to some of the rigors of self-employment qualification including income averaging and an examination of all applicable income documents.

The reason for this is the underwriting concern that a borrower may offset some of the variable income earned with tax deductible expenses reducing the actual income. If the variable income does not result in deductions by the borrower, then there is no problem. However, if the borrower does have significant deductions which adversely affect qualifying every effort should be made to limit the amount of variable income attributed to the borrower for qualifying purposes to less than 25% of the overall qualifying income. One can even include a co-borrower's income to increase the proportion of variable income that can be utilized before invoking the 25% rule.

Getting the most of Overtime, Bonus, & Commissions

Overtime, Bonuses and Commissions are three areas in which a salaried or base income employee can enhance their qualifying income. The most important aspect of utilizing these is past history of receiving the type of income, the current level, and the probability of its continuance. The circumstances surrounding each are different so its treatment and maximization are different.

Overtime

Overtime is paid out at a multiple of base earnings. The trick in maximizing overtime income is to extract the amount of hours of overtime worked for

Year	Pay/Hr.	Hrs/wk.	Base		O.T.Weekly	Annual
1993	6.50	46 Hrs	260.00	58.50	318.50	16,552
1994	6.83	46 Hrs	273.20	61.47	334.67	17,402
1995	7.18	46 Hrs	287.20	64.62	351.82	11,258
(8 Months in 1995)					Total	45,212

averaging, as opposed to averaging the dollar amount. The reason for this is that averaging the dollar amount reflects past earnings, whereas averaging the hours allows you to take advantage of the current rate of pay and utilize income going forward. This takes into account increases in the base or hourly rate as cost of living and other raises are applied.

The most fundamental issue for overtime maximization is establishing the average number of hours worked per week. The greater the number of hours worked the larger the income for qualifying. If; 1.) There is nothing that prevents an employee from working more hours, such as a second job, school, or a demonstrated need to care for a family, and 2.) The employer states that the employee is eligible to work more hours and states an average number of hours of overtime worked per week, it may then be possible to use additional income available for qualifying.

Approach	Conservative - Average Earnings		Maximized - Average Hours Worked	
Example	Total Income Divided By Number of Months (12+12+8) Qualifying Income	45,212 32 = 1,412.87/mo.	Current Overtime Rate (7.18 x 1.5) Multiply by Average Hours of O.T.x Qualifying Weekly Overtime Plus Base Weekly Income Total x52 =18,294/yr divided by 12 =	$ 10.77/hr 6 $ 64.62 $287.20 $351.82 $1524/mo

Bonus, Tips and Commission

With overtime you can establish qualifying income with some certainty; the number of hours and the rate of pay, in addition to a historical performance, can all be demonstrated. The only thing that can be reasonably quantified about Bonus, Tips and Commission income is that it will continue. In these cases a historical average is the accepted method of determining qualifying income. There are some circumstances in which a larger amount of income might be acceptable, depending on whether the situation is compelling and compensating factors are in place. Unfortunately, even under the most lenient guidelines, credence will never be given for income that has not yet been received - referred to as prospective income.

Income Type	Conservative Treatment	Optimal Treatment	Maximized Treatment
Commissions	Average 2 Years Tax Returns	Utilize 24 months exactly. Example: 8 months Year to Date, 12 months past year and 4 months previous year	If there is a trend of increasing commissions, utilize a shorter average. For instance previous full year and year to date. Must show previous earnings were irrelevant/not comparable. (See self-employment)
Bonuses	Average past 2 years	Use previous bonus alone with letter from employer that future bonus will be higher	Use guaranteed bonus if it can be shown that similar employees received similar bonus.
Tips	Average Past 2 Years	Average previous 24 months exactly, if beneficial for qualifying	Utilize bank statements to show deposits of tips above base. Utilize previous year and year to date

Other Arguments for Using a Shorter Average

When a borrower needs to utilize a higher level of income to qualify, and a using the methods shown above do not provide enough help for the case, another strategy is to show the progression of a borrower's income. A case can be made that the current income (from the previous year's tax return and year to date income statement) can be used in the example of 1.) a borrower that has had income which has increased regularly for 5 years and can provide substantiation that it will continue at least at the same level at a minimum. In the previous example, we assume that the borrower doesn't qualify for the loan requested based on 1994 and 1995 income averaged over 24 months (47,000 + 58,000 ÷ 24 = 4375/mo.).

Year	Income	(%Increase)
1990	20,000	N/A
1991	25,000	25%
1992	31,000	24%
1993	38,000	22%
1994	47,000	23%
1995	58,000	23%
YTD	58,000	25%

By showing that the income has increased consistently, we might be able to utilize the past year and year to date income (58,000 + 58,000 ÷ 21 = 5523/mo) increasing the qualifying income by nearly 1175/mo.

Another scenario for using a shorter average, might actually be where the lender needs to omit a recent year. If there was a personal tragedy, or the borrower was working on something unrelated, which caused the income to drop it might be unfair to hold the decrease against the borrower. In this case, the same strategy is utilized, except the year that was unfavorable is minimized or omitted. If 1994 was the documented bad year, the traditional approach would yield income of only (18,000 +

Year	Income	(%Increase)
1990	45,000	N/A
1991	47,000	5%
1992	40,000	(10%)
1993	50,000	18%
1994	18,000	-53%
1995	58,000	(18%)322%
YTD	58,000	25%

58,000 ÷ 24 = 3166/mo.) while going back further and averaging (50,000 + 18,000 + 58,000 ÷ 36 = 3500/mo.) still penalizes a borrower whose income decrease was really an anomaly. Omitting the income and including year to date income (50,000 + 58,000 + 58,000 ÷ 33 = 5030/mo.) greatly enhances the average or stable monthly income.

Future Raises

Something that is scheduled to happen in the future is never certain. Things change, as we all know, and this is one of the truths in underwriting. Anything that is proposed is prospective and is automatically discounted. Since prospective income can never really be included for qualifying income, don't ever refer to it as such. Call it something different, like pro-forma income. It means the same thing, but doesn't have the negative connotations. An argument can be made for counting future raises if there is a history of past raises and the new pay will start reasonably soon (within 6 months) of closing. A future bonus may fall under the same category.

There are specific instances where a future raise can definitely be used. Government workers, armed forces servicemen, or employees of institutions which have regularly scheduled cost of living increases which are a matter of record can compellingly prove that their raise will be effective. In this case a future raise can be used as a matter of course. If an employee obtains a copy of a performance review which indicates a promotion, or a grade increase, then it is possible to utilize the higher figure. Again, it is a matter of how compelling the information is.

Verification of Employment/Income

When income is in question, the best way of clarifying issues is the use of the direct employment verification. Direct Employment Verification, referred to as a VOE, is a pre-printed form which is sent directly from the processor to the employer. It may not pass through the hands of any financially interested person or the borrower. VOEs are particularly useful in clarifying

- Variable income, such as bonuses or overtime hours
- Job changes within a company
- Borrowers who are re-hired

[Form image: Request for Verification of Employment, form 0501EM000010]

Verifying Variable Income: The form requests information on number of hours worked, the likelihood of continuance, future pay increases

Verifying Other Qualifying Income: Items such as Housing Allowances, Rations or other military pay can be used as qualifying income.

Verifying Previous Employment: The form requests previous employment information. This can answer concerns about gaps in employment.

Dividends & Interest

One frequent pre qualification error is in utilizing assets as income bearing that will be liquidated as part of the transaction. Just as prospective income cannot be used, income from an asset that no longer exists cannot be used. If a portion of the assets yielding income is to be liquidated it may benefit the borrower to determine the percentage of assets remaining and then take a percentage of the previous income.

Mutual Fund Account	$100,000
Portion Liquidated	$ 50,000
Percentage	50%
Income - 1994	8,125
Income - 1995	13,150
Total	21,275
Divided by 24 Months	$886
Multiply by 50%	$443

Self-Employment

There exists a quandary for the self-employed borrower. It is based upon the premise of risk and reward. Small business drives economic growth and the entrepreneurial spirit has created many wealthy people. But there are some stunning and sobering statistics:

- Self-employed borrowers are more than 200% as likely to default on their obligations. In Southern California self-employed borrowers are 400% as likely to default.
- 90% of all start-up businesses fail within the first two years

These are daunting odds and present a special challenge in qualifying, processing and approving self-employed borrowers. The case will be reviewed far more thoroughly than the average borrower for a number of reasons:

- The borrower's income stream, even if it appears stable, is based upon the company's performance, which may vary. There are two levels of income to review.
- Self-employment income is taxable on a "net of expenses" basis. Since paying taxes decreases income, one of the benefits of self-employment is deducting expenses from gross income to reduce a tax bill. In this situation the most substantiate form of income documentation - the tax return - suddenly becomes the enemy because every conceivable legitimate deduction is utilized to reduce the tax burden.
- In a closely held company, where does the company end and the self-employed borrower begin? Is a company car really the company's? What expenses are really just personal expenses that are taken into consideration by general underwriting guidelines for the populace?

2 Years!!

Because of the high number of failures of start up businesses someone who is considered self-employed must have been in business for at least 2 years to even be eligible for a mortgage. A case can be made for considering a borrower who has been self-employed for less than two years if there is sufficient documentation to show that the income going forward has a reasonable probability of continuing.

Obviously, if the borrower has been in business for 22 or 23 months, and shows signs of success, it is probably close enough. If a borrower could go back to a salaried position, such as a lawyer, doctor or other professional, the risk is mitigated particularly if the income being used for qualifying is lower than the salary being earned before and the business and clients are the same. One could also make the argument that an existing businesses previous cash flow could be attributed towards the borrower who recently acquired it - if it were a franchise or other established business.

Who is Self-Employed?

An individual who owns 25% or more of a business would be defined as self-employed. In addition to income averaging at this level you must now analyze the business as well as the borrower. The first level of understanding is what kind of a business it is, because this determines what documentation is required and how the income is averaged.

Sole Proprietor	An 100% individually owned business with no separate legal entity or identity. There is no separation between the individual and the business. The only way to separate the person and the business accounts is if separate bank accounts are maintained. The benefit of this business form is its simplicity.	Schedule C Personal Tax Return
Partnership	A partnership is created with a legal contract that binds at least two people. There are stratification, or levels, of Partnership participation. A General Partner makes decisions concerning the operation of the business, and is liable for the business's debts. The General Partner may deduct certain items for tax purposes but are limited to the amount of capital that they have contributed and the amount that they have "at risk". A Limited Partner does not participate in the operation of business and is liable only to the extent that their investment in the partnership is at risk. K-1 will detail ownership interest, General or Limited Partner, Capital Contributions.	Partnership Return is Federal 1065. Personal Income on K-1 and Schedule E of 1040's
"C" Corporation	A corporation is a legal entity created within a specific state for which shares of stock are issued. The stock may be sold to the public or privately to get money for the business operation. Owner(s) of stock are entitled to participate in the profit of the company. A Board of Directors controls decisions over the operation of the business. Owners of stock are liable only for their initial investment, not for business debts. The corporation may retain or disburse income at its discretion. In addition, there may be a fiscal year different than a calendar year, which may make year to year analysis difficult	Corporation Tax Return is Form 1120. Personal Income is W-2.
"S" Corporation	"S" Corporations are a hybrid combination of Partnerships and Corporations. Business income must be claimed within a calendar year (like a partnership) and cannot be carried forward. However, shares of stock are issued and owners are limited in liability to their initial investment.	1120S Federal Tax Return, K-1 from 1040
LLC & LLP	"Limited Liability Corporations" and "Limited Liability Partnerships" are recent innovations. From a tax perspective, they will mirror the business form of Corporation and Partnership. The benefit of this form is that Officers and Partners will have less personal liability.	
Trader	An individual who buys and sells on his or her own account, such as a stock investor or real estate speculator.	Schedule D 1040
Investor	An individual who owns and rents real estate, or other income producing assets.	Schedule E 1040

Treatment of Self-Employment Income.

One of the primary benefits of self-employment is that there are expenses, allowable write-offs, deductions, and deferments that reduce taxable income can offset many ways income. The fewer taxes you pay, the more money you keep - simple! Taxable income is net income. Often there is confusion when a self-employed borrower reports Gross Income, which is not the income the lender will use for qualifying. In addition, companies themselves are vehicles for storing money or assets necessary for operation of the business. This money does not get taken out until it is needed or the business is liquidated. This is legitimate tax avoidance - not tax evasion. There are many wealthy self-employed people who pay far less in taxes than their employed counterparts. By it's very nature self-employment income verification is in direct contradiction to the goals of the loan officer. The borrower wants to show the best possible picture to the lender, but the worst picture to the IRS. The problem here is that both the IRS and the lender have to use the same source of information - the Federal Tax Forms. Tax avoidance is one of the biggest businesses in the country, and the playing field is littered with the most well educated lawyers and accountants whose own livelihood depends on saving their clients money.

Because each self-employed borrower is unique, many lending personnel have a phobia of analyzing this income. Every lending manual prescribing varying methods of how to do it exacerbates this phobia. The underwriters at FNMA probably thought that they were helping when they designed 3 different self-employed income analysis forms for lenders to use in assisting evaluating tax returns. In fact the forms themselves raise other quandaries; should I use the Adjusted Gross Income Method or the Schedule Analysis Method? Why do you need a comparative income analysis - can't you just see whether the income is increasing or decreasing? The problem with these forms is that they try and provide the same treatment for all forms of self-employment. So to be comprehensive the worksheet is very long and daunting. In addition, they give the impression that there are some types of income that must be excluded.

The truth is that every self-employed borrower is different. You can't use a pre-printed form and fairly maximize the income. The only method that works is to **actually read the entire tax return!!** The depth of the analysis goes back to the first question asked in this chapter - How much income does the borrower need to show to qualify for the loan they want? If they qualify based on a 2-year average of the adjusted gross income from the first page of the tax returns, you don't need to perform a further analysis. If they are challenged at that level, though, get out a pencil and be prepared to read and write. The philosophy of self-employed income analysis is to find all of the deferred income, deductions, non-cash losses, and duplicative expenses deducted by the business and held against the borrower **and add them on back to, or on top of,** taxable income. The result should be tallied in column form, by year, and averaged for the period analyzed (generally two years) to result in qualifying income.

Start With the Personal Returns

The most frequent complaint we encounter in analyzing self-employed borrowers is the complexity. Like many things, the way to tackle a complex task is to break it down into its components and work from there. Break apart the personal returns from the business as a beginning and begin analyzing where the income comes from. The Federal 1040 will be the basis of the income analysis, so always start the analysis here, even though additional information and/or returns may be needed to complete the review. Take a blank piece of paper, or a spreadsheet, make the first column the most recent year, write down the source of each piece of income from the first page. As you note the income from the 1040, to see what deductions have been taken that can be added back in go to the corresponding schedule.

Income Sources & "Addbacks"

The general theory of adding deductions back to the taxable income is based on the fact that these deductions did not actually affect the bottom line of the business. They are allowable "Paper" Deductions. You can almost always add back depreciation. A gray area is the concept of "non-recurring expenses". If, for instance there is a large deduction for attorney's fees, and the applicant's position is that this suit was settled and won't occur again, how do you know that it won't?

In isolated cases the borrower may have income which is paid to him - a schedule E

Source	Description & Addback Rationale
W-2, 1099, Tips	Salary & Other Income - Compare to Company Return for Consistency
Schedule B, Interest/Dividends	Asset be verified and remain after closing. Non-Taxable income can be added back in and "grossed-up", if necessary. Notes receivable must continue for 3 years.
Schedule C - Sole Proprietor	Since the borrower and the entity are one and the same, look for duplicative expenses. Car Expenses - is a car loan paid by the business? If yes deduct it from the debts. Add back Business use of the home, Depreciation. "Optional" expenses like contributions, pension/profit sharing can be added back. If there will be a home office and rent will be eliminated, add the rent back.
Schedule D	Capital Gains can only be counted as income if there is a history of assets purchased and sold, and if the assets remain. Deductions from gain, exclusions and non-cash losses can be added back.
Schedule E - Rent and Royalty Income	Two Methods: 1.) Ignore Tax Returns, Take Rental Income supported by leases, deduct 25% and subtract Debt Service. 2.) Analyze Schedule E for Addbacks - Depreciation, Anomolies such as tenant evictions, and eliminate properties sold. Newly added properties must utilize 1st method. Partnership and S Corporation Income is also reported here, but addbacks come from the K-1 or business returns.
Schedule F - Farm Income	An active farm may not be eligible for financing. Depreciation, interest payments accounted for in the ratios can be added back.

Property (it may even be a vehicle he leases back to himself) which he pays the rent on. It may make sense to look for an add-back here, but is must be done in the context of which works better for qualifying. If it is added back as a non-cash loss, then there may be a mortgage to be added to debts.

Partnership and S Corporation Tax Returns and Income Analysis

If the borrower's income is from a partnership or S Corporation the **K-1 Form** will determine the ownership interest. If the interest is more than **25%** the entity's returns must be analyzed. Unlike C Corporations, Partnerships and S Corporations must operate on a calendar year and their specific purpose is as a vehicle to disburse all income to the owners to avoid duplicate taxation. The K-1 Form itself will give the partners' share of deductible expenses which can be added back - depreciation, charitable contributions, and tax credits. An analysis of the tax returns can reveal other add-backs, non-cash deductions, and non-recurring expenses. A partner would generally not receive a salary from the partnership. If it is referred to as salary, it is more likely that it is a guaranteed draw or distribution. Conversely, an S Corporation can pay its officers a salary. In addition it may not be clear that there is an ownership interest if the borrower does not have a corporate title. Caution must be taken to identify that, if the borrower is an officer, the K-1 Statement be requested to determine if there is ownership interest. If there is ownership interest, the borrower is not considered salaried and must submit to income averaging.

Limited Partnerships may be treated differently if the purpose of the entity is to provide a tax shelter. These are investments, generally, and do not represent the individual's primary source of income. If there are limited partnership losses that reduce income these should be added back in because the limited partner is only liable up to the extent of his initial investment. In other words, the loss doesn't represent a negative going forward, it is an expression of the deteriorating value of the initial investment.

Analyzing the US Corporation Income Tax Return

One of the unique advantages of the Corporation ("C Corporation" as opposed to "Subchapter S Corporation") is the ability to operate on a fiscal year that is different from the fiscal year. This is referred to as "Straddling". Because C Corporations have the highest income tax rate of any form, this straddling allows the company to declare income over two years, or offset a loss in one year against income in another to reduce the impact of taxation. The benefit for the corporation, however, becomes a challenge for the underwriter. This is because the fiscal year has to be reconciled with the calendar year of the individual returns

The borrower's income will appear under officer's compensation. This is the W-2 income accounted for on the personal tax returns. The corporation's net income is also income to the borrower. To determine how much income from the corporation can be attributed to the borrower take taxable income and start **adding back non-cash losses, depreciation, depletion, duplicative expenses, discretionary or voluntary expenses, and contributions to profit sharing plans.** The result is the corporation income that the borrower can utilize for qualifying. This amount is multiplied by the ownership percentage of the borrower.

Retained earnings are a curious phenomenon. It is income that was previously declared but not paid out and has been added to the corporation's balance sheet. As a result it is possible to count this as income if it can be shown that it resulted in a year that is not being utilized in the income computation. In other words, if you were analyzing 1995 and 1996 returns and there were retained earnings in 1996, and not in 1995, that income has already been accounted for in the average. However, if retained earnings are carried forward to 1995 and not 1996, a case can be made to utilize the 1995 portion, because it hasn't been counted anywhere else.

The **balance sheet** is a part of the corporation return. It shows positives such as retained earnings. But it may also show negatives such as a deterioration of cash position from the beginning to the end of the year. Also, loans that come due within 12 months must be deducted from corporate income.

Borrowers who do not take income from the corporation, but loan themselves money are avoiding tax consequences. The loans may show as assets for the company. This cannot be counted as income. However, if the borrower decides to repay the corporation and it can be documented with copies of the promissory notes, checks payable to the borrower, and a letter from the accountant, it is possible to increase the corporation's income, which would then be attributable to the borrower.

The Profit and Loss Statement

An Income Statement, Profit and Loss, or other bookkeeping record is required to cover the period between the end of the most recent tax period and document the business performance up to the current time - within 90 days. It is a concern as to whether an accountant must prepare the statement. The extent of preparation of this document is contingent upon how much weight the underwriter needs to give the income from this period. If the reliance on the income statement is just to show that the business is on track, it can be self-prepared. If the income is needed for qualification, either because of a short business experience or to document an increasing income stream, an account prepared statement is necessary. The same treatment for the profit and loss should be taken as with the tax returns - non-cash losses, duplicative expenses, and tax treatment deductions such as depreciation, depletion and amortization, as well as any discretionary contributions should be added back to the year to date income, for qualifying.

Level	Description
Self-Prepared	The borrower or internal accounting mechanism may prepare the document. It must be signed and accompanied by a perjury statement
Compilation	An accountant takes the borrower's information, and presents it in proper format, addressing apparent issues
Audit	An accountant reviews all inflows and outgoes independently and presents a thorough view of the operation's financial condition. Because of the time and expense involved, an audit is not mandatory.

The Balance Sheet

As part of the profit and loss statement of the borrower's company, there should be a section dealing with the assets and liabilities of a company called the balance sheet. There are some useful aspects of this. Since a company is often a vehicle to keep wealth from being taxed, there may be a **large net worth** that can be added to the borrowers net worth. In addition, liquid assets that the borrower might have access to or even retirement funds would appear here. On the other hand, the balance sheet can reveal weaknesses. Most importantly **notes and loans receivable within one year** are counted against the company's income.

Self Employment Analysis Tools

There are a number of tools that you can use to make the process of income analysis more a matter of discovering facts and less making numerical calculations. The spreadsheets on the following pages are available to modify as you like.

Simple Analysis

The simple analysis is for situations when the larger self-employment calculations are not appropriate and we are simply trying to average income over a period.

Income Analysis
Simple Income Analysis

	2006	**2007**	**2008**
Net Income	$15,014.00	$5,662.00	$12,322.00
Add Back:			
Depreciation	$0.00	$11,257.00	$580.00
Home Office Expense	$695.00	$852.00	$0.00
Qualifying Income	$15,709.00	$17,771.00	$12,902.00
Total	$46,382.00		
Averaged over	$34.00 Months		
Stable Monthly Income	**$1,364.18**		

Self-Employed Income Analysis - Adjusted Gross Income Method

This is the traditional self-employed analysis, where you take the bottom line, and add back in certain standard deductions. While there is a version of this form in POINT under SEIA, it is not as flexible as a stand-alone form

---

Fannie Mae
Self-Employed Income Analysis

Borrower Name

Property Address

General Instructions: This form is to be used as a guide in Underwriting the Self-Employed Borrower. The underwriter has a choice in analyzing the Individual Tax Return by either the Schedule Analysis Method or the Adjusted Gross Income (AGI) Method.

The AGI Method begins with adjusted gross income from the individual tax returns and either increases or decreases that figure after analyzing specific lines and schedules of the return. This method derives total income (both business and non-business)
If the borrower has passive activity unallowed losses or loss carryovers, use the Schedule Analysis Method of analyzing income.

Adjusted Gross Income (AGI) Method

	+/-	1996	1997	1998
A. Individual Tax Return (Form 1040)				
1. Adjusted Gross Income:				
INCOME SECTION				
2. Wages, salary considered elsewhere	(-)			
3. Taxable Interest Income *Only deducted if asset is liquidated to close*	(-)			
4. Tax-Exempt Interest Income	(+)			
5. Dividend Income *Only deducted if asset is liquidated to close*	(-)			
6. Taxable Refunds	(-)			
7. Alimony	(-)			
8. Business Income or Loss - Schedule C				
a. Depletion	(+)			
b. Depreciation	(+)			
c. 20% Meals and Entertainment Exclusion	(-)			
9. (-) Capital Gain or (+) Capital Loss - Schedule D				
10. IRA Distributions (Non-Taxable)	(+)			
11. Pensions and Annuities (Non-taxable)	(+)			
12. Schedule E - Depreciation	(+)			
13. Schedule F - Depreciation	(+)			
14. Unemployment Compensation	(-)			
15. Social Security Benefits (Non-taxable)	(+)			
16. Other - Schedule E, Loss Carryforwards				
Adjustment Section				
17. IRA Deduction	(+)			
18. One Half of Self-employed Tax	(+)			
19. Self-Employed Health Insurance	(+)			
20. Keogh Retirement Plan	(+)			
21. Penalty for Early Withdrawal	(+)			
22. Alimony Paid	(+)			
Additional Schedules				
23. Form 2106 Unreimbursed Expenses	(-)			
24. Form 4562 Amortization	(+)			
Total Income				
Year to Date				
1. Salary/Draws to Individual				

Self-Employed Income Analysis - Schedule Analysis

This method addresses the various schedules that comprise the self-employed borrower's tax returns. This method allows for more subjective analysis of various components and is more appropriate for borrowers who have "non-natural" business forms, like partnerships and corporations.

Income "Red Flags"

In some situations a borrower's documentation simply raises questions that have to be addressed. In others, discrepancies may be an indication of a borrower trying to conceal facts or perpetrate fraud. Being aware of these warning signs can eliminate problems later in the loan process.

Fannie Mae
Self-Employed Income Analysis

Borrower Name

Property Address

General Instructions: This form is to be used as a guide in Underwriting the Self-Employed Borrower. The underwriter has a choice in analyzing the Individual Tax Return by either the Schedule Analysis Method or the Adjusted Gross Income (AGI) Method.

The Schedule Analysis Method derives total income by analyzing Schedule C, D, E and F for stable continuing self-employed income.

Schedule Analysis Method

A. Individual Tax Return (Form 1040)   19___   19___   19___
   1. Schedule C:
     a. Net Profit or (Loss)
     b. Depletion   +
     c. Depreciation   +
     d. Less 20% Exclusion For Meals & Entertainment   (-)
     e. Home Office Expense   +
   2. Schedule D
     Recurring Capital Gains   +
   3. Partnership S Corporation Income (Loss)
     a. Section 179 Deduction   +
   4. Schedule E
     a. Net Profit or Loss
     b. Depreciation   +
   5. Schedule 2106
     Total Expenses   (-)
   6. W-2 Income From Corporation   +
   7. Total

B. Corporate Tax Return Form (1120) - Corporate Income to Qualify the borrower will only be considered if the borrower can provide evidence of access to the funds.
   1. Taxable Income (Tax & Payments Section)   +
   2. Total Tax (Tax & Payments Section)   (-)
   3. Depreciation   +
   4. Depletion   +
   5. Mortgages, notes, bonds payable in less than one year   (-)
     (Balance Sheet Section)
   6. Subtotal
   7. Times Individual Percentage of Ownership   x
   8. Subtotal
   9. Dividend Income reflected on borrower's individual   (-)
     income tax returns
   10. Total income available to borrower

C. S Corporation Tax Returns (Form 1120S) or Partnership Tax Returns (Form 1065) - Partnership or S Corporation income to qualify the borrower will be considered only if the borrower can provided evidence of access to the funds.
   1. Depreciation (Deductions Section)   +
   2. Amortization (Deductions Section)   +
   2.a. Nondeductible Shareholder Benefits
   3. Mortgages, notes, bonds payable in less than one year
     (Balance Sheets Section)   (-)
   4. Subtotal
   5. Times individual percentage of ownership   x   * %age already consider
   6. Total income available to borrower

EMPLOYMENT / EMPLOYMENT VERIFICATION

- Employee is paid monthly
- No prior year earnings on VOE
- Gross earnings per VOE for commission-only employees should not be used (see IRS Form 1040 Schedule C)
- Borrower is a business professional (may be self-employed)
- Answering machine or service at place of business (may be self-employed)
- Prior employer "out of business"
- Seller has same address as employer
- Employer signs VOE prior to date it was mailed by the lender
- Borrower uses employer's letterhead for letters of explanation
- Employment verified by someone other than personnel department
- Pay stubs are not preprinted for a large employer
- Pay stubs are handwritten for a large employer
- Current and prior employment overlap
- Date of hire is weekend or holiday
- Income is primarily commissions or consulting fees (Self-employment)
- Employer uses mail drop or post office box for conducting business
- Change in profession from previous to current employer
- Borrower is a professional employee not registered/licensed (doctor, lawyer, architect, real estate broker, etc)

- Illegible employer signature with no further identification
- Inappropriate verification source (secretary, relative, etc.)
- Document is not folded (never mailed)
- Evidence of ink eradicator (whiteout) or other alterations
- Verification "returned to sender" for any reason
- Inappropriate salary with respect to amount of loan

SELF EMPLOYED
- (Some "red flags" are indicators that someone may be self employed, these are important if a borrower has not revealed themselves to be self employed)
- Business entity not registered or in good standing with the applicable regulatory agencies.
- Address and/or profession does not agree with other information submitted on the loan application
- Tax computation does not agree with tax tables
- No estimated tax payments made by self-employed borrower (Schedule SE required)
- No FICA taxes paid by self-employed borrower (Schedule SE required)
- Self employment income shown as wages and salaries
- Income or deductions in even dollar amounts
- High bracket taxpayer with few or no deductions or tax shelters
- High bracket taxpayer does not use a professional tax preparer.
- Paid preparer signs taxpayer's copy
- Paid preparer hand-writes tax return

TAX RETURNS
- Schedule A – Real estate taxes paid but no property owned
- Schedule A – No interest expense paid when borrower shows ownership of property (or vice versa)
- Schedule A – Employee who deducts business expenses (check against Form 2106)
- Schedule B – Amount or source of income doesn't agree with information submitted on loan application
- Schedule B – No dividends earned on stock owned (may be closely held)
- Schedule B – Borrower with substantial cash in bank shows little or no related interest income
- Schedule C – Gross income does not agree with total income per Form 1099
- Schedule C – Borrower shows interest expense but no related loan (business loans with personal liability)
- Schedule C – Borrower takes a depreciation deduction for real estate no disclosed (or vice versa)
- Schedule C – No IRA or Keogh deduction
- Schedule C – No salaries paid on non-service companies
- Schedule C – No "cost of goods sole" on retail or similar operations
- Schedule C – No schedule SE filed (computation of self-employed tax)
- Schedule E – Net income from rents plus depreciation does not equal cash flow as submitted by borrower.
- Schedule E – Additional properties listed by not on loan application
- Schedule E – Borrower shows partnership income (may be liable as a general partner for partnership's debts)
- Form W-2 – Invalid employer identification number
- Form W2 – FICA and local taxes withheld (where applicable) exceed ceilings
- Form W2 – Copy submitted is not "Employee's Copy" (Copy C)
- Form W2 – Large employer has handwritten or typed W-2

Chapter 6 – Document Review Asset Verification

Verifying Assets

Assets, down payment and closing costs are inextricably linked. Accurately assessing the sufficiency of assets to consummate a transaction requires an understanding of the components. This process is called qualifying for assets. Understanding what the costs are made up of allows you to quickly estimate and manipulate the numbers, tailoring the transaction for its requirements. It should be stated that one of the strongest factors in the loan approval process is the level of assets. Often, having a large amount of residual cash can make up for a shortfall in income.

What These Costs Represent

Understanding what the actual costs represent and who they are paid to can also help to explain the Good Faith Estimate and Settlement Statement.

Line	Paid to	Paid By - Description
700. Sales/Broker's Commission	Real Estate Broker	Seller - This is the total dollar amount of the real estate broker's sales commission, which is usually paid by the seller. This commission is typically a percentage of the selling price of the home
800 Section - Items Payable in Connection with Loan. These are the fees that lenders charge to process, approve and make the mortgage loan.		
801. Loan Origination	Lender or Broker	Buyer - This fee is usually known as a loan origination fee but sometimes is called a "point" or "points." It covers the lender's administrative costs in processing the loan and the costs of commissioned sales people. Often expressed as a percentage of the loan, the fee will vary among lenders. Generally, the buyer pays the fee, unless otherwise negotiated.

Line	Paid to	Paid By - Description
802. Loan Discount	Lender	Buyer/Seller - Also often called "points" or "discount points," a loan discount is a one-time charge imposed by the lender or broker to lower the rate at which the lender or broker would otherwise offer the loan to you. Each "point" is equal to one percent of the mortgage amount.
803. Appraisal Fee	Appraiser	Buyer - This charge pays for an appraisal report made by an appraiser
804. Credit Report Fee	Credit Bureau	Buyer - This fee covers the cost of a credit report, which shows your credit history. The lender uses the information in a credit report to help decide whether or not to approve your loan.
805. Lender's Inspection Fee	Lender	Buyer - This charge covers inspections, often of newly constructed housing, made by employees of your lender or by an outside inspector.
807. Assumption Fee	Lender	This is a fee which is charged when a buyer "assumes" or takes over the duty to pay the seller's existing mortgage loan.
808. Mortgage Broker Fee	Mortgage Broker	Buyer/Borrower, Seller, Lender - Often, lenders will not allow brokers to charge an origination fee and will insert the fee as a mortgage broker fee. In some cases, the fee paid to the broker is a yield spread premium and does not come out of the borrower's funds at all. If this is the case, the fee may show up as P.O.C. – (Paid Outside Closing)
809. Tax Service Fee	Tax Service Company	Buyer/Borrower – The Tax Service Contract runs for the life of the loan and reports to the lender when real estate taxes go past due. This is important because delinquent taxes allow the government to force the sale of the property without the lender's consent to satisfy back taxes.
810. Flood Certification	Flood Service Company	Buyer/Borrower – Also known as a "Flood Zone Determination" a flood certification is an independent confirmation as to whether a property is in a flood hazard area. If it is, the lender will require Federal Flood Insurance.
Section 900. Prepaid Items Required by Lender to Be Paid in Advance: You may be required to prepaycertain items at the time of settlement, such as accrued interest, mortgage insurance premiums and hazard insurance premiums.		
901. Interest	Lender	Borrower – Also known as per diem interest, this is the pro-rated amount of interest from the date of closing until regular principal and interest payments begin to accrue under the terms of the note.
902. Mortgage Insurance Premium	Lender - Mortgage Insurer	Borrower – Lenders require that the first year's private mortgage insurance premium or FHA Mortgage Insurance Premium, be paid in advance. Even if the premium will be financed, it will still appear as a charge here – the increased loan proceeds cover the cost.
903. Hazard Insurance Premium	Hazard Insurance Company	Buyer/Borrower - Hazard insurance protects against loss due to fire, windstorm, and natural hazards. Lenders often require the borrower to bring a paid-up first year's policy to the settlement or to pay for the first year's premium at settlement.
904. Flood Insurance	FEMA	Buyer – If the flood certification indicates a flood hazard, the lender will require flood insurance.
1000. Section - RESERVES DEPOSITED WITH LENDER		

Line	Paid to	Paid By - Description
1001. Hazard Insurance 1002. Mortgage insurance 1003. City property taxes 1004. County property taxes	Insurer or Municipality Collected by Lender	Buyer – Lines 1000 – 1008 are Escrow Account Deposits. These lines identify the payment of taxes and/or insurance and other items that must be made at settlement to set up an escrow account. The lender is not allowed to exceed a cushion of 2 months.
Section 1100. Title Charges: Title charges may cover a variety of services performed by title companies and others to conduct the closing. These costs for these services/items may vary widely from provider to provider.		
1101. Settlement or Closing Fee	Title, Escrow Company or Attorney	This fee is paid to the settlement agent or escrow company. Responsibility for payment of this fee should be negotiated between the seller and the buyer.
1102-1104 Abstract of Title Search, Title Examination, Title Insurance Binder	Title, Escrow Company or Attorney	The charges on these lines cover the costs of the title search and examination, so that the closing agent can perfect the clear title for the property.
1105. Document Preparation	Title, Escrow Company or Attorney	This is a separate fee to cover the costs of preparation of final legal papers, such as a settlement statement, mortgage, deed of trust, note, transfer or deed
1106. Notary Fee	Title, Escrow Company or Attorney	A Notary Public takes oaths and, in the case of the real estate closing, attests to the fact that the persons named in the documents did, in fact, sign them.
1107. Attorney's Fees	Title, Escrow Company or Attorney	An attorney is traditionally required to review any drafting of legal documents. Since most loan documents are pre-printed forms, an attorney may not be required for the closing. Attorney's fees are, however, compensable settlement services. Occasionally, a vendor may place their Closing or Escrow fee here.
1108. Title Insurance	Title, Escrow Company or Attorney	Lender's Title Insurance covering the loan amount, is a normal a requirement of a lender. Owner's title insurance, which insures the owner's equity based on the sales price less the loan amount, is not. The charge is variable based on the size of the policy.
Section 1200. Government Recording and Transfer Charges		
1201. Recording Fee	Jurisdiction Courthouse	Buyer/Borrower- The fees for accepting for record the new deed and mortgage/trust. Normally a per page charge.
1202 and 1203. Transfer Taxes, Tax Stamps	State/Local Government	Buyer/Seller/Borrower - Transfer taxes may be collected whenever property changes hands or a mortgage loan is made. These are taxes on the transaction and are set by state and/or local governments. These may be referred to as tax stamps, recording stamps, recording taxes or other names.
Section 1300. Additional Settlement Charges:		
1301. Survey	Surveyor	Buyer/Borrower – Technically part of the title insurance, a survey examines whether any property line violations exist that could impact the marketability of the title.
1302. Pest and Other Inspections	Inspection Company	Termite or Wood Destroying Pest Inspections assure there is no active infestation or damage. Well/Septic for non public water/sewer property. Final Completion for new construction or repairs.

Seller Contributions

Depending on the loan program, a seller may assist by paying for closing costs on behalf of a buyer. This is called a contribution because it is a standard practice and pays for actual costs normally incurred by a buyer. This is acceptable because the lender still assures that the borrower is making an equity contribution in the form of a down payment.

Seller Concessions Reduce Sales Price	
Sales Price	100,000
Down Payment (5%)	5,000
Loan Amount	95,000
Concession	-10,000
Actual Sales Price after Concession	90,000
Borrower Equity	- 5,000

There are limitations as to what the seller can pay for. The reason for this is that excessive seller contributions may artificially inflate the sales price. Excessive contributions are called concessions. For instance, a seller trying to sell a house without a swimming pool to a buyer who wants a swimming pool agrees to give the buyer $10,000 to pay for a swimming pool to be installed. The reality is that the house price is being inflated to pay for a swimming pool that does not yet exist. The danger in an inflated sales price is that the financing is based upon a certain amount of equity contribution - or down payment - from the buyer as a personal investment. The seller's concession may erode the buyer's equity contribution to the point where the loan balance is greater than the value of the house. As a result concessions may be allowed, but the underwriter/lender should make a downward adjustment to the loan amount to compensate for a lower equity contribution.

It may seem a contradictory technicality that a seller contribution of 3% of the sales price towards closing costs is acceptable, but a 3% decorator's allowance is not. To a certain extent it is, because everyone accepts the fact that seller assistance is based upon a certain amount of price inflation. From the seller's perspective it is all the same. A sales price of $100,000 in a transaction with no contribution as opposed to a $103,000 sales price with a 3% contribution nets the seller approximately the same amount of money. The distinction is one of valuation. If the contribution is traditional in the marketplace, and the inflated selling price is supported by other comparable sales, then the lender has some certainty that the borrower's equity contribution/down payment is bona fide.

Avoiding Problems with Seller Contributions

- **Watch for concessions**, especially on transactions where a reduced sales price could have an impact on the loan approval. An 80% LTV loan with a concession could push the loan into a PMI requirement. Decorator/repair allowances are concessions.
- **Don't specify what can and cannot be paid** with the seller contribution. Specify a flat dollar amount. This allows the buyer the maximum flexibility in structuring financing. In addition, this will avoid disputes at closing regarding who is responsible for paying certain fees.
-

Assets for Down Payment, Closing Costs and Reserves

The borrower may have saved cash over time, or may be selling a current home and reinvesting the proceeds. In fact, the borrower may have waited until he or she has a surplus of cash beyond what is needed to close and if this is the case, a discussion of assets isn't really necessary. It is when the borrower doesn't have the appropriate sufficient funds that a loan officer earns the commission. Here is a listing of some possible alternative sources of down payment funds.

Source	Description/Treatment
Gift	Gifts from family are an acceptable source of funds. With FNMA/FHLMC financing, the borrowers must document that they have 5% of the sales price of their own funds invested into the transaction. If the down payment is 20% or more, the 5% limitation does not apply. FNMA/FHLMC requires that the source, transfer, and receipt of the gift be verified. "No income verification" loans do not generally allow the use of gift funds. FHA/VA does not limit the amount of the gift and does not care who the source is, provided there is no business relationship. SEE GIFT TIPS!
Sale of Asset	If a borrower has any property that could be sold, such as coin or stamp collection, jewelry, used cars, artwork, rugs, or anything of durable value, this can be used as a source of funds for closing. A sales receipt is required, along with a copy of the payment to authenticate the sale. The asset may also be used to meet post closing reserve requirements, if a reputable dealer ascertains the item's value and what the dealer would pay for it - to demonstrate its liquidity. An insurance policy stating the value of an asset is also substantiation of value.
Borrowing	Borrowing against an asset is an acceptable source of down payment funds. Loans include 401(k), life insurance policy or other retirement savings plan loans that provide for partial liquidation in emergency or home purchase. <u>Pawnshops are excellent sources of secured loans</u>, lending on everything from musical instruments, technical equipment, jewelry, cars, silverware, or anything of durable value, and you get a receipt. Many stock accounts have margin options, which is a loan secured by stock. A credit union may lend you money on an unsecured basis and take something of value as security for the purposes of a home loan. With the exception of VA, loans for down payment and closing costs must be secured. FHA/VA - Borrowing is not an acceptable way of making up the difference between the sales price and appraised value. **YOU MUST ALWAYS QUALIFY CARRYING THE LOAN PAYMENT!**
Side Jobs	If a borrower needs to make up a small cash shortfall to meet the requirement to provide 5% of the funds, consider performing some personal services, such as house sitting, painting, dog walking, lawn mowing, catering, etc. Because these are not subject to withholding taxes, and because they are paid immediately and usually by personal check, these funds can quickly absorb cash shortfalls. These cannot be counted as income, but are acceptable sources of cash if documented properly. Handicraft sales can achieve the same goal.
Rental/Deposits	Often the rental security deposit is overlooked as a source of cash reserves. A letter from the landlord stating that a security deposit refund is due can substantiate the amount of money underwriting may use as a reserve.
Repayment of Personal Loans	You lent someone money 5 years ago, but have been letting it go because you are friends. They didn't sign a note, but you wrote them a check. Get them to pay you back, at least partially. A letter from the borrower, a copy of the original check and copy of the repayment are required.

Source	Description/Treatment
Gambling Earnings	When you gamble and win a large amount of money, a casino may write you a check in lieu of cash. Again, while this is not a source of income, it can be acceptable documentation of funds.

Borrower's Own Funds

The guideline that the borrower must have 5% of his or her own funds is a reflection of the fact that as lenders we want to show that the borrower has some attachment to the property. If they are leveraging a purchase to the point that they do not have any real investment of money and are receiving all gift funds, then there is little inclination for the borrower to sacrifice and make the payment of the mortgage a priority. Some Community Homebuyer programs allow as little as 0%, 2% or 3% of the borrower's own funds to be invested into a transaction. The portfolio performance of borrowers having less than 5% of their own funds invested into the property is roughly 300% worse than traditional 95% LTV programs. Expect that this is an issue that is heavily scrutinized when the borrower's funds situation is very close.

Reserves

One of the last trip wires you may encounter in qualifying is that there are insufficient funds in reserve. Reserves are moneys lenders require to offset any unseen cash shortfalls and to show that, after the transaction, the borrower isn't broke. The standard guideline is to have 2 months' PITI remaining after all down payment, closing costs and prepaid items are met. This is because there are costs outside of the transaction (moving expenses, necessary sundries like shower curtains and garbage cans, inspections, etc.) that will absorb some cash flow ordinarily devoted to making the payment. Any of the sources mentioned above would suffice for reserves and wouldn't have to be liquidated. FHA requires only 15 days of interest in reserve. VA doesn't care and some Community Homebuyer programs waive the reserve requirements if the case is strong.

> **Qualifying Tip:** To offset any projected qualifying cash shortfall, consider adding the borrower's name to a relative or friend's bank account. The statements can be shown and counted towards cash or reserves as long as a letter is obtained stating that the borrower has complete access to those funds.

Lender Credits for "Above Par" Pricing Towards Closing Costs

You can use the "above par," rebate, or yield spread towards some of the purchaser's closing costs, prepaid items, or other fees. In certain cases, the amount of the premium is limited to the amount of the seller contribution allowed under the specific loan plan.

Using Yield Spread to Contribute to Closing Costs		
Sales Price	$	100,000
Loan Amount	$	95,000
Down Payment	$	5,000
Closing Costs	$	1,500
Total Cash Required	$	6,500
Price on Loan Sale ("above par")		103.50%
Cash from "Yield Spread"	$	3,325
Less Lender Cost of Loan	$	1,425
Cash Available to Borrower	$	1,900

Tips for Gifts

The gift letter form is designed to state the intention that funds received are a "bona fide" gift, and that there is no explicit, or implicit, requirement for repayment. To substantiate that there is no implicit repayment required and to confirm that the funds received are, in fact, gift funds and not funds from another source, we require that the following documentation be provided in addition to the actual gift letter:

Donor's Ability to Give	This shows that the person giving the gift actually has the funds to give. This can be accomplished two ways. • The donor can provide a complete bank statement showing that the funds are available in their depository institution, or • The donor can take the gift letter form, when Section A is complete, and have the depository institution complete Section B.

Proof of Transfer	The "paper trail" of funds must be established to document that the funds received are actually from the donor and not an undisclosed or borrowed source. To do this the following must be provided:
	1. Proof of withdrawal of funds from donor. This can be accomplished by providing
	    a. A copy of the cancelled check from the donor,
	    b. A copy of the withdrawal slip from the donor's account,
	    c. Copies of the wire transfer advice. If a broker or 3rd party is liquidating funds on behalf of the donor, copies of this transaction must be made (i.e., debit memo, inter account transfer, etc.).
	2. Proof of receipt of gift funds. This can be provided in the form of
	    a. A copy of the recipient's deposit slip,
	    b. A copy of the wire transfer advice or
	    c. A copy of the credit memorandum from the bank

Verification of New Balance	Once the gift funds have been received, we need to prove that the funds, now received, are sufficient to complete the transaction. To accomplish this, when the gift is deposited, please have your bank provide a letter with the following verbiage: *PLEASE BE ADVISED THAT $_____ (gift sum) HAS BEEN DEPOSITED INTO THE ACCOUNT OF _____ (recipient's name) ACCOUNT NUMBER _____ (recipient's account). THIS DEPOSIT IS IN ADDITION TO THE CURRENT BALANCE OF $ _____ (recipient's current account balance). THIS WILL RESULT IN A NEW BALANCE OF $_____ (gift deposit combined with current balance)* *Signature of Depository, Date*

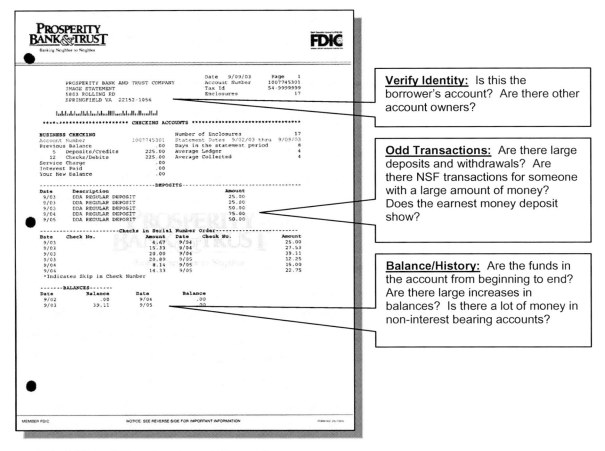

"Red Flags" for Assets and Deposits

Review the asset portion of the borrower's application closely for inconsistencies. Asset documentation is one of the most difficult to track areas in the mortgage process. These warning signs can help you avoid pitfalls in the loan process.

VERIFICATION OF ASSETS /DEPOSIT / BANK STATEMENT
- Regular deposits (payroll) significantly at odds with reported income
- Earnest Money Deposit not debited to checking account
- NSF items require explanation.
- Large withdrawals may indicate undisclosed financial obligations or investments
- Lower income borrower with recent large accumulation of cash
- Bank account is not in borrower's name (business entity, trust funds, etc.)
- Evidence of ink eradicator (whiteout) or other alterations
- Verification "returned to sender" for any reason
- High income borrower with little or no cash (undisclosed liabilities)
- IRA is shown as a liquid asset or a source of down payment
- Non-depository "depository" (escrow trust account, title company, etc.)
- Credit union for small employer
- Borrower's funds are security for a loan
- Illegible bank employee signature with no further identification
- Source of funds consist of (unverified) note, equity exchange or sale of residence
- Cash in bank not sufficient to close escrow
- New bank account

- Gift letters must be carefully reviewed (canceled checks, bank statements)
- Borrower has no bank accounts (doesn't believe in banks)
- Document is not folded (never mailed)
- Young borrower with large accumulation of unsubstantiated assets
- Young borrowers with substantial cash in bank

The Earnest Money Deposit

In a purchase transaction, the borrower normally makes a deposit towards the purchase of the property. Verifying the earnest money deposit can be challenging because of the timing of the transaction. If the borrower made the deposit well in advance of loan application, the check may have cleared the bank.

Status of Deposit	Proof	Verified?
Paid prior to application - Cleared	Copy of deposit check to Real estate Broker and copy of Bank Statement	<ul><li>Identify bank statement where check has cleared by placing behind copy of earnest money deposit and on top of purchase contract copy in file.</li><li>Highlight check number and amount and</li><li>Give borrower credit for deposit paid under "Deposits – Other on 1003".</li><li>Do NOT give borrower credit for Statement Balance including Deposit.</li></ul>
Paid at time of Application - Cleared	Copy of Deposit check and Verification of Deposit	<ul><li>Request VOD</li><li>On VOD type specific language which asks Depository to "Please verify that Check #_____ in amount of $ _____ has/has not cleared. Date Cleared _____"</li><li>Give borrower credit for deposit paid under "Deposits – Other on 1003". Do not double count</li><li>Place copy of VOD behind earnest money check and on top of Purchase Contract</li><li>Do NOT give borrower credit for Statement Balance AND earnest money deposit. Use Statement Balance, less deposit or VOD balance – whichever is more advantageous to borrower.</li></ul>
Paid at Application – Not Cleared	Copy of Deposit Check	<ul><li>Place copy of deposit check on top of contract</li><li>Give borrower credit for Statement Balance</li><li>Do NOT give borrower credit for Deposit Check Balance</li></ul>

Using Direct Verifications to Solve Asset Problems

A direct verification of deposit is very useful to solve problems with asset verification. It is not unusual for buyers to move money around, have influx or outflow of cash, or consolidate funds prior to the purchase of a home. Underwriting guidelines are focus on verification to uncover any undisclosed debt. When the movement of funds is just an issue of convenience, the processor can avoid unnecessary questions may be raised by this activity with deposit verification. In addition, verification of the receipt of funds, and credits like a cancelled or paid earnest money deposit can be accomplished with the VOD.

Deposit Verifications may not pass through the hands of anyone who has a financial interest in the transaction, like the loan officer, realtor or borrower.

Avoid Confusing Bank Statements: Often, manually computing an average balance from statements can understate the actual average balance. Deposit Verification solves this problem.

Request Specific Information: Request the proof that the earnest money deposit has cleared, or that a gift has been received.

Chapter 7 - Documentation Review - Property Information Appraisals, Projects and New Construction

Understanding Property Types

We have learned that different types of borrowers present special risks. The loan program, down payment or other characteristics may be reasons a loan may not meet guidelines. One major facet of risk is the type of property being given as security or collateral. Primarily, there are two sources of risk that drive property underwriting: 1.) what kind of risk is the lender taking if they have to re-sell the property after a foreclosure? and 2.) What kind of risk is the borrower accepting by living in a certain property type?

Usually, property risk begins when the density of units increases. When someone buys a single-family house, with public streets and no common areas, there is limited risk as to outside forces impacting the borrower. However, risk increases when the property is part of a Homeowner's Association that is responsible for maintaining common areas such as roads, pools, tennis courts, landscape, etc. In a situation like this, for instance, someone might slip and fall on a community road, and sue the homeowner's association. If the association lost the suit and there wasn't sufficient insurance, they might go bankrupt which would adversely impact property values.

There are numerous forms of property ownership, each impacting the risk of the individual loan. In addition, within each type of property ownership, there may be sub-types of property, which impact the risk, such as a mobile home project, a log cabin or historic home, or a condominium with a commercial/retail influence. Property Types by Ownership Form

Property Type	Description
PUD (Planned Unit Development)	This refers to a property comprised of Single Family Homes, Town Houses or Condominiums. The individual homes and land are privately owned, but common elements such as roads, open areas and recreational facilities are owned and maintained by a mandatory Homeowner's Association. Individuals owners in PUDs are required to be members in and pay for the Homeowners Association.

Property Type	Description
Condominium	A Condominium is created out of vertical air space. Instead of owning a parcel of land, you purchase a subdivided piece of space contained within a condominium regime, which might be an apartment or a townhouse. The walls, common elements and all improvements are owned and maintained by the condominium.
Cooperative	A cooperative is a corporation that owns real estate. To purchase a cooperative unit the owner actually purchases a pro rata share of the corporation stock. The corporation is responsible for paying real estate taxes, underlying mortgages, and maintenance of all common elements.
Leasehold	A leasehold estate is a long-term ground lease. Renting land out for unencumbered use instead of selling creates a ground lease. At the end of the lease term the land is returned, in its improved state, to the landlord.
Fee Simple	Also referred to as SFD (single family detached) property, this means that the land is unencumbered by any covenant requiring ownership in an association. An attached home can be Fee Simple as well.

Why Condos are Hard to Finance

Like many forms of property ownership, the development of condominium ownership and the lending guidelines surrounding it have evolved to reflect the industry's experience. Condominium ownership creates a high density of individually owned units. The risks and guidelines are based on common sense. Unlike a Planned Unit Development, where the owner maintains each individual house, the owner's association maintains a condominium building. Unlike a cooperative, where the board of directors of the corporation can be selective about who can live there, condominiums cannot have restrictive covenants. They cannot exclude people who might default on the maintenance obligations (a condominium unit that is owned by an investor who rents out the unit would have less of a vested interest in project maintenance) such as absentee owners. Because project maintenance relies on owner's contributions, a project's soundness is impacted by the overall ability of the unit owners to pay for the operation of the condominium.

Conforming Guidelines

Keep in mind that, just like in underwriting a loan, a project underwriter may decide that a project has superior factors and merits an exception. As a result, particularly with new projects, the agencies may make exceptions to their standard guidelines. FNMA and FHLMC both have guidelines for condominium projects. The classifications address the level of risk and approval.

Effective 5/1/05 FNMA has eliminated the approval classifications known as A, B, and C. It has replaced these approval criteria with new processes. The announcement was met with much elation, but a closer examination showed that the guidelines were only moderated somewhat. Most importantly was a slightly lower pre-sale and investor concentration requirement. A major modification was the release of FNMA's Condo Project Manager (CPM) program which automated the approval process and allowed lenders to save time in managing condominium project lists and documents.

Condominium Classifications by Agency

	FNMA	FHLMC
New Project	**"Formerly" Type C** - Direct FNMA approval required. 1028 - is a form issued by FNMA that indicates project phase has been underwritten and approved by FNMA. Form 1027 is conditional project approval. Requirements for approval: 1.) 50 % of units within a phase must be sold or under contract to settle. Unit appraisals must address market absorption and sales plan (Addendum A) and budget adequacy (Addendum B). 2.) Attorney's opinion letter addressing condominium documents. 3.) Conversions require engineering structural survey. CPM approval is valid for 6 months	**Class I** - Direct FHLMC approval required. Requirements for approval: 1.) 70% of units within a phase must be sold or under contract to settle. Of those 70% must be sold to owner-occupants. Unit appraisals must address market absorption and sales plan (Addendum A) and budget adequacy (Addendum B). 2.) Attorney's opinion letter addressing condominium documents. 3.) Conversions require engineering structural survey.
Existing Project Not Fully Sold Out	**"Formerly" Type B** - Project is 1.) Complete and no additional phasing 2.) 60% Sold and 70% of those are owner occupied/2nd homes. 3.) Still under developer control. 4.) No more than 10% of units owned by single entity. **Required for Approval:** Attorney's opinion letter; Addendum B.	**Class II** - Project is 1.) Complete and no additional phasing 2.) 70% Sold and 60% of those are owner occupied/2nd homes. 3.) Project turned over to Owner's Association **Required for Approval:** Attorney's Opinion letter; Addendum B.
Existing Project	**"Formerly" Type A** - Project is 1.) 100% completed, no additional phasing, 2.) Owner's association is in control for one year, 3.) 90% sold/50% owner occupied, 4.) No entity owns 10% or more **Type A - Limited Project Review** - For down payments of 25% (20% for DU) or more - Project is 1.) 100% Complete 2.) No other restrictions	**Class III** - Project is 1.) 100% completed, no additional phasing, 2.) Owner's association has been in control for two years, 3.) 90% sold, 4.) 90% individual unit owners - multiple sales to one owner counted toward % of individual owners. 60% owner occupied.
FHA Approved	**Type D** - Project is 1.) On FHA Approved Condo List 2.) 51% Owner Occupied 3.) No entity owns 10% or more 4.) Project is not otherwise ineligible	

As this table demonstrates, as a project becomes more established, the guidelines for approval become less rigorous. This is because the lender's risk is mitigated as the project proves that it is acceptable in the marketplace and people continue to buy units there. You will note that there is considerable influence placed on the percentage of owner occupants within a project. There are two reasons for this:

1. Owners who live in a project tend to have a greater "pride in ownership," and thereby - theoretically - will take better care of the project. They will vote to spend money for

items that may become necessary to maintain the project such as a special assessment. An absentee owner would only care that the rent charged covered the expenses.
2. If the economy turns down, investors would not necessarily make the sacrifices required to maintain mortgage payments, resulting in defaults and foreclosures that would adversely affect the market value of other units within the project.

For instance, if there were a project with 100 units and the monthly assessment fees were $100, and one individual owned 30 of these units, what would happen if that person went bankrupt? Monthly revenue for project operation would go from (100 x $100 = $10,000) to (70 x $100 = $7,000) for a $3,000 per month shortfall. In order to keep the project viable, the association would have to spread the $3,000 shortfall out over the remaining 70 units ($3,000 divided by 70 = $42.85/mo additional levy). This is an increase of nearly 50%! Such a dramatic increase could create a domino effect where other unit owners could no longer afford the maintenance obligation and collapse the entire project.

Private Mortgage Insurance

While the agencies have established guidelines for condominiums, so have the Private Mortgage Insurance companies (MIs). During the introduction of condominium ownership, many MI's did not evaluate condominiums any differently than individual home loans. As a result, some companies became over exposed insuring large percentages of units within individual projects. It was the MI's that were significantly hurt when the real estate market softened dramatically with the rise in interest rates in the early 1980's. As a result, many of the MI companies have developed guidelines that are even more restrictive than agency guidelines (as with all guidelines, exceptions can be made). To summarize there are a number of specific rules which may apply:

- Square footage limitations - Efficiency condominiums are cheaper to buy and require a smaller down payment investment than a house. In addition, the smaller the unit the more difficult it is to sell (a phenomenon which may be linked to the fact that the agents involved can only earn a small amount of commission). Finally, because the equity investment is so small, there is more chance of the lender taking a loss. As a result, the smaller the condominium, the more likely the owner is to walk away from the initial investment during bad economic times. Minimum square footage is considered to be approximately 600-square feet, or one bedroom.
- Owner occupancy - Because condominium apartment projects mirror the appeal of rental apartments, they hold investment potential. These tend to turn into largely investor-held buildings - and because many MI's hold to the belief that pride in ownership is a critical part of risk analysis - investor concentration in condominiums is a huge issue for MIs. Twenty to Thirty percent investor to owner occupant ratio is generally acceptable, with some higher concentrations allowed for established projects.
- Risk exposure - The MI's track exposure in projects and will only accept a certain number of units or a percentage. Always check ahead of time to assure a slot remains. In addition, some MIs will perform their own project review prior to insuring the first loan in a condominium.
- There is currently a movement in underwriting away from traditional subjective underwriting

guidelines toward the process of predictive credit scoring. In cases such as this project eligibility may not be an issue. Several of the insurers have stipulated that with scores of over 700, no other underwriting criterion needs to be met.

Regardless of project status, the following information will always be required in conjunction with condominium financing:

Documentation Required for Project Approval

Legal Documents	___ ___ ___	Recorded Declarations, By-Laws, Amendments Covenants, Easements and Restrictions Horizontal Plat/Survey
Insurance	___ ___ ___ ___ ___	Master Policy Declarations If Professional Management firm handles Association funds Fidelity Bond equal to 6 Months HOA fees, naming Management Company as insured and HOA as payee If HOA handles funds, Director's & Officer's Liability If High Rise, Elevator Insurance Certificate of Insurance for specific unit being given as collateral
Financial	___	Current and Past Years' Budget

Treatment of Condominium Fee for Qualifying Purposes

When you are using income and debt ratios in trying to qualify someone to buy a house, do you add in the amount they would be paying for utilities such as electricity, water, gas, sewer, heat and air conditioning? These are not factors in normal underwriting, but they can be large components of the housing expense for a condominium. In fact you can "net out" the utility portion of the condominium fee from the amount used for qualifying. To do this, analyze the project's budget to determine the percentage of the total budget attributed towards utilities, and subtract that percentage from the total fee for qualifying. The appraiser may make your job easier by indicating the percentage of utilities included on the report on page two, project information.

Approved Lists

FHA and VA do approve each individual condominium phase and unit. Project approval through FHA requires an attorney's opinion letter, budget, engineering report, environmental impact analysis and 51% owner occupancy. When a project or phase is FHA or VA approved, it appears on the "approved list." When there is an existing project where it is unlikely that the association will go to the expense of complying with the FHA/VA requirements, it is possible that the individual units could qualify for "spot loan" financing. No more than 10% of the units (20% for projects with less than 30 units) are eligible for spot financing, and the project must still meet the 51% owner occupancy percentage.

FNMA publishes a "list" of condominiums that it has issued 1028 and 1027 approvals for. Until recently, they required the lender to prove that a project, other than a newly approved project, was eligible. FNMA has release Condo Project Manager (CPM), a portal which allows lenders to investigate and request approvals on condominium projects.

> When a project has a high investor concentration according to the Management Company, consider seeking alternative sources of information. Tax records, appraisers data sources, even direct mail campaigns within projects can be a good way to override management company statistics. Second homes are considered owner occupied.

FHLMC issues a list of condominiums that it has purchased loans in and for projects that it has declined project loans. These lists, however, do not necessarily mean that financing is available. Having a loan in a project that is on a "list" indicates that there is a better chance that the project meets guidelines, but is more useful for locating projects in which a declination has been issued. On most loans in existing condominiums it is up to lenders to "warrant" or guarantee that the condominium meets the agency guidelines.

Termite Reports - If the condominium budget shows a line item for pest control, often the requirement for a termite report can be waived. In addition, because termites need water to digest wood, units above the 3rd floor are normally considered exempt from this requirement. This is because the industry has determined that termites can only climb about 3 floors before they have to turn back to get a drink. However, if a specific unit has a fireplace or wood storage area, a termite report might be prudent to determine if any wood destroying insects have been introduced by imported firewood.

Owner Occupancy Ratios/Individual Unit Owner Concentration

Normally, the person who completes the pre-sale questionnaire has done so repeatedly and often. It is a mundane task. Often the individual may memorize certain responses or may not update pertinent information. This may be detrimental to the ability of a lender to obtain financing. Press the individual for the source of their information regarding this and how recently it was compiled. There are a number of additional questions to ask beyond the standard responses.

> **Standard Condominium Questionnaire**
>
> 1. How many units are in this condominium?
> 2. How many units are sold?
> 3. How many units are closed?
> 4. How many units are owner occupied?
> 5. How many units are second homes?
> 6. How many units are rented?
> 7. Are all units and common areas completed?
> 8. When was the control of the condominium turned over to the unit owner's association?
> 9. What percentage of the monthly association fees are more than one-month delinquent?
> 10. Are there any special assessments now planned or have there been in the past year?
> 11. How many individual unit owners, other than the developer, exist in this project? In other words, how many different unit owners are there? (If there are 10 units, and one person owns 2 units, there would be 9 individual owners.)
> 12. Does any one individual own more than 10% of the units?
> 13. Is there any additional phasing or annexation for the project?
> 14. Is the project leasehold?
> 15. Is the project a party in any legal actions?
> 16. Is the project a conversion? If so, was the conversion in the last 3 years?
> 17. Are there short-term rentals, or rental desks within the project?
> 18. Are there cleaning services provided to the unit owners?
> 19. What percentage of the project is devoted to commercial space?
> 20. Is the project professionally managed or self-managed? If professionally managed, does the management contract have a 90-day right to cancel with no penalty?

1.) Are any of the non-occupant units second homes or occupied by the unit owners for at least two weeks of the year?

2.) Consult the tax records - Are tax bills still being sent to the property? If so, there is a chance that current owners intend to return and a compelling argument for a lower investment owner ratio.
3.) Is the current unit a rental being purchased by an owner occupant?
4.) If there is a concentration of units owned by an individual or firm, are the units being actively marketed? Perhaps the underwriter can meet a pre-sale requirement instead of a owner occupancy requirement.

PUD/Classifications & Requirements

There are fewer risks relative to Planned Unit Development Financing. Obviously if the project is complete, there is less risk. Concerns arise from the failure to complete a project, examples of which abound. The impact then is on the marketability of the units that are complete, when common elements aren't finished or do not materialize. Again, FHLMC, FHA, VA and FNMA all have varying requirements.

	FNMA	FHLMC	FHA	VA
New Projects, Proposed or under Construction	50% pre-sold for attached housing. All common areas must be complete. No 2-4 family units. Project may not be a conversion. Fidelity and liability insurance required. Fee simple ownership, budget review. Project may not be otherwise ineligible. 1028 - project approval is acceptable in lieu of meeting warranties.	No pre-sale requirement May not be a conversion, contain commercial or multifamily or 2-4's. Liability, flood and hazard insurance required. No fidelity. Need comparables outside project.	Approved list	Approved list
Existing Projects	Control of HOA turned over to owners association. Not ineligible. Liability/fidelity Insurance.	Same as FNMA.	Fee simple - no requirements.	Approved list

New Construction- Construction Permanent

With new homes there are other considerations for the loan officer. Aside from the project approval issues above, the financing process is very different when there is no developer present. In this case, the buyer or borrower becomes the developer and the loan officer is the construction lender and the permanent lender.

Mortgage lenders do not generally make construction loans because they are inherently short-term loans - intended to be used for the construction period (usually 3-9 months) and then retired. These are ideal loans for bank or savings and loans to make. The loan needs to be structured so that money from the loan is made available over a period of time as the construction proceeds. The loan amount is not fully disbursed at closing, like a permanent loan.

Rather the proceeds are disbursed in a series of draws based upon a pre-arranged construction schedule. Because of this Construction Loans are almost always interest only transactions.

Construction Permanent Financing

Land Price	$	50,000.00					
Construction Contract	$	200,000.00					
Total Costs	$	250,000.00		Maximum Loan			$ 225,000.00
Down Payment		10%		Construction Loan Rate			8.50%
Draw Schedule	**Funds Needed**		**Cash In**	**Loan Balance**		**Number of Days**	**Interest Carry**
Closing	$	50,000.00	$ 25,000.00	$	25,000.00	15	$ 88.54
1st Construction Draw (40%)	$	80,000.00	$ -	$	105,088.54	30	$ 744.38
2nd ConstructionDraw (15%)	$	30,000.00	$ -	$	135,832.92	30	$ 962.15
3rd Construction Draw (15%)	$	30,000.00	$ -	$	166,795.07	30	$ 1,181.47
4th Construction Draw (15%)	$	30,000.00	$ -	$	197,976.53	30	$ 1,402.33
Final Draw	$	27,023.47	$ 4,378.87	$	225,000.00	30	$ 1,593.75
Total	$	247,023.47	$ 29,378.87	$	225,000.00	165	$ 4,378.87
Final Interest Payment	$	1,593.75					

The process begins with the raw land. Raw land is either purchased in cash or financed. This has a bearing on the transaction because land equity is considered a part of the down payment for the construction lender. In addition, when converting the construction loan into a permanent loan, the permanent lender may require that the valuation be based upon the acquisition cost, as opposed to the final value of the home. This acquisition cost formula may be a problem for the borrower with permanent financing because of loan-to-value restrictions and issues such as cash out to recapture the initial investment. Often, to escape this dilemma, borrowers elect to do one of two things with a permanent loan: 1.) Arrange the permanent financing (end-loan) at the time of the construction loan closing (referred to as a construction-permanent loan); or 2.) Wait until the property is seasoned to escape the loan to value restrictions imposed by the acquisition cost formula.

The advantage of a construction permanent transaction is that the entire package is wrapped up into one closing, and the buyer/builder doesn't have to worry about the end loan. The disadvantage is that, because the construction loan and permanent loan are tied together, the borrower's end loan terms may not be the most favorable. However, construction lenders are able to force this type of arrangement because they can facilitate a "modification" which is the altering of the final construction loan documents. The modification proceeds like refinances in that new document are executed; however, because the funds transfer is internal, there are no closing costs or taxes.

The disadvantage of seeking permanent financing outside of the construction lender is there will have to be a refinance closing, unless an unlikely arrangement can be made with the construction lender to have the construction loan terms modified. The second disadvantage is that the loan to value limitations may impact the borrower, particularly when the borrower wishes to capitalize the very valuable property he has just built.

This can be overcome by seasoning the loan - waiting until the property has been complete for one year - or by financing through a lender who doesn't have a seasoning requirement.

Investment Property

When an area real estate market becomes dynamic, property values fluctuate rapidly. Often the purchase of an investment property can provide for both income and equity growth. The major challenges in financing investment property are determining appropriate source of funds for down payment and, at the same time, assuring adequate cash flow.

Rental Properties: Income properties often create problems for potential homebuyers. Aside from the difficulties of managing rental real estate, lenders may have a disparaging view of the impact rental real estate has on the prospective borrower. Restrictions on rental income include:
- Exclusion of 25% of the gross rental income as a vacancy/loss factor. Although a property may carry a positive cash flow, lenders adjust this income significantly to take into account the potential for the property being vacant with no rental income for an extended period of time. This is known as a vacancy/expense factor. While most rental properties experience a 5 - 10% vacancy factor, an additional expense must generally be considered to determine the wear and tear on the property. The exception to this is FHA/VA loans, in which the borrower can demonstrate a lower vacancy factor, or previous experience as a landlord. Then the vacancy expense factor can be as low as 7%. If this is the case, then examine the actual cash flow of the property. Has it been rented for more than two years? If so, can you examine the borrower's Schedule E, Rental and Royalty income, from his or her tax returns? Adding the actual income, less actual expenses (depreciation and depletion added in) may result in a more favorable net rental income than a 25% vacancy factor.
- In many lease situations, properties are rented on a month-to-month basis. If this is the case, the tenant must be contacted to provide a letter attesting to the fact that they intend to continue residing in the property.
- How many properties are financed? If a purchaser owns more than four 1-4 family properties that are financed, and the subject property is an investment property, they are generally ineligible for financing on conforming loans.
- Each property's mortgage must be verified. Also, the taxes and insurance must be obtained separately, either by proving that they are held in escrow, or by providing copies of the paid bills for the obligation.

Requirements for Investment Property Financing

- **Leases:** A current lease showing the monthly rental repayment, lease ending date, and names of landlord and tenant. If the lease is expired, a "tenant letter" will suffice along with the expired lease. The tenant letter is a statement by the tenant giving their occupancy terms and intent to continue occupancy. In certain situations, two years of tax returns may be substituted for leases. A two-year average will be utilized.
- **Insurance:** Rental dwelling coverage is required for all investment property. If the dwelling has more than one unit, rent loss coverage in an amount equal to 6 months PITI is required.
- **Schedule of Rental Comparables** is required to be completed by an appraiser. This is used to substantiate market rents.

- **Operating Income Statement** is required to be completed by an appraiser. This is a line-by-line analysis of the property's expenses. The underwriter will use the net income from the operating income statement to determine income for qualification if the net income number is lower than the net rent shown on the property's lease.

Appraisals

You will note that not much time is spent discussing appraisals and appraisal technology in this course. The reason for this is that the loan officer's expertise is much more effectively applied towards structuring transactions. Misguided trainers often bring the very complex issues of market value and comparable analysis into the curriculum as a way of adding bulk, not substance, to a curriculum. The issues that arise from appraisals are most often value related from the perspective of the market – something the loan officer has no control over. In fact, the loan officer is legally prohibited from exerting any influence over the value conclusion of the appraiser. The loan officer's best interests are served by developing a close vendor relationship with an appraiser or appraisal department and cultivating a dialogue over which appraised value and property condition issues may be discussed with an eye towards compromise.

Appraisal Basics

An appraisal of the real estate is requested to support the transaction. An appraisal is an estimated value – an opinion - of property by a trained professional to indicate whether the property is adequate to serve as security for a loan.

Loan Officer Knowledge of appraisal technology and underwriting is given an inordinate amount of weight training resources and regulatory authorities. The problem with this is that there is very little, if anything, that a loan officer can do to anticipate or fix problems that arise in this area. Loan officers are expressly prohibited from influencing the value conclusion.

Value Conclusion Methodology

Approach	Description – Weight in Valuation
The Cost Approach	**LEAST WEIGHT** – used for confirmation purposes. The cost to replace or rebuild the existing structure and site improvements based on construction industry estimates is the approach that is given the least emphasis. It is most useful when appraising a property to be built.
The Income Approach	**INDICATIVE WEIGHT** – if an investment property. Used for income-producing (rental) property. In addition to reviewing market rents, the appraiser capitalizes the property (determines if the rental income would recapture the cost of the property). The appraiser must consider future revenue and expenses.
The Market Approach	**MOST WEIGHT** - A comparison of the subject property to similar recent sales using the principle of substitution. Similar properties are called comparable sales or "comps". The appraiser starts with the sales price of a comparable and reduces or increases the relative value of the comparable based upon aspects of the subject that are superior or inferior. In "adjusting" the value of the comparables, the appraiser arrives at a scientific conclusion of the indicated value of a property. This is the approach that is given the most weight in the value conclusion.

States license appraisers, but appraisers may also have designations from industry associations that advance their credentials, such as the SRA (Senior Residential Appraisal) or MAI (Member Appraisal Institute) issued by the Appraisal Institute of America.

Simple Approaches to Resolving Valuation Problems

Concern	Possible Solution
Circumstance – Possible error	Get the appraiser to go back out and re-evaluate the property? Do you have evidence that he or she overlooked something? Did he or she do most of the report at a desk and spend little time at the property? Was it a "rush" order?
Comparable Data	Check the comparable properties listed on the report. Is there someone, like an agent or builder who can provide additional comparables for the appraiser to consider?
New Data	Are there pending or recent sales that might support a different conclusion? Ask an agent or builder in the area of the property if there is any "inside" or soon to be released information that could change the value conclusion. New comparables are very powerful tools, because they don't indicate that the appraiser "missed" something – it is new data.
Desk, Drive by or Limited Appraisal (Short Form Appraisals)	Short form appraisals can be useful if the value conclusion would be better if the basis for the value assessment was tax records – over assessed property. If there is significant equity in the property, or the purchaser is putting a lot of money down, is there even a need for a full appraisal? Did DU/LP require a full appraisal? Will the investor accept a short form appraisal?
Confirm the value independently FIRST	Check the property value independently. One web-site offering this service is domania.com, but there many valuation sites, including tax assessor's offices. A value that appears unobtainable here will be even more difficult to obtain through a full appraisal.
Motivated buyer or seller	Even with a low value, the transaction can still work. The purchaser has to make a larger down payment. If the contract is contingent upon loan approval, the buyer may use this as leverage to extract a concession in sales price or costs from the seller. The buyer may cancel a contract that is contingent upon financing, if the financing approved does not meet the terms of the sales agreement.
Excessive Seller contributions	Excessive seller concessions, particularly those that drive the sales price over the list price, can cause value problems. Can the loan be restructured to eliminate these?
New Appraisal	If there were serious flaws in a prior appraisal, the borrower may be willing to pay for a new appraisal. The new appraiser may arrive at the same value conclusion, but you have satisfied the borrowers need for confirmation.
Borrower Provided Appraisals	It is very rare that a customer will be able to use an existing appraisal. Loan officers should be wary of a customer who wants to use an appraisal from a non-approved vendor. What if the borrower were to abandon the loan process or provide a faulty appraisal?

Adjustment Issues	
Net and Gross Adjustments	Net and Gross adjustments are reviewed carefully. Net adjustments should be less than 15% and gross adjustments less than 25%. Site Adjustments over 30% require explanation
Across-the-board	If all-positive or all-negative adjustments exist across a line for particular property characteristics like location, age, quality condition, rooms, and living area, contact the appraiser for additional comps.
Date of Sale	Comps sales values should be no more than six months old, although recent comps may not be available. If all comps are older than six months, contact the appraiser for explanation or for more-recent comps.
Room Count	Bedroom count should be similar
Amenities	Adjustments for special amenities - at least one comp must have same amenity.

Fraud Alert

Be conscious of strategies outside of normal influences as to valuation. These can be indicative of problems and can cause delays or problems in a transaction.

APPRAISAL
- Ordered by a party to the transaction (seller, buyer, broker, etc.)
- Comps are not verified as recorded or submitted by potentially biased party (seller, real estate broker)
- Tenant shown to be contact on owner-occupied property
- Income approach not used on tenant-occupied SFR
- Appraiser uses FNMA number as sole credential (discontinued program)
- Market approach substantially exceeds replacement cost approach
- "For Sale" sign on the photos of the subject (in refinance loans)
- HUD-1 or grant deed on original purchase is less than two years old (for refinance loans)

Real Estate Contracts

At the time of application, the loan officer and processor should review the sales contract. The standard purchase contract should include the terms and conditions of the purchase.

Purchase Contract Review

Item	Description
Buyer and Seller	Signatures of all parties
Property Description	Property Address Complete Legal Description
Transaction Details	Purchase Price Financing Amount and terms Earnest Money Deposit and Down Payment Amount Identity of Party Holding Deposit Closing Cost Concessions/Contributions
Dates	Contract Date Initial Contingency Date – Property Inspection and Repairs Final Contingency Date Closing Date

Chapter 8 – Underwriting Submission and Approval

The processor has been working diligently to assemble all of the exhibits for the loan file. The loan file may be ready for submission to underwriting immediately after loan setup, opening or intake. Alternately, the file may be held for the receipt of conditions.

Basic Underwriting Preparations

The underwriter is, in most cases, an individual with extensive experience in reviewing loans from a processing perspective. In fact, most underwriters were processors at one point and have been promoted to their positions as a result of their expertise. Thinking of it from that perspective, there is probably nothing the processor could do to raise the contempt of an underwriter more than to present a sloppily processed loan. Essentially this tells the underwriter, "Here. YOU figure it out..." It reflects poorly on everyone.

"Memo"-izing

As a result, take care to make sure the case is comprehensible. When documentation is missing that is forthcoming, let the underwriter know by putting a memorandum to this effect in the file, or make a comment on the submission summary.

If the case has marginal attributes, someone on the origination side needs to make the argument as to why the loan should be approved. It is not the job of the underwriter to look past file weaknesses to approve the loan. It is much more difficult to reverse a declination that to argue for an approval initially.

The standard cover memo should come from the loan officer. It should:

- briefly describe the transaction (owner occupied purchase)
- concede file weaknesses (ratios, credit problem, unusual cash)
- describe why weaknesses do not present a guideline problem, or why an exception is warranted

- what the compensating or overriding factors on the case are - why the underwriter shouldn't worry about the exception

This is more true when the borrower has an unusual income scenario. If you do not explain how the income number was derived, expect the underwriter to arrive at a different number.

Memorandum

To: Underwriting/File

Date: February 1, 2006

Subject: Joe Smith

This is an owner occupied refinance transaction. Joe had a heart attack (minor) a couple of years ago and as a result his architectural practice has suffered somewhat. Otherwise, the borrower has perfect assets, credit and a great loan to value. By credit score only, this case passes. The income analysis is difficult because of the slow down in 1995 and 1994. We have taken 1995 out of the averaging scenario for income purposes. But this is only part of his income. He receives social security, interest and dividends, and rental income. Taken together, Joe has more than sufficient income to cover the mortgage payment. And this is evident since he has been able to manage it for an extended period of time at this income level, and this refinance will simply allow him to reduce his payments.

Your consideration is appreciated.

If the file is held for receipt of conditions, the status is considered "Open – In Process". The case will be reviewed weekly by the processor and the loan officer for receipt of conditions to determine file readiness. The processor reviews the file **every time information is received** to determine if the last piece of missing information has been received.

The impetus of the processing staff is not to arrest the loan, but to expedite its movement from "Open – In Process" to "Submitted". As a result, processing reports are generated by the loan processing system to track certain key information.

Detailed Credit Package Order

CONVENTIONAL LOANS – Stack Order from Top to Bottom

CREDIT

_____ Program Disclosure - Registration
_____ 1008 – Transmittal Summary
_____ URLA (1003) (Typed Loan Application)
_____ Handwritten Loan Application (Photocopy)
_____ Schedule of Real Estate
_____ Purpose of Refinance Statement Motivational/Responsibility/Relationship Statement Commute Letter
_____ Credit Report
_____ Debt Payoff Evidence
_____ Letters Regarding Credit
_____ Canceled Checks Showing Payments
_____ Subordination Agreement Equity Line Agreement
_____ Bankruptcy
_____ Landlord Rating
_____ Property Disposition
_____ Mortgage Ratings
_____ Demand Statement/Payoff Statement
_____ Note/Deed (Not subject property/not current loan)
_____ HUD-1 (Not subject property/not current loan)
_____ Appraisal (Not subject property/not current loan)
_____ Divorce Documents Divorce Letters

EMPLOYMENT

_____ Verification of Employment
_____ Paycheck Stubs
_____ W-2
_____ Letters Regarding Employment
_____ Income Tax Returns
_____ Profit and Loss Statements
_____ Balance Sheet
_____ IRS Form 8821/4506 (Copy only)

FINANCIAL

_____ Verification of Deposit
_____ Bank Statements
_____ Credit Union Information
_____ Cash on Hand Statements
_____ Gift Letter / Gift Money Information
_____ Copy of Stock or Statements
_____ Copy of Savings Bonds
_____ Letters From Bank Regarding Location of Funds

PURCHASE/PROPERTY

_____ Purchase Agreement
_____ Sales Contract
_____ Escrow Instructions
_____ Grant Deed
_____ Quit Claim
_____ Closing Statement/Settlement Statement (Estimate)
_____ Re-certification of Value
_____ Appraisal & Addenda
_____ Form 998
_____ Form 1000
_____ Property Photos
_____ Property Drawings
_____ Property Location Map
_____ 442/Photos – Final Inspection
_____ Appraisal Letters
_____ Homeowners Association – Condo Statements / Information
_____ Fidelity Bond – Certificate of Insurance
_____ Project Approval Warranty
_____ Road Maintenance Agreement
_____ Health Authority
_____ Termite Report
_____ Septic Certification
_____ Well Certification

Disclosures

_____ Truth-in-Lending
_____ Good Faith Estimate
_____ ARM/Buydown/GEM Disclosure
_____ Equal Credit Opportunity Act
_____ Appraisal Copy Notice
_____ PMI Cancellation
_____ Mortgage Loan Lock-In Agreement/Service Agreement/ (Copy – Original Kept in Broker/Servicing File
_____ IRS 4506
_____ Transfer of Servicing
_____ Borrower's Certification & Authorization

GOVERNMENT LOANS – Stack Order – Top to Bottom

CREDIT

_____ Assignment Letter (Case Assignment)
_____ HUD 54133
_____ Statement Of Account - RBMIP - FHA
_____ Funding Fee 26-8998 - VA
_____ Certificate Of Eligibility - VA
_____ DD-214 - VA
_____ VA Entitlement Certification - VA
_____ VA Report And Certification Of Loan Disbursement 26-1820 - VA
_____ Verification Of VA Benefit-Related Indebtedness 26-8937 - VA
_____ Debt Questionnaire 26-0551 - VA
_____ Federal Collection Policy Notice 26-0503 - VA
_____ HUD-1 Certification (Borrower, Seller, Agent)- FHA
_____ HUD-92900-A (pages 1-4) - FHA
_____ VA 26-1802a (pages 1-4)- VA
_____ URLA (1003) (Typed Loan Application)
_____ Schedule Of Real Estate
_____ Disclosure HUD-92900-B - FHA
_____ HUD ARM disclosure - FHA
_____ VA ARM Disclosure - VA
_____ Interest Rate & Discount Disclosure Statement - VA
_____ Loan Analysis VA 26-6393 - VA
_____ Interest Rate Reduction Refinancing Worksheet 26-8823 - VA
_____ Mortgage Credit Analysis Worksheet HUD-92900-WS - FHA
_____ Upfront MIP Credit Worksheet - FHA
_____ Good Faith Estimate (photocopy)
_____ Purpose Of Refinance Statement
_____ Motivation / Responsibility / Relationship Statement / Commute Letter
_____ Credit Report
_____ Debt Payoff Evidence
_____ Letters Regarding Credit
_____ Canceled Checks Showing payments
_____ Subordination Agreement/Equity Line Agreement
_____ Bankruptcy
_____ Landlord Rating
_____ Property Disposition
_____ Veteran Rate Reduction Refinance Certification - VA
_____ Mortgage Ratings
_____ Demand Statement
_____ Note/Deed (Not subject property/not current loan)
_____ HUD-1 (Not subject property/not current loan)
_____ Child Care Statement
_____ Divorce Documents Divorce Letters

EMPLOYMENT

_____ Verification of Employment
_____ Off-Base Housing Authorization - VA
_____ Paycheck Stubs

_____ W-2
_____ Letters Regarding Employment
_____ Income Tax Returns
_____ Profit and Loss Statements
_____ Balance Sheet
_____ IRS Form 1821/4506 (Copy only)

FINANCIAL

_____ Verification of Deposit
_____ Bank Statements
_____ Credit Union Information
_____ Cash on Hand Statements
_____ Gift Letter/ Gift Money Information
_____ Copy of Stock or Statements
_____ Copy of Savings Bonds
_____ Letters From Bank Regarding Location of Funds

PURCHASE/PROPERTY

_____ Purchase Agreement
_____ Sales Contract
_____ HUD Certification (Buyer, Seller, Broker)- FHA
_____ Escrow Amendatory/Escape Clause
_____ Grant Deed
_____ Quit Claim
_____ Closing Statement/Settlement Statement (Estimate)
_____ Social Security Card (Photocopy)- FHA
_____ Letters Regarding Social Security Card
_____ Drivers License (Photocopy)- FHA
_____ Identification with Photograph of Borrower (Copy) - FHA
_____ Handwritten Loan Application (Photocopy) Prelim

APPRAISAL

_____ Appraisal & Addenda
_____ Property Photos
_____ Property Drawings
_____ Property Location Map
_____ Inspections Photo Related to Inspections
_____ Affirmative Fair Marketing
_____ Builder Warranty
_____ Home Buyers Warranty / HOW / 2-10
_____ Lead Paint Notice
_____ Road Maintenance Agreement
_____ Health Authority Termite Report
_____ Termite Soil Report (Signed by Veteran Only - VA)
_____ Well Certification
_____ Septic Certification
_____ Borrower Signed Statements Regarding Property

Loan Submission

A file is ready for submission to underwriting when substantially all of the items required by the base review have been provided. However, it is more critical to analyze whether items which are outstanding actually are important in determining approval.

If the borrower meets underwriting criteria, but there is a piece (or pieces) of missing documentation, the processor should substitute a memo to file acknowledging the missing documentation. In this way, we show that we have reviewed the file but feel that the missing documentation is not critical to the loan decision. This allows the underwriter to address items that are critical to loan approval.

When submitting a case, the processor should assure that the case meets basic underwriting guidelines. To do this, review the case against the base processing checklist.

In addition, there are clerical tasks to be performed in conjunction with the submission. Utilize the Submission Checklist to assure that the basic requirements have been met.

Basic Loan Submission Checklist

Basic Loan Submission Checklist

☐	Assemble File In Stack Order (see File Stack Order Form)
☐	Stamp Documents "Certified True"
☐	Data Correct -At each set of Documents, the processor should verify the information that is entered in the loan file against the information entered into the loan processing system. The Documents should not be stamped until the information in the system is confirmed to be correct
☐	Note missing documentation
	• If missing documentation is not substantive, insert memo to file regarding each item
☐	Verbal Verifications of Employment
☐	Print 1003/1008
	Quick Check
	☐ • Ratios in Line?
	☐ • LTV O.K.?
	☐ • Cash to Close O.K.?
☐	Copy File
	☐ • Place one copy in Origination File
	☐ • Original on Right Side of Submission File
	☐ • Copy on Left Side of Submission File
	☐ If 2nd Copy package is required, it should be paper fastened together and included with file
☐	PMI Submission form
☐	Register Loan
☐	Print Assignment Letter
☐	Prepare Fee Sheet
☐	Package in Local/Overnight Delivery for Submission or upload to DU/LP and submit file to document review

Base Processing Checklist

General Items

	Registration/lock sheet • Lock Still Valid? • LTV within Guidelines • Within Maximum/Minimum Loan Amount?
	fee sheet
	signed lock-in agreement
	assignment letter
	Occupancy • All borrowers occupy • Non-Occupant Co-borrower Guidelines Met
	PMI Required? • Coverage Correct • Payment Correct on 1003/1008 • copy package for PMI/pool insurance if Jumbo Loan

Loan Analysis - 1008, 92900WS, 6393

	Borrower information correct, same as original & typed 1003
	PITI correct and same as 1003 and addendum - if arm or buydown, indicate qualify rate – Buydown/ARM Disclosure – Are ratios different for buydowns? – Borrower Qualification
	all debts as listed on credit report and verifications
	1003 ratios in line with loan program
	cavir #'s – fha/va
	Maximum Number of Properties Financed
	Secondary Financing • Is 2nd Allowed Under Program • Is CLTV in Guidelines • Are terms of 2nd Acceptable

FINAL TYPED LOAN APPLICATION (1003/URLA)

	ss#'s match paystubs, w-2's, Photo id, credit report and original 1003
	2 years employment/residency
	assets/liabilities in line with original 1003 and loan analysis
	home, time share or land owned free and clear - do you have evidence - have you counted taxes, insurance, condo, hoa, management fees as debts
	government monitoring completed original/typed 1003
	final typed original 1003 signed by loan officer prior to submission
	green card if resident alien
	Property Address, Legal Agree with Title, Sales Contract

Credit Report - Liabilities

	ss#'s names, match original/typed 1003 and photo id (FHA only)
	2 years residency verified with 12 month current payment history
	debts on credit report match original/typed 1003/loan analysis – if not explanation for undisclosed debts
	12 months reviewed on all mortgage/installment loans-balances w/in 90 days
	12 months cancelled checks on co-signed loans-balances within 90 days
	open judgements/collections/past due/charge offs - must clear PTC
	all "creditor declines" or "written verification to update" are verified
	satisfactory explanation with documentation for all derogatory credit
	satisfactory explanation for credit inquiries with new accounts verified
	If using vom/vor/vol or paid mortgage, please state "see vom, etc on Credit Report.
	business credit report for FHA/FHLMC
	alimony/child support/child care counted as debt as documented by separation agreement/divorce decree
	If line of credit subordinated, need full terms, count maximum line and payment
	WRITTEN PAYOFF STATEMENT accurate/current written payoff statement for all loans. Payoff may be updated verbally with processor cert. however the initial written payoff cannot be more than 90 days from UW

EMPLOYMENT/INCOME

	2 year history/explain gaps
	If income is inconsistent, provide satisfactory documentation from employer on their letterhead
	explain how income derived
	Overtime/bonus/commission - 25% of total earnings? Need 2 years complete tax returns and continuance verified
	Un-reimbursed business expenses? calculated and income reduced
	Any loan on pay stub?
	FULL DOCUMENTATION • fully completed, signed, dated V.O.E. all information is completed, initialed • current y-t-d pay stub - FHA no older than 30 days at time of approval • w-2's for past two years
	ALTERNATE DOCUMENTATION • verbal verification certification signed by processor • current year to date pay stubs to cover 30 day period (biweekly employees ~ 3 pay stubs) W-2's for past two years
	SELF EMPLOYED • two years personal/corporate/partnership tax returns • k-1's, with all schedules and signed by borrowers • IRS form 4506 signed • Current year to date profit and loss, balance sheet signed by preparer • FNMA 1084 (self employment analysis) completed
	RETIREMENT VA DISABILITY PENSION CHILDS SUPPORT ALIMONY, NOTE INCOME • 2 years 1099's • evidence of receipt for last 12 months • is income going to continue for 3 years for fnma/5 years va/fha • award letter • divorce decree, separation agreement
	DIVIDEND/INTEREST • 2 years tax returns • ytd dividend/interest earnings from bank • deduct money for closing
	LEASE INCOME • 2 years tax returns • current leases required on all properties • expenses counted • real estate owned schedule • fha/va streamline income verification not necessary as long as borrowers remain as listed on original loan

ASSETS

	are adequate funds for closing/reserves verified
	any large deposits explained/documented
	Gift funds adequately documented? • completed, signed gift letter • transfer of funds • receipt of funds • updated bank balance, ATM RECEIPT NOT ACCEPTABLE
	3 consecutive current bank statements for ALT DOC must be certified true copies(not allowed on va loans)
	verification of deposit with 2 month average balance or, • two months current bank statements • does borrower have own 5k (FNMA / fhlmc)
	earnest money deposit adequately verified
	all accounts are updated stock/bonds/ira/cd/40lk/thrift savings plan
	3 consecutive current statements/or most current quarterly statement
	IRA/401(k) • if there is a penalty for liquidation, are funds sufficient to cover all costs • is liquidation properly documented • properly document whether repayment IS or IS NOT required
	one month bank statement dated within 45 days for FHA/VA streamline

Property

	Is property complete? • did you order final • do you need a recertification • Are repairs required?
	Are required? • Private road • flood insurance • well/septic
	fha/va project approval letter condo/pud
	fnma/fhlmc warranty for condo/pud
	condo/hoa association management letter
	investment property - completed operating income statement and rent comparable schedule (fhlmc/fnma)
	Make sure with realtor/builder no changes Final Sales Price made
	Sales Contract and all addenda to sales contract - signed
	Contract - check seller paid items; closing costs, points, allowances, do they conform to program guidelines
	all contingencies satisfied and removed
	Relocation Agreement – Terms Highlighted

DISCLOSURES

	initial GFE and TIL within 3 days of loan application
	redisclosed TIL/GFE and Financing Agreement if initial amount, type of financing changed
	ECOA - Disclosure
	loan servicing disclosure
	borrower certification and authorization
	financing agreement
	occupancy statement
	appropriate program disclosures

Refinance

	IS LTV acceptable
	Cash Out? • is $ amount allowed • is seasoning met
	effects of refinance statement
	Deed/Title matches borrowers

FHA/VA LOAN SUBMISSIONS

	Photo identification (FHA only)
	FHA underwriter's certification
	FHA/VA addendum to URLA
	FHA refinance worksheet maximum loan amount calculation
	VA interest rate reduction worksheet
	Closing cost/prepaid worksheet (is there a lender credit?)
	VA indebtedness letter
	VA award letter dated within past year if applicable
	Original certificate of eligibility
	LH# on COE matches payoff statement/Deed Note
	veteran to take title, 1003 as on COE
	copy of case number assignment from VA/FHA (comp. printout)
	FHA case binders as required by FHA
	evidence condo/pud approved by FHA/VA
	conditional commitment/vc sheets-FHA
	FHA-new construction - need builder certification
	Lapp notification to veteran, signed by authorized Lapp individual and Veteran
	complete mcrv with evidence all conditions met • if using mcrv on FHA loan - fha conversion form • if mcrv need option sheet
	appraisal not needed for fha/va streamline (unless financing cc on fha or cashout)

	Disclosures • HUD interest rate and discount point disclosure • HUD assumption disclosure • fact sheet Lead Paint Notice • FHA arm disclosure terms • VA arm disclosure if applicable • VA interest rate and discount point notice • VA federal collection notice • VA loan assumption Notice • VA credit counseling notice • VA occupancy notice if active duty • Veteran Purchaser multiple use of entitlement disclosure • Acknowledgement of increase in VA funding fee • VA debt questionnaire (not the indebtedness letter)

Forms – Assignment Letter

The Assignment letter allows you to use the investors stored in the processing system instead of checking again and again for investor addresses. The assignment letter is only prepared if the loan is being assigned to an outside investor for underwriting and closing.

Verbal Verification of Employment

The purpose of the verbal employment verification is to confirm the borrower's employment data

«Lender_Name1»
«Lender_Address»
«Lender_City», «Lender_State» «Lender_Zip»
«Lender_phone1»
«Lender_Fax»

September 2, 1999

«lender_name»
«lender_address_1»
«lender_address_2»

     Re: «bor_first_name» «bor_last_name»
       «subject_address»
       «subject_city», «subject_state» «subject_zip»
       Loan Amount: «loan_amount»

Dear Sir or Madam:

«Lender_Name1» hereby assigns all right, title and interest in and to the referenced loan file to:

«lender_name»
«lender_address_1»
«lender_address_2»

Please feel free to contact me should you have any questions.

Sincerely,

«loan_processor»

in the event written employment verification was not obtained - such as is the case when utilizing alternative documentation. In addition, it is used to confirm that the borrower's employment status hasn't changed since the date of the loan approval.

Procedure

Step 1 Form	Prepare the employment verification form by printing the Verbal VOE document. Have the application form available in the event you need to change or confirm information or otherwise identify the applicant.
Step 2 Independent Verification	Independently verify the name, address and telephone number of the employer. Identify the information source utilized, i.e.; 411, yellow pages, internet, etc.
Step 3 Attempt Verification	Contact the employer through the number verified. State the purpose of the call to whoever answers the telephone and request to speak with the individual responsible for verifying employment. Record the responses when they involve re-directing the call to another number or office.
Step 4 Interview	When the correct authority is contacted, note their direct dial number, their name and title. Request the information that needs to be verified. Often the information cannot be volunteered, the verifier must provide the information the borrower supplied and have the authority confirm it. If they cannot give exact information, record what the authority does provide - such as "over 5 years", etc.
Step 5 Findings	Record the information and sign the form. If there is an adverse finding in the information, or if there are questions as to the authenticity of the verifier, report these incidents to management - do not attempt to confront the borrower regarding this.

Probability of Continued Employment is the most critical question to be answered. Often the authority doesn't volunteer this information. If this is the case ask if there is any reason to question continued employment. If the employer can state that there is no reason to question, simply record "no reason to question".

In addition, the requestor may find the authority intractable as to providing information. In this case, call directly to the individual's office and verify through an administrative personnel staff member the borrower's employment.

Forms – Verbal Verification of Employment

«lender_name»
«lender_address_1»
«lender_address_2»
«lender_phone»

Verbal Verification of Employment

Borrower:	«bor_first_name» «bor_last_name»
Property Address:	«subject_address»
	«subject_city», «subject_state» «subject_zip»
Employee ID/SS#	«borrower_ssn»

Employer:
Employer Phone: «bor_bus_phone»
Directory Assistance:
Person Contacted:
Title:
Date of Employment:
Position:
Employment Status (full/pt)
Probability of Continued Employment
Eligible for Bonus/Overtime/Incentive
Current Salary
Per (year/month/bi-monthly/bi-weekly/hrly)
If Income was not verified state reason

I hereby certify that this information was personally verified by me and is true and correct to the best of my knowledge and belief.

By:_____
   «lender_name»

Reviewing the Application

Each individual loan officer develops a unique way of interacting with customers - explaining, questioning, developing an accurate profile of the borrower. This initial interview is critical, because during the first meeting customers tend to be more compliant and receptive to requests for additional information or explanations. The loan officer is in control and can manage the customer's expectations. One of the most frequent complaints customers have with lenders is that they receive frequent requests for additional information. The application interview is the loan officer's last opportunity to ask for information without the customer providing resistance, so it is important to be thorough.

The application form actually works like a tickler - ALL THE BLANKS SHOULD BE FILLED IN! If something can't be filled in, you are missing information!

Sections 1 & 2 of Application

Uniform Residential Loan Application [form image]

Use the mini checklists to review sections 1 & 2 for compliance.

Read the sales contract. How much is the earnest money deposit? Record this information not

> Section I&II - Property Information Checklist
> **Check the Sales Contract for**
> ❏ Loan Amount/Down Payment Correct (can you do the loan?)
> ❏ Settlement Date Reasonable
> ❏ Contract Signed by all?
> ❏ Seller Contributions w/in Guidelines
> ❏ No Decorator/Repair Allowance
> ❏ Interest Rate/Points Available
> **Audit Property for**
> ❏ Condo/PUD/Coop/Property Info **If Refinance**
> ❏ Check Deed for Titling
> ❏ Legal Description
> ❏ Ask for Survey
> ❏ Construction Permanent - Land Cost/Value –
> ❏ Construction Costs Documented?
> ❏ 2nd Mortgage to be subordinated?

only on Section 6 Assets, but also in section 11, Details of Transaction. Did the earnest money deposit check clear?

Section 3 – Personal Information

Here we analyze whether the borrower has any potential areas of discrepancy. If they have moved a lot, there may be numerous landlords or mortgages to verify. If you are collecting their previous address, GET THEIR rental data – write down the name, address and phone number of the landlord so that you can have the credit bureau verify it later. *(There is a 4th page of the application designed specifically for when you run out of room on the page.)*

Section 4 – Employment Data

While collecting employment data verify the income documentation. Check the names, addresses and social security numbers against the documents provided for information that doesn't make sense such as:

- A W-2 from an employer that is not listed.
- A missing W-2 for a listed employer.
- If there is a job that has been going on all year with a very small year-to-date income number.
- A 1099 instead of a W-2 – indicating self-employment.

Section III & IV - Borrower Information & Employment
- ❑ Borrower's Complete Name, Jr., Sr. ID Variance?
- ❑ Social Security Number Match
- ❑ 30 Days' Pay stubs
- ❑ 2 Years W-2's
- ❑ Self-Employed at least 2 years?
- ❑ Two Years 1040's/1120/1065
- ❑ Non-Schedule C business credit report necessary?
- ❑ Any Job Gaps/Different Employers? get letter

Incongruent information caught early can save trouble down the line. These are all substantial examples of items that can be caught at the time of application.

V. MONTHLY INCOME AND COMBINED HOUSING EXPENSE INFORMATION						
Gross Monthly Income	Borrower	Co-Borrower	Total	Combined Monthly Housing Expense	Present	Proposed
Base Empl. Income*	$	$	$	Rent	$	$
Overtime				First Mortgage (P&I)		
Bonuses				Other Financing (P&I)		
Commissions				Hazard Insurance		
Dividends/Interest				Real Estate Taxes		
Net Rental Income				Mortgage Insurance		
Other (before completing, see the notice in "describe other income," below)				Homeowner Assn. Dues		
				Other		
Total	$	$	$	Total	$	$

*Self Employed Borrower(s) may be required to provide additional documentation such as tax returns and financial statements.

Describe Other Income Notice: Alimony, child support, or separate maintenance income need not be revealed if the Borrower(B) or Co-Borrower(C) does not choose to have it considered for repaying this loan.

B/C		Monthly Amount
		$

Section V - Income & Housing Expense

In the employment section we check dates. Here, we need to check the numbers. The borrower may state a certain income, but may intend to tell you the net income after taxes as opposed to the gross. They may offer additional income such as benefits, which cannot be counted. Again, there is space for all types of income to be noted, SO NOTE THEM. As to the housing expense, if they are currently renting, ask for the name, address and phone number of their landlord. Is the mortgage on the credit report? If not, get 12 months checks!

> **Section V - Income & Housing Expense**
> ❑ Examine Pay stub
> ❑ Salary evident from pay stub?
> ❑ Yr. to Date Higher/Lower than base salary? - Document/Explain
> ❑ Deductions - Any Loans? Shown on Credit Report? if not request rating
> ❑ Retirement? - Get Statement
> ❑ Bonus/Overtime/Commissions 25%
> ❑ Rent amount? - Get Landlord Name & Number
> ❑ Mortgage Amount - Shown on Credit Report? - if no, need 12 months checks

Remember

❑ **NO Income/NO Ratio Verification Loans.** Do not state income here or anywhere else on the application.
❑ Rental Property – Put primary housing expense where PITI goes

Section VI - Assets & Liabilities

Collecting asset and liability information is critical for the success of the application. If there are liabilities listed here which are not verified on the credit report, verifying them may become a chore later. Anything listed or disclosed on the application must be verified, so listing inconsequential accounts can lead to wasted time tracking verification. This is why we always want to take a credit report with us prior to the application interview. In addition, this is your only real opportunity to really question large deposits or other transactions on the deposit verifications – bank statements. It is tedious, but before you write anything down, check to make sure you review all pages of any document BEFORE you commit it to the application.

> **Section VI - Assets & Liabilities**
> ☐ Copy of Earnest Money Check - Agrees with Contract?
> ☐ Review Bank Statements
> ☐ Funds for Closing Evident? - When received & What
> ☐ Any large withdrawals, deposits? - Explain & Document
> ☐ Net Worth Business? Self-employed P&L
> ☐ Cars owned free & clear? Titles?
> ☐ Other assets? Anything? Anything?
> ☐ Liabilities Reported not reported or verified?
> ☐ Credit explanations needed?
> ☐ Proof of Payoff?
> ☐ Real Estate Schedule - Rental Property on Tax Returns?
> ☐ Leases for Rentals

(Callout: List IRA's, Savings Bonds, 401(k)'s)

(Callout: Carries over from Real Estate Schedule)

The "Schedule of Real Estate Owned" is a continuation of Section VI – Assets and Liabilities. It presents an opportunity and a challenge. If the borrower has sold an existing property, and there is a question about net proceeds, the amount of the sales price should be inflated to keep the underwriter from minimizing net proceeds. In addition, if a property is pending sale, and may be rented to allow the customer to qualify for a new mortgage, the borrower should be advised now that the amount of the rent will be reduced by a vacancy/expense factor of 25%. To offset the vacancy factor the borrower must rent the property for a higher amount - at least 125% of the mortgage payment is required to negate the effect of not having sold the property.

Section VII - Cash Requirements and the First Disclosure - The Good Faith Estimate

VII. DETAILS OF TRANSACTION	
a. Purchase price	$
b. Alterations, improvements, repairs	
c. Land (if acquired separately)	
d. Refinance (incl. debts to be paid off)	
e. Estimated prepaid items	
f. Estimated closing costs	
g. PMI, MIP, Funding Fee	
h. Discount (if Borrower will pay)	
i. **Total costs (add items a through h)**	
j. Subordinate financing	
k. Borrower's closing costs paid by Seller	
l. Other Credits (explain)	
m. Loan amount (exclude PMI, MIP, Funding Fee financed)	
n. PMI, MIP, Funding Fee financed	
o. Loan amount (add m & n)	
p. Cash from/to Borrower (subtract j, k, l & o from i)	

(From the Good Faith Estimate: items d, e)

Sufficiency of assets for closing is a critical concern. The borrower will receive many differing accounts of how much cash they need to bring to closing. At this point you can set them greatly at ease by accurately completing the "Good Faith Estimate of Closing Costs."

Essentially, you are adding all of the costs and coming up with the total transaction costs. Then you subtract all of the items that will be paid for by the seller, the funds from the loan transaction and items, like the deposit that the borrower has already paid. This results in the borrower's net cash requirement for closing. Hopefully the borrower has sufficient funds for closing. In a refinancing transaction and closing costs are being financed, you will go through this process to determine what the appropriate loan amount should be.

The Approval Process

Depending on whether an investor on a whole loan basis is purchasing the loan, or being sold off into a security by a mortgage banker, the underwriter may be an employee of the company or an employee of another company. There may be more or less leniency as a result of this. It may impact the amount of time it takes to obtain an approval. In addition, depending on the loan size, there may be a loan committee or a pool insurance underwriter. Most underwriting today is what is called compliance underwriting - assuring that the loan meets guidelines. The approval process isn't very subjective if the loan meets guidelines - it meets the guidelines, it's approved. If the loan doesn't meet guidelines then there comes the process of determining whether there are sufficient compensating factors to approve the loan. It is the loan officer's job to intervene in a situation where there is difficulty and act as the borrowers advocate. There may be much advice and consent in this process.

If there is mortgage insurance, the PMI Company will also have to approve the loan. PMI underwriters generally underwrite on a risk basis. They look both subjectively at whether they have a good feeling about the case and whether the case meets risk profiles established in their risk scoring.

Government Agencies (FHA/VA and Bond Programs) do approve loans directly, and in some cases must, approve loans directly. FHA allows approved underwriters to approve loans through the "Direct Endorsement" program. VA offers the same thing called the "Automatic" underwriting program. State Agencies have their own underwriting, or may accept a FHA Direct or VA Automatic approval.

A new trend in underwriting is the "contract" underwriter. This may be a PMI underwriter who is authorized to approve loans for various lenders, saving the lenders the expense of maintaining a large staff of underwriters.

Recently most loans are being approved by computers - through the FNMA Desktop Underwriter or FHLMC's Loan Prospector - or directly by the investor's own proprietary underwriting mechanism. In this case the underwriting preparation is even more critical, because if there is a problem with the submission the only way to correct the problem is to cancel the loan completely and resubmit it. However, automated underwriting does ease some of the paperwork pressures. Some cases may not require an appraisal or a credit report, and certain guidelines are relaxed for certain borrowers.

The bottom line is the same. The underwriter is a person who is subject to the pressure of balancing the need to make loans and the need to make loans that will not default or on be ineligible for purchase in the secondary market. Only one default or one non-saleable loan can be a huge problem for a small or mid-sized lender.

Desktop Underwriter and Loan Prospector

Many people projected that the era of the traditional loan officer would be over when the mortgage process evolved into a fully automated system. Those people did not understand the business, as it exists on a practical basis. Automation only eliminates the underwriter. The loan still needs to be structured correctly. The customer also needs an advocate in process. Most importantly, automated underwriting only provides acceptable initial results in about 25% of all applications because:

- The supporting documentation varies from what was entered into the system initially. Automated Underwriting relies on the information that humans enter into the model. If that information does not conform to the documentation requirements, the loan is denied and must be manually underwritten or re-submitted to Automated Underwriting
- The program specifications require manual underwriting.
- The loan does not meet eligibility criteria for other reasons, such as credit, loan parameters, or other factors.

If you have access to automated underwriting it can simplify the process tremendously. Even though Automated Underwriting protocols sometimes reduce the documentation required for approval, this does not mean that you should not collect as much application documentation as possible. If simply to give a borrower the opportunity for a better rate through another source, or to cover tracks in case a further review of information is required, there is no excuse for not collecting as much information as possible from the borrower. Remember that once the borrowers sign applications, they think they are done. Don't put yourself in the position of chasing conditions simply because it was easier to get the application in the door. Ultimately, the complete application remains the "Holy Grail" of the mortgage business. Strive for complete applications.

Automated Underwriting – Electronic Decision Engines

	Approved	Suspended	Declined
Desktop Underwriter – "D.U." – FNMA Conventional Loans, some Jumbo Loans	**Approve – Eligible**: The loan is approved and a live underwriter must simply review required conditions or exhibits.	**Approve – Ineligible**: The loan meets guidelines and receives an approval recommendation, but due to one or more characteristics, a human underwriter must approve it.	**Ineligible**: The loan does not meet A.U. parameters and must be underwritten and approved by a human underwriter.
Loan Prospector – "L.P." – FHLMC Conventional Loans, some Jumbo Loans, FHA and VA Loans	**Accept**: The loan is approved and a live underwriter must simply review required conditions or exhibits.	**Refer**: The loan meets guidelines and receives an approval recommendation, but due to one or more characteristics, a human underwriter must approve it.	**Decline**: The loan is ineligible for sale to FHLMC; must be underwritten to other guidelines by a human.

These are the results you can expect from Desktop Underwriter or Loan Prospector. Most Major lenders have adopted some sort of credit decision engine and have a private label for it. If a file does not meet the decision engine's credit guidelines, the loan is then underwritten to more rigorous "manual" underwriting guidelines.

Simple Troubleshooting Strategies

A common error made by new loan officers is to rely on the initial approval from the engine as a "firm" approval. The approval really is still subject to underwriter review of the underlying documentation.

When an adverse decision is received from one of the engines, the common approach is to re-submit the request to another approval engine hoping for a more favorable outcome. For example a loan officer may submit to Desktop Underwriter and receive a decline. To attempt to solve the problem, the loan is submitted to Loan Prospector in order to reverse the decision. While this occasionally works it is detrimental to the company and to the ultimate destiny of the loan if there is a subsequent rejection from the 2nd engine. It is best to analyze the information input to the system, make any corrections, and resubmit before seeking alternative approvals.

Most often a loan is declined or referred by A.U. due to one negative characteristic in combination with maximum financing (the borrower is putting 5% or less down). Changing the loan term to 25 years reduces the statistical risk of the loan and may render it approve/accept upon resubmission.

Understanding FHLMC Loan Prospector Results

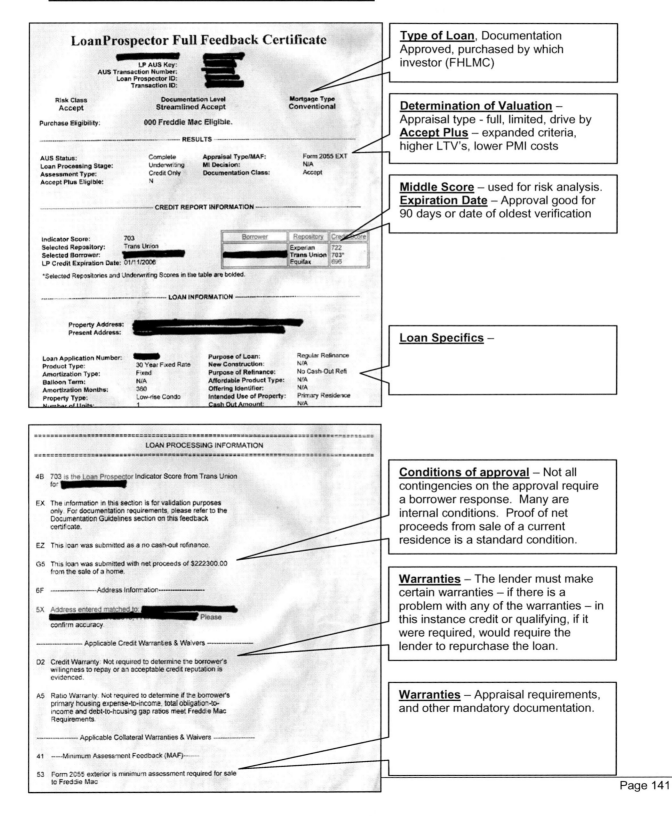

1S Verify property unit number and resubmit to determine eligibility for reduced MAF.

---------- Documentation Guidelines ----------

EW Lender is responsible for documenting any situation not addressed on this feedback certificate according to the LP User Guide, Seller Servicer Guide and/or Master Agreement.

EU ----------Employment Information----------

AS Obtain most recent YTD paystub documenting 1 full month earnings to verify current employment for ▬▬▬▬.

CV Obtain most recent tax year W-2(s) to verify current and previous employment for ▬▬▬▬.

4R If any borrower is self-employed, most recent 1 year complete individual federal tax returns are required to determine what effect the business income or loss has on other types of income, even if self-employed income is not being used to qualify the borrower.

CX For an employed borrower who receives commission income, income on a per-job basis or contract basis, or is employed by the property seller, real estate broker or a closely held family business, obtain most recent year signed individual complete federal income tax returns.

1K If tax returns are used to document source of income or to verify income, obtain signed IRS Form 8821/4506 covering most recent year from borrower.

EV ----------Asset Information----------

4U Revolving or open-end accounts: When the required monthly payment does not appear on the credit report, you may use five percent of the outstanding balance for qualifying or provide documentation from another source.

AX If the contingent liability is an assumed mortgage, obtain a copy of the documents transferring the property and the assumption agreement executed by the transferee in order to exclude the payment from the monthly debts. The payment on a secured debt or mortgage can also be excluded from the monthly debts if the obligation has been assigned to another by a court order; document the file with the court order and the transfer of title.

4X To exclude payment on a contingent liability from the monthly debts, obtain evidence that all payments have been made on time by someone other than the Borrower for the most recent 12 months, and document who makes the payments by obtaining copies of canceled checks or a statement from the lender.

AN ----------Documentation Alternatives----------

CC Standard forms of documentation (such as written VOE, VOD, income information obtained directly from IRS) may be used as addressed in the Seller/Servicer Guide, LP AUS Training and User Guide.

CW W-2(s) are not required if current employer confirms 1 year history and only base pay is used to qualify.

6E ----------Affordable Product Information----------

6B This loan meets Affordable Gold income limits based on property location for address entered. If you choose to deliver this loan as an Affordable Gold loan, it must meet all requirements of the Affordable Gold program selected.

JT This loan meets Home Possible income limits based on property location for address entered. If you choose to deliver this loan as a Home Possible loan, it must meet all program requirements of the Home Possible program selected.

Warranties – The lender is still responsible for addressing any issue not addressed by the underwriting engine.

Employment and Asset Documentation – LP may reduce the documentation requirement in the initial approval. This does not mean the standard documentation should not be requested – it should be in the event further questions are asked.

Additional Underwriting Conditions – Standard boiler plate guidelines to be satisfied by the processor.

Documentation Alternatives – In this case the underwriting results allow the borrower to substitute written employment verification, or limit the documentation required of the borrower. The processor should maintain the documentation already obtained in the file in the event of underwriting status changes

Fannie Mae Underwriting Findings

SUMMARY

Recommendation	Approve/Eligible		
Primary Borrower		Co-Borrower	
Lender Loan Number	███████	Casefile ID	███████
Underwriting Run Date	10/19/2005 04:02PM	Submitted By	███████

Mortgage Information

LTV/CLTV	80.00% / 95.00%	Note Rate	5.875%
Housing Expense Ratio	23.48%	Loan Type	Conventional
Total Expense Ratio	46.69%	Loan Term	360
Total Loan Amount	$189500.00	Amortization Type	Fixed Rate
Sales Price	$236900.00	Loan Purpose	Purchase
Appraised Value	$236900.00	Refi Purpose	

Property Information

Address ███████
Woodbridge, VA 22191

Property Type   Condominium

[Annotation: **Loan Approval Terms** – Identifies the assumptions the model made to approve the loan. If any of these circumstances change – ratios, LTV, Interest Rate – the loan must be re-approved.]

RISK/ELIGIBILITY

1. The risk profile of this case meets Fannie Mae's guidelines.
2. This case meets Fannie Mae's eligibility requirements.
3. This recommendation is valid up to a note rate of 6.875 percent.

FINDINGS

4. The following risk factors represent strengths in the borrower's loan application: Credit Profile

VERIFICATION MESSAGES/APPROVAL CONDITIONS

5. This loan is also subject to all other lender specified conditions and must comply with all applicable federal, state, and local laws and regulations.
6. Verify the terms of the subordinate financing for compliance with the Fannie Mae Selling Guide. (Selling Guide Part VII, Chptr. 1, Sect. 104.08)
7. Based on the credit report obtained through Desktop Underwriter, this loan must close on or before 02/15/2006. All verification documents must be dated within 120 days of the closing date. For new construction, documents must be dated within 180 days of the closing date.
8. There is a loan-level price adjustment associated with this product.
9. If there is a home equity line of credit secured against the subject property, the maximum allowable HCLTV is 100 percent. The HCLTV calculation is based on the maximum credit

[Annotation: **Contingencies of Approval** – The conditions identify documentation issues that must be satisfied prior to or at closing.]

Employment and Income

10. ███████ income must be supported by a paystub and a telephone confirmation of employment, or by a standard Verification of Employment (1005). The paystub must be dated no earlier than 30 days from the application date and it must include at least 30 days of year-to-date earnings. In lieu of obtaining the telephone confirmation, an additional paystub dated within 30 days of closing may be obtained.

[Annotation: **Income Verification** - may be waived or limited from standard documentation.]

Assets

11. Assets totaling ███████ must be verified. From the liquid assets listed on the 1003, at a minimum verify those accounts that are needed to satisfy this amount.
12. If depository assets are needed to support the amount of funds required for closing and reserves, verify these assets with a verification of deposit or bank statements covering a one-month period. A satisfactory explanation and documentation should be provided for large deposits.
13. Based on the data provided, Desktop Underwriter has determined that the borrower has the assets to make the required minimum down payment from their own funds. However, verify that any additional credits to be applied at closing, such as premium pricing and down payment assistance, which have not been entered on the Details of Transaction, have been documented and reviewed and that the borrower still meets the minimum borrower funds down payment requirement.
14. Earnest money is listed as an other credit on the details of transaction. If the deposit is used to make any part of the borrower's down payment that must come from his or her own funds, the source of funds for the deposit must be verified. (Selling Guide Part X, Chptr. 6, Sect. 603.01)

Property and Appraisal Information

15. This property is located in either a condominium or PUD project. A limited review can be performed if the project is 100 percent complete and not ineligible as defined in Part XII, Section 102 of the Fannie Mae Selling Guide. If the property is a detached condo, a limited review according to Sections 102 and 104.02 is acceptable. Otherwise, a full review according to Part XII is required. If the property is a detached PUD, a project review is not required.
16. Desktop Underwriter could not verify the submitted subject property address for this transaction. Fannie Mae will accept delivery of this case with an appraisal based on an interior and exterior property inspection reported on Form 2055 for single-family properties, Form 1004 with Form 1004c for manufactured homes, or Form 2095 for cooperative properties. Alternatively, you can modify the subject address and resubmit to verify if the system can offer a more streamlined property fieldwork recommendation.

[Annotation: **Additional Underwriting** – Even though the loan is approved, additional underwriting is required. The computer can't see that the details behind the information reported, so guidelines must be adhered to and this is where subjectivity re-enters the decision process.]

Loan Approval Notification

This is the best part of the process. If it was a difficult case, it may proceed quite rapidly to closing. Understanding the mechanics of closing will allow you to "grease the runway" for a case that has been languishing in underwriting.

```
«lender_name»
«lender_address_1»
«lender_address_2»
«lender_phone»

September 2, 1999


«bor_first_name» «bor_last_name»
«cobor_first_name» «cobor_last_name»
«mailing_address»
«mailing_city», «mailing_state»  «mailing_zip»


                    Re:     «purpose_of_loan» of
                            «subject_address»

Dear «bor_first_name»:

We are pleased to advise you that your application for financing has been pre-approved for the following terms:

Loan Amount:          «loan_amount»
Interest Rate:        «note_rate»
Loan Type:            «loan_type»
Loan to Value:        «LTV_ratio»
Appraised Value:      «appraised_value»
Loan Term:            «term»
Lien Position:        «lien_position»
Occupancy Status:     «residency»

Prior to closing the following Closing Conditions must be met:

1.) Satisfactory evidence of Hazard Insurance and Paid Receipt
2.) Termite Inspection Report
3.) Title Binder and Survey

Prior to the release of the file to the closing department the following items must be received and accepted by the underwriter:

«condition_1»
«condition_2»
«condition_3»
«condition_4»
«condition_5»
«condition_6»
«condition_7»
«condition_8»
«condition_9»
«condition_10»

This is not a Lock-in Agreement. Your lock-in agreement takes precedence over the approval notification as to rate and terms. You will receive the firm commitment once all of the referenced conditions have been released by the underwriter. Please feel free to contact your loan officer or processor if you have any questions.

Sincerely,



«loan_rep»
Relationship Banker
```

But first the conditions of the underwriter's approval must be met. The best way to assure the borrower is notified of ALL the contingencies is to provide a written approval notification. The conditions of the approval are entered in the "Loan Tracking", "Conditions" screen in point and replace any contingencies which previously were there. From this screen, export the data to the Loan Approval Notification letter.

Chapter 9 –
The Closing and Requirements

There are two processes for closing preparation, depending on whether the loan is brokered or closed directly. The requirements are similar in terms of the underlying documentation, but time frames are different and the extent to which there is processor involvement in the closing is different.

Brokered Transactions vs. Funded Transactions

A brokered transaction usually indicates that the loan has been approved by an outside investor and will be closed by the investor's closing department. This means that the closer works for a different company and will have formal procedures in place for scheduling and required documentation. In this situation the processor acts as a closing coordinator - collecting and directing information between the closing agent and the investors closing department.

Responsible Party	Description
Settlement Agent	Schedules closing - advises borrower, investor's closing department and processor of anticipated closing date. Settlement agent is responsible for providing the closing department with: ❏ Title Binder ❏ Insured Closing Service Letter ❏ Survey - If required ❏ Wiring Instructions ❏ Tax Information
Processor	Final Conditions of Approval - If there are any remaining contingencies, the processor utilizes this as an opportunity to obtain these in conjunction with the closing requirements which the borrower or borrower's agent must provide ❏ Homeowner's Insurance Policy and Paid Receipt ❏ Termite Report - If Required ❏ Final Inspection ❏ Well & Septic Inspections
Loan Officer	Lock-In - If the loan is not locked-in (floating), or if the lock-in has expired, the loan officer is responsible for insuring this is met in a timely manner.

Processor	Review lock-in Agreement - against lock-in confirmation from investor. ❏ Is the rate correct ❏ Are the points correct ❏ Is the lock-in period sufficient to take the loan through closing and disbursement (if refinance)
Processor	Prepare "Fee/Cost" Reconciliation - Reconcile fees due from applicant against application deposit.
Processor/ Operations Manager	Prepare "Fee Sheet"
Processor	Prepare and Deliver Attorney "Pre-Closing Notification and Broker Demand Letter"

Preparing the "Fee Sheet"

The most important requirement in fee sheet preparation is to assure that the correct amounts of fees are collected at closing. Errors occur when

❏ the processor/loan officer wait until the last moment to lock-in a loan
❏ the processor doesn't compare the lock in agreement/lock-in confirmation and the fee sheet
❏ the settlement agent doesn't correctly collect all the fees
❏ the closing department doesn't correctly asses all broker charges.

To avoid these situations there are a number of checks to perform:

1. Correctly reconcile the customer fees
2. Have the fee sheet double checked
3. Send the Broker Demand Letter to the closing agent and the investor

Preparing the Broker Demand Letter

The broker demand is one last piece of recourse a broker can have against the closing agent or closing department when fees are not correctly attributed. The Data in this letter comes from Loan Origination System – usually in the fees section. This page is where all of the closing coordinating information can be drawn - Attorney, closing department, lender name and, most importantly, fees.

Since the investors and wholesalers control the funding for mortgage brokers transactions, the collecting of the mortgage broker fee is one of the most delicate areas of the process. Surprisingly, this task is often delegated to processors, even though a simple mistake can cost thousands of dollars. If the processor is responsible for preparing the fee request, broker demand or other fee related process, the financial service agreement, mortgage broker contract or business agreement must be followed precisely. The fee agreement is very explicit about what the broker can charge.

The fees are entered in the Loan Submission/Fee Summary page in the LOS. This is the Section that describes fees and charges, and pre-rates the charges between lender borrower and broker.

Determining the Net Charges on the Broker Demand Screen

There are 3 versions of the "Loan Related Fees" Screen - Lender (or the investor or wholesaler who is funding the loan) - Broker (which will be blank) - and Borrower.

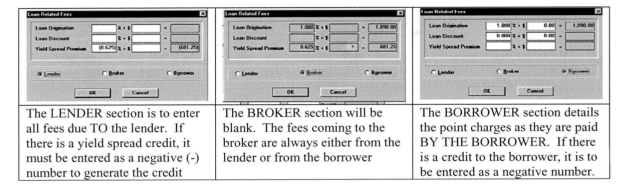

The LENDER section is to enter all fees due TO the lender. If there is a yield spread credit, it must be entered as a negative (-) number to generate the credit	The BROKER section will be blank. The fees coming to the broker are always either from the lender or from the borrower	The BORROWER section details the point charges as they are paid BY THE BORROWER. If there is a credit to the borrower, it is to be entered as a negative number.

From this data you can export to a template and create a broker demand letter. Alternately, the processor can print the fee screen from the loan origination system and forward a copy of the broker agreement, to the settlement agent with a cover letter.

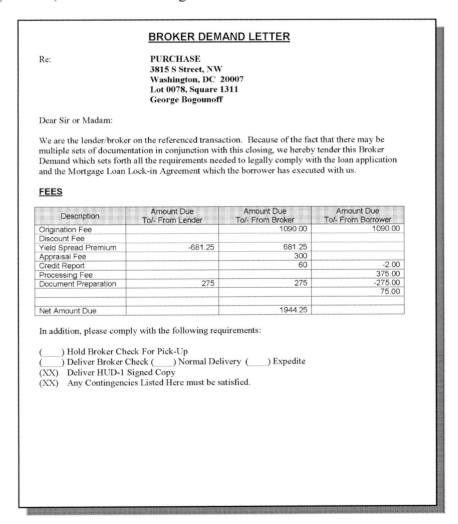

The Fee/Cost Reconciliation

The process of completing this form assures that the processor/closer has documented fees received against the costs of processing. All fees that are incurred in conjunction with the loan should be documented on this form under other fees. Most difficult to track are Overnight Shipping charges and Long Distance Phone Records because, most often, these are charges which can't be reconciled with concise dollar amounts. This is the reason that most lenders charge a "document preparation" or "lender inspection" or "processing fee" - to account somehow in the process for these charges. All documented expenses should be recorded on the fee cost reconciliation.

Closed Loan Checklist

Borrower:
Loan Closed:
Investor:
Funds Received:
Application Date:
Good Faith Date:
T-I-L Date:
Mortgage Loan Agreement Date:

Fee Cost Reconciliation

Application Fees Received: (Attach Check)	+$
Appraisal Fee (Attach Bill)	-$
Credit Report Fee (Attach Bill)	-$
Other Fees Describe:	-$
Other Fees Describe:	-$
Amount to Collect (-) Refund (+)	

Record Retention Checklist

- ✓ Original Mortgage Loan Lock-in Agreement.
- ✓ Settlement Statement
- ✓ Copies of Checks Received from Borrower
- ✓ Copies of All Invoices in Case for Appraisal Credit Report, Review Appraisal, Final Inspections, Condominium Documents, Courier Receipts, Federal Express Bills, Telephone Logs for Long Distance, etc.
- ✓ Copies of Funding Check(s)
- ✓ Good Faith Estimate of Closing Costs.

In addition to the fee reconciliation, this form is used to preliminarily audit the file for items that the regulatory authorities require to audit the file. Attach the checklist items for record retention purposes.

Settlement Agent – Document Requirements

A settlement agent is also known as a closing attorney, title company or escrow company. The settlement agent is responsible for scheduling settlement and provides 1.) Title Binder 2.) Survey and 3.) Insured Closing Protection Letter.

Title Binder

A title "binder" is a commitment to issue title insurance. The binder states that a policy will be issued in accordance with coverage outlined in the binder if all the requirements are met. As lenders we only care about the Lender's Title Insurance. Buyers are offered the opportunity to purchase OPTIONAL Owner's Title Insurance to protect the equity in the home being financing. This policy is in addition to the **mandatory** lender's policy.

If the transaction is a refinance and there is a Title Insurance Policy in force, the settlement agent may be able to reissue the policy. In addition, with the old Title Policy, a full title search may not be necessary - a "present owner bring down" simply researches the title from the date of the last title search.

Survey

A house location survey shows the location of the property improvements relative to the lot lines. If a borrower is refinancing it may not be necessary to obtain a new survey if 1.) The title is insurable without a new survey, and 2.) No changes have been made to the exterior of a house (you must sign an affidavit stating this). If these requirements can't be met an existing survey may be recertified as a cost savings. Surveys are not required for condominiums.

Insured Closing Protection Letter

An insured closing protect must normally be provided with each new closing agent. Some closing departments require a new letter each time. The letter must be from the same company that issues the title insurance binder/policy.

Required Closing Conditions

Homeowner's Insurance Policy

The basic standards for Homeowner's (Hazard/Fire Insurance) are that the company should be Bests Rated A- or better and meet the following:

- Dwelling Coverage in the amount of the Loan
- Dated within the same month, but prior to the date of settlement
- Paid receipt for the first year's premium
- Correct property address
- Names shown as they are shown on your loan application or property title
- Mortgagee/Loss Payee Clause
- Investment Properties must carry rent loss coverage equal to 6 months rent.

Condominiums

The Management Company provides a certificate of insurance showing owner's names, the condominium unit number and Loss/Payee (lender) clause as shown above. The settlement agent, real estate agent or borrower may provide this. The processor may obtain this as part of the loan file set up during condo questionnaire completion.

Planned Unit Developments

If there is a Homeowner's Association fee for maintenance of Common Elements, such as roads, recreational facilities or other amenities the property is in a Planned Unit Development (PUD). If the association maintains the common elements, a fidelity bond or employee dishonesty policy may be required. In addition, liability coverage in the amount of $1,000,000 may be required. The processor normally obtains this in conjunction with the loan file set-up during appraisal ordering.

Termite Report

A termite report, showing no damage or infestation, is required. Refinances MAY be exempt from this requirement. The original form dated within 30-60 days of settlement must be provided. Condominiums MAY be exempt from this requirement, if the association shows a line item in the budget for pest control, or the property is located above the 4th floor. New Construction requires a soil treatment certificate.

Well/Septic Certification

If the property is serviced by a well and/or septic system, the local health department must provide a certification as to the safety of water. Take caution if the property is newly construction and a Termite Soil Treatment is performed. Water safety must not be affected. A certification from the Health Department to this effect is required. Refinances MAY be exempt from this.

Flood Certification

The processor obtains a Flood Zone Determination. Ideally, the property is an area of minimal flooding. If the property is located in a Flood Plain, the processor advises the borrower that Flood Insurance is required. In some cases, a risk assessment can be performed to define if the flood certificate is accurate.

New Construction

A Residential Use Permit (RUP), Certificate of Occupancy or Completion is required from the code compliance authority in the jurisdiction is required. When the property is complete must be notified so that we order the final inspection be the appraiser.

Vesting of Title – Application vs. Closing

When you buy a house, you get a Title to the property. This may be referred to as a Deed of Bargain and Sale, Fee Simple Deed, or a Title. This is the original loan document that is recorded at the local land records in the jurisdiction where the property is located. You notice that on the first page of the application there is a section that requests "Manner in which title will be held". There are 4 common forms of ownership.

> **Joint Tenants with Right of Survivorship** means that when one owner dies, the survivors automatically become the owner of the property.
> **Tenants by Entirety** is a form of ownership reserved for married couples. The property reverts to the survivor but shields the owner from claims of individual creditors
> **Tenants in Common** allows the owners to assign percentage of ownership to each owner. When one owner dies, it creates an estate, which will be distributed under the terms of the owner's will
> **Sole & Separate** means there is no other titleholder

In addition, the type of Deed that the owner receives may affect the owner's interest. A General Warranty Deed conveys the property with the seller's guarantee that the title is good. A Special Warranty Deed is basically a statement from the seller of the property that as far as he knows, the title is good. A "Quit-Claim" Deed sets forth some probability of a problem with the title. For instance, in Massachusetts much of the eastern part of the state is subject to Indian tribe land claims. If ever enforced, there is a possibility you loose your title. Thus, by accepting a "Quit-Claim", you are releasing a seller of any liability in the event of forfeiture.

When encountering property rights, it is important to know what kind of community property laws your region has. Common Law States give spouses rights of Dower & Curtsey that may have to be addressed at closing.

Disclosures at Closing - HUD-1 Settlement Statement

The borrower has a right to obtain the HUD-1 Settlement Statement 24 hours in advance of closing. It is the final accounting for all the fees and charges in conjunction with the transaction.

Lender Sends Loan Instructions to Settlement Agent

The lender will not normally go to settlement, but sends closing instructions to the settlement agent who will prepare a settlement statement. This is an exact summary of the costs of the transaction. Once prepared, the settlement statement will show exactly what you will be required to pay at closing. Borrowers should bring a certified check for the remainder of the down payment (if any) and closing costs. Loan officers are encouraged to read all of their company's closing documents as well as attend a number of settlements to become familiar with the mechanics of real estate transactions. Some people recommend that loan officers attend settlement as a customer service and sales opportunity. Loan Officers should not attend a settlement that is anticipated to be difficult.

It is at the closing that questions may be raised about the disparity of fees disclosed on the Good Faith Estimate and the total charges on the settlement statement. Of course no one is concerned when the fees are lower. When they are higher, however, there is usually a panicked call to the loan officer to explain. Obviously the good faith estimate is just that - an estimate.

> Pro-rated Condo Fees
> New Construction Assessments/Partial Levy
> Termite Treatment
> Reimbursement of Seller Paid Real Estate Taxes
> More Days of Per Diem Interest
> Optional Owner's Title Insurance Purchased
> Refinance - Most recent payment not accounted for in Payoff

Look at all the numbers. Isolating the lender's charges from the overall closing costs can often defuse a situation where a borrower is attributing the higher number to variances in the closing costs.

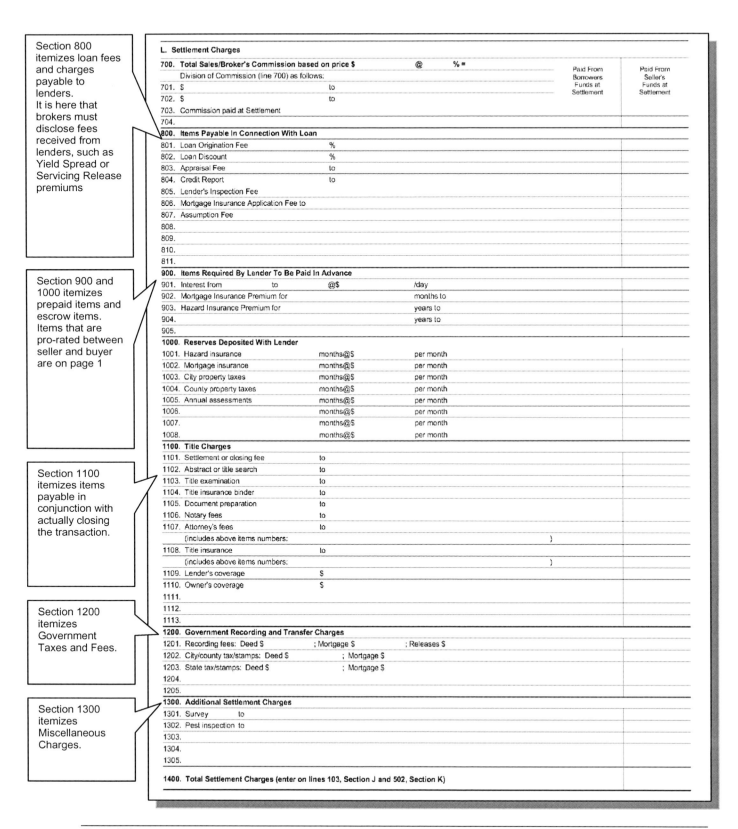

> The first page of the HUD-1 is a summary of the transaction. On a refinance, there is no seller, so that side is often omitted.

> The borrower Can be confused about the "costs" of a transaction because the cash requirement is affected by items the borrower has to "pay back" to the seller.

A. Settlement Statement

U.S. Department of Housing and Urban Development

OMB Approval No. 2502-0265

B. Type of Loan

1. ☐ FHA 2. ☐ FmHA 3. ☐ Conv. Unins.
4. ☐ VA   5. ☐ Conv. Ins.

6. File Number:
7. Loan Number:
8. Mortgage Insurance Case Number:

C. Note: This form is furnished to give you a statement of actual settlement costs. Amounts paid to and by the settlement agent are shown. Items marked "(p.o.c.)" were paid outside the closing; they are shown here for informational purposes and are not included in the totals.

D. Name & Address of Borrower:
E. Name & Address of Seller:
F. Name & Address of Lender:

G. Property Location:
H. Settlement Agent:
Place of Settlement:
I. Settlement Date:

J. Summary of Borrower's Transaction		K. Summary of Seller's Transaction	
100. Gross Amount Due From Borrower		400. Gross Amount Due To Seller	
101. Contract sales price		401. Contract sales price	
102. Personal property		402. Personal property	
103. Settlement charges to borrower (line 1400)		403.	
104.		404.	
105.		405.	
Adjustments for items paid by seller in advance		Adjustments for items paid by seller in advance	
106. City/town taxes to		406. City/town taxes to	
107. County taxes to		407. County taxes to	
108. Assessments to		408. Assessments to	
109.		409.	
110.		410.	
111.		411.	
112.		412.	
120. Gross Amount Due From Borrower		420. Gross Amount Due To Seller	
200. Amounts Paid By Or In Behalf Of Borrower		500. Reductions In Amount Due To Seller	
201. Deposit or earnest money		501. Excess deposit (see instructions)	
202. Principal amount of new loan(s)		502. Settlement charges to seller (line 1400)	
203. Existing loan(s) taken subject to		503. Existing loan(s) taken subject to	
204.		504. Payoff of first mortgage loan	
205.		505. Payoff of second mortgage loan	
206.		506.	
207.		507.	
208.		508.	
209.		509.	
Adjustments for items unpaid by seller		Adjustments for items unpaid by seller	
210. City/town taxes to		510. City/town taxes to	
211. County taxes to		511. County taxes to	
212. Assessments to		512. Assessments to	
213.		513.	
214.		514.	
215.		515.	
216.		516.	
217.		517.	
218.		518.	
219.		519.	
220. Total Paid By/For Borrower		520. Total Reduction Amount Due Seller	
300. Cash At Settlement From/To Borrower		600. Cash At Settlement To/From Seller	
301. Gross Amount due from borrower (line 120)		601. Gross amount due to seller (line 420)	
302. Less amounts paid by/for borrower (line 220)	( )	602. Less reductions in amt. due seller (line 520)	( )
303. Cash ☐ From ☐ To Borrower		603. Cash ☐ To ☐ From Seller	

Wet and Dry Settlements

The "Wet Settlement" Act requires that actual cash or "good funds" be at the closing table. This is designed to assure that all the accounting be based on actual receipts and disbursements so that the settlement agent may accurately disburse all funds at the closing. The settlement agent acts as a conduit for all of the funds accounted for at the transaction. So the settlement statement is a bucket where all the money goes and comes out of. When all the parties meet at the closing table, this is referred to as a round table closing. In certain parts of the country, closings are conducted in escrow. This means the same thing, basically, except that not all parties are at the table at the same time - and the buyer doesn't usually know what the sellers summary is, and vice versa.

The Right of Rescission - Refinances

Although this information is not an early disclosure requirement, it affects any extension of additional credit on a borrower's primary residence. This is part of the Truth-in-Lending Regulation and it provides a 3 full day "right to cancel" the transaction. Because of this on refinance and home equity loans documents are signed but funds do not disburse until after the period expires.

Chapter 10 – Time Management Strategies for Processors

Pipeline Management - Loan Tracking Reports

Managing the processing caseload is the responsibility of the operations manager and the individual processor. The objective of the processor is to obtain loan approval and prepare files for closing. To achieve this objective with limited resources there are 4 benchmarks that need to be addressed, and everything is prioritized from the scheduled closing date. These are reviewed in the context of a closing month. The objective of this management system is to assure that cases are approved a minimum of one week prior to closing.

Processing Status Benchmarks

- **To Go/Ready** - This indicates a case which is scheduled to close within a given month and needs to be worked up and reviewed prior to submission. This is generally an unknown status. These are the most dangerous cases because there could be substantial omissions which the processor and loan officer are not aware of. These cases have no status, and are simply scheduled to close.
- **Worked/Pending** - This status indicates that the processor has prepared the file for submission and that the case is either ready for submission or is pending information prior to submission.
- **Submitted** - The loan has been submitted to underwriting or the investor and is waiting for approval. The goal is to have all cases submitted 2 full weeks prior to closing.
- **Approved** - This indicates that the file is underwriting approved. There may be conditions of the approval, but all parties have been notified and are working towards satisfaction. Loans which are "conditionally approved" subject to substantial underwriting review should not be placed in Approved status, since they will have to be fully reviewed by underwriting. These loans should remain in submitted status

Processing Reports

New Loan Set Up – Pipeline/Loan Source/Processor

This report is to make sure that new loans are being set up in proper time frame. The date opened and the date of Truth-in-Lending/Disclosure package (which coincides with the Welcome Package) should be no more than 3 days. This report should be generated daily and reviewed by the origination and processing manager. For the processor who works closely with referral sources, such as a builder or a busy real estate agent, to create a report broken out by source so that all of the sources loans can be status updated at one time.

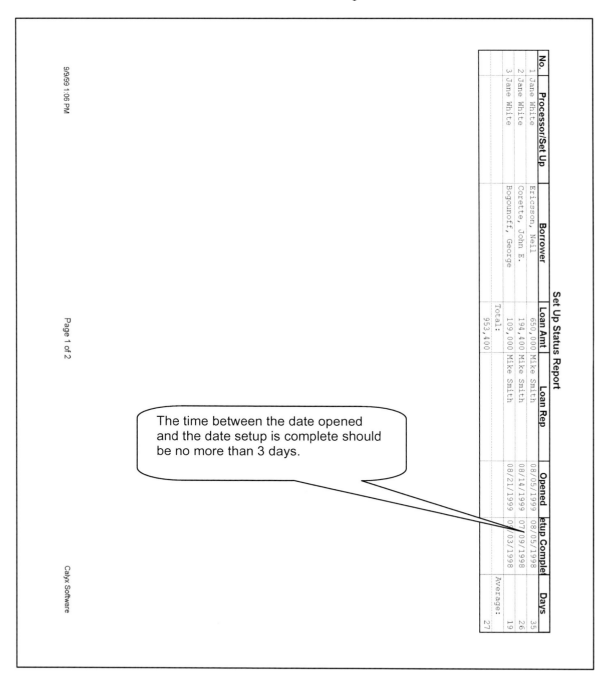

Loan Status Report – Pipeline/Loan Source/Processor

This report show all loans that the processor has in the pipeline, regardless of status. This allows an overall management of case status and the ability to see if all cases due for settlement are progressing as necessary.

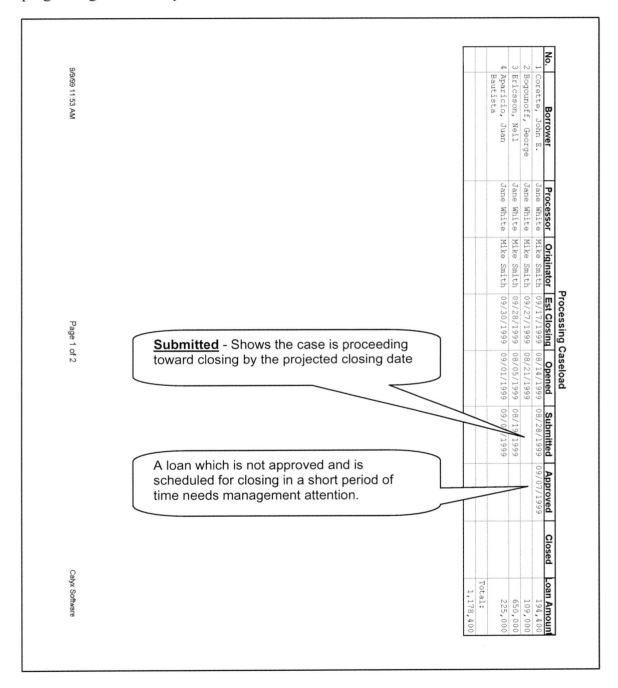

Conditions Outstanding

This report allows the loan officer and processor to communicate regarding conditions which need to be satisfied. This should be as a supplement, not a replacement of, the weekly status review process.

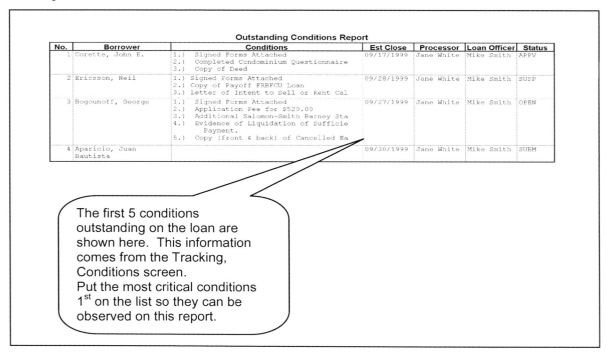

The first 5 conditions outstanding on the loan are shown here. This information comes from the Tracking, Conditions screen.
Put the most critical conditions 1st on the list so they can be observed on this report.

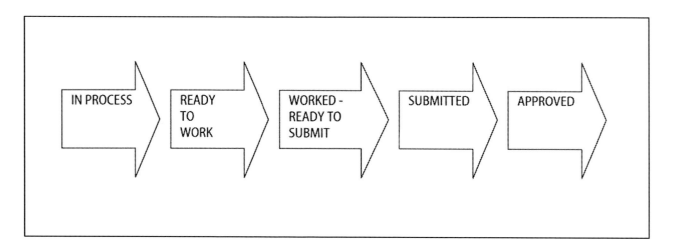

Processor Time Management Techniques

The loan process is a very detailed progression and assembly of paperwork. Sloppy or incomplete documentation is the single largest cause of problems in the process. To avoid issues with loan processing, every loan officer should have systems in place to manage a caseload.

These systems insure that the loan officer spends time generating business, not following up on individual loans. Systems also reduce interruptions for processing. Interruptions are a processor's largest time management challenge.

System 1 - Pipeline Review

Weekly pipeline review may seem redundant in an era of automated approvals and fast decisions. You can simply forward an e-mail that the loan is approved or the appraisal is in. What else is there to check? As this book shows, there are many things that can and do go wrong in the process.

As loan officers, we are responsible for the loan process. When a customer or referral source calls and asks what the loan status is, the loan officer will typically call or e-mail the processor. The processor has to stop what he or she was doing and investigate the status. This interruption can cost the processor 15 minutes of productive time. In addition, because the loan officer doesn't know what the status is, the customer or referral source isn't convinced of the loan officer's professionalism. It also creates a time management issue for the loan officer, because returning phone calls takes 15 minutes of productive time. In this case, one phone call costs 75 minutes of time for the loan officer and processor.

Loan Status Calls Waste Time	
Action	Minutes Spent
Customer Call to Loan Officer	15
Call to Processor	15
Investigation	15
Call back to Loan Officer	15
Call back to Customer	15
Total Time Per Call	75
vs Loan Status	
Minutes Per Loan	5
Status Meeting with Client	15
Total Time Per Loan	20

Loan Status Procedure

It is in the interest of the loan transaction to have all parties who are participating or responsible for the processing of a loan application to meet and agree an action plan to meet all requirements. While there is ample reason to schedule this loosely around a loan officer's schedule - since most often the loan officer is an outside sales person and the processing staff are inside support - the idea is to manage limited resources by planning. Weekly meetings between loan officer and processor are mandatory to review the status of outstanding items and to determine who is responsible for follow up.

Status Process - Conducting Pipeline Review

We "prove" excellent customer service by providing the results of conducting a weekly pipeline review. The written reports resulting from the review show the customer that the loan officer is in control of the pipeline. Referral sources receiving weekly reports do not badger support staff for status on their transactions. Delivering weekly reports is also an excellent opportunity for the loan officer to generate additional business. Finally, a weekly status review is a time management tool for the loan officer and processor alike. A loan officer who conducts status weekly, instead of every time a customer asks what the status is, controls the number of interrupting telephone calls received by himself and his processor. Pipeline review is an amazing time management tool for production and production support personnel.

Management has even more critical reasons to insist on loan officers performing a weekly review. By insisting on this as part of the corporate culture, the company is not directly responsible for the smooth outcome of a transaction – it is the loan officer's responsibility. In addition, the company can assure that the employee is reviewing each case appropriately by requiring a copy of the weekly pipeline review. When a problem arises on a case, the company's first question should be "has the loan officer properly managed this case?" by reviewing status logs.

The temptation is to allow customers to access loan status via the internet. This is particularly true when there has been a significant technology investment on the part of the company. The availability of status reports through an internet portal does not preclude the need for the loan officer to conduct a weekly status review.

Conducting Weekly Status Reviews

Responsible Party	Description
Loan Officer	Schedules meeting with each processor handling cases. Time allotted for meeting should be 2-5 Minutes for each case in process
Processor	Assembles all of the loan officer's files regardless of status, in the order defined by the processor. The file should not be "prepared" for status. The loan officer should witness the actual condition of the loan file.
Loan Officer/Processor	Meet at the scheduled time to review all cases in process. Either processor or Loan Officer is charged with the responsibility of completing the status log.
Loan Officer	Assumes responsibility for external related documentation on case 1. Customer contacts for additional information 2. Referral source calls for items required on the transaction 3. Any qualification issues must be resolved by the loan officer 4. Loan Program or lock-in issues are the loan officer's responsibility.

Processor	Assumes responsibility for internal related documentation on the case
	1. Closing Department or closing agent related documentation
	2. Underwriting Department flow related issues, condition/stipulation satisfaction
	3. Vendor issues
	    a. Credit Report ordering/correction
	    b. Appraisal ordering/correction
	    c. PMI
	    d. Flood Certification
	    e. Insurance Policy

Processor	During the week, incoming loan documentation is fastened on top of the file. During the loan status meeting, loose (received) documents are reviewed together with the Loan Officer and marked on the status report to determine whether document is sufficient or if 2nd request is necessary.
Loan Officer/Processor	Take completed Status Log and make one copy for loan officer, processor and branch manager.

Responsible Party	Description
Loan Officer	Take copies of each individual loan's updated status report and deliver to all referral sources the following day.

Sample Status Log

Status Log
Loan Officer _____
Processor _____
Date Completed _____

Borrower	Processor to Handle	Loan Officer to Handle	Checklist
			Appraisal Ordered Credit O.K. Lock Expiration VOE O.K. VOA O.K. Complete Application Docs In?
Borrower	Processor to Handle	Loan Officer to Handle	Checklist
			Appraisal Ordered Credit O.K. Lock Expiration VOE O.K. VOA O.K. Complete Application Docs In?
Borrower	Processor to Handle	Loan Officer to Handle	Checklist
			Appraisal Ordered Credit O.K. Lock Expiration VOE O.K. VOA O.K. Complete Application Docs In?
Borrower	Processor to Handle	Loan Officer to Handle	Checklist
			Appraisal Ordered Credit O.K. Lock Expiration VOE O.K. VOA O.K. Complete Application Docs In?
Borrower	Processor to Handle	Loan Officer to Handle	Checklist
			Appraisal Ordered Credit O.K. Lock Expiration VOE O.K. VOA O.K.

Status Logs, Status Reports and Detailed Status Process is available in the "Loan Officer's Practical Guide to Marketing at www.lendertraining.com

Step/Responsible Party	Action
Loan Officer	Weekly - Prepare and review the loans in process report to assure programs are correct, lock-in dates, estimated closing dates are entered.
Processor	Weekly - Prepare and review the outstanding conditions report and the Processing Caseload Report. Assemble the cases for the respective loan officer.
Processor	Daily - File and Log in mail. Requested items, such as verifications, borrower documentation, closing items and other correspondence is to be logged into the computer as received, but left loose in the proper file.
Loan Officer and Processor	Weekly - Formal meeting to review cases. Go over 1. Received Underwriting & Closing conditions - review for problems 2. Identify potential problems with Conditions, such as qualification issues, sufficiency of funds, and identify whether conditions are internal (operations staff/appraisal/credit report) or external (additional information or borrower clarification) to determine if processor or loan officer is more suited to address issue and whether it is urgent. If there is no urgency, probably the information can be requested in writing by processor. If expediting is required, the loan officer is more suited. 3. Scheduled Closings: Is the case on target for settlement?
Loan Officer and Processor	During meeting prepare written list of items to follow up on, and who is responsible. Bring list to subsequent status meetings to evaluate

Step/Responsible Party	Action
	progress and whether obligations are being fulfilled by both parties.
Loan Officer	Distribute written Status Reports to all parties, referral sources, closing agents, borrower.

General Division of Duties – Loan Status

Loan Officer	Processor
Rate/Lock-in Issues Customer or Client Issues Qualification Issues Program Issues Cover Letters Status Updates	Internal Issues ❑ Underwriting ❑ Processing Priorities ❑ Closing Appraisal/Credit Report/Vendors Written Customer Communication ❑ Additional Information Requests ❑ Approval Notification ❑ Closing Scheduling

The loan officer and processor should reserve a block of time -typically 5 minutes for each case in process - to meet and review all cases. In this meeting there should be a pipeline report for the loan officer and a "conditions outstanding" report for the processor.

This process is merely an outline. Individuals working together may devise their own system for processing status as long as they result in a complete weekly review of entire pipeline and a written status report to all interested parties.

Instead of reacting to customer requests, move pro-actively to deliver loan status reports to interested parties. This is a sales opportunity for the loan officer. The pipeline review meeting saves the processor's time by avoiding interruptions. The loan officer saves time by staying out of the return phone call loop.

System 2 - The Complete Application System

Despite the advances in automation, missing documentation is the biggest problem the mortgage business faces. The problem begins when a loan officer accepts an application that is missing information. This puts the responsibility of obtaining the documentation on the loan officer, instead of the borrower. The loan officer, who is now in a defensive position, begins the process of mostly undocumented follow-up.

Even though a borrower may be aware of additional documentation requirements, once the application is submitted, there is pushback for providing more. The borrower says, "I thought I sent you that." Then, when the loan officer receives the missing documentation, it raises other questions - such as a pay stub that shows variable income, a bank statement with unexplained deposits or other problems. When this happens there is a question as to whether the loan can be granted. A negative feedback loop begins as the referral source may become involved, and documentation requests are followed by more documentation requests. The customer becomes frustrated or angry. This situation is caused by the incomplete application

The solution is obvious – don't accept incomplete applications. Loan Officers must have a complete application system.

A Pre-Application Kit, or other open ended information collection device, such as the one on the following page, can meet this need. When utilizing this system, the loan officer can arrest the application process until he or she is satisfied that there is enough documentation to proceed. With this in hand, the loan officer can turn in a complete application and not have to revisit the loan until it closes. This frees the loan officer to originate loans and make more money, not chase documentation.

System 3 – Time Blocking

It's hard to start each day with the fresh challenge of deciding what to do. Without a schedule you allow de-motivating thoughts to prevail in your mind and control your plans. Scheduled activities are the easiest target for cancellations when you get busy. But it is easy to lose sight of the forest for the trees and begin reacting instead of managing your business.

What Should My Week Look Like?

	Monday	Tuesday	Wednesday	Thursday	Friday
a.m.	**8:30 – 10:30 – Quiet Time –** Review mail, work up income solutions, follow up on status items, and submit cases. **10:30 – 12:30** Return Phone Calls – Follow up on Status/Pipeline review items	**8:30 – 10:30 – Quiet Time –** Review mail, work up income solutions, follow up on status items, and submit cases. **10:30 – 12:30** Return Phone Calls – Follow up on Status/Pipeline review items	**8:30 – 10:30 – Quiet Time –** Review mail, work up income solutions, follow up on status items, and submit cases. **10:30 – 12:30** Return Phone Calls – Follow up on Status/Pipeline review items	**9:30 – Office** Meeting **11:00 – Review** Loan Status with Loan Officers	**8:30 – 10:30 – Quiet Time –** Review mail, work up income solutions, follow up on status items, and submit cases. **10:30 – 12:30** Return Phone Calls – Follow up on Status/Pipeline review items
p.m.	**Routine Maintenance –** Closing Calls to settlement agents, appraisers, credit bureaus. Copying Copy Packages Out	**Routine Maintenance –** Closing Calls to settlement agents, appraisers, credit bureaus. Copying Copy Packages Out	**Routine Maintenance –** Closing Calls to settlement agents, appraisers, credit bureaus. Copying Copy Packages Out	**1:00** – meet or call underwriters with outstanding conditions – review closings pending with closer/funder	**Routine Maintenance –** Closing Calls to settlement agents, appraisers, credit bureaus. Copying Copy Packages Out

System 4 – Forms Management

There are many, many forms utilized in the mortgage business. Often, processors spend a significant amount of time in search of the correct form. Having all the correct forms at your desk or on your computer can save substantial time.

System 5 – Do Redundant Tasks Once a Day

Instead of getting up and opening the mail every time a document is delivered to your desk, have an "in-box". Once a day, file those documents into the appropriate loan file. Remember not to fasten them in until the loan has been reviewed by the loan officer during loan status.

Don't get up to copy every time there is a document that needs to be copied. Set a stack of documents aside that require copying – such as loan file submissions – and do them all at once.

Software Introduction

All mortgage companies utilize some form of loan processing software, also known as a Loan Origination System or Loan Origination Software (LOS). The mortgage industry is a form filling intensive business and the best way of filling forms is to capture the data once and use that same data to prepare the forms over and over. For the processor, understand that there is always an initial investment in time - setting it up and learning to use it. Once you have made that investment, there is no other tool that will save you more time than a functional literacy of the LOS. **Make that time investment.**

All LOSs work the same way – data is captured into "fields". Those fields are called to be used in blanks in forms or for calculations. If you put bad information into the system, it can create problems later in the process. This is the old adage "garbage in - garbage out".

Using Data In the System

The process of using Data already compiled in the processing system is referred to as "Data Export". Once exported, the information from any borrower file can be utilized in any other application. This makes it a perfect way to create custom forms, letters, labels and reports.

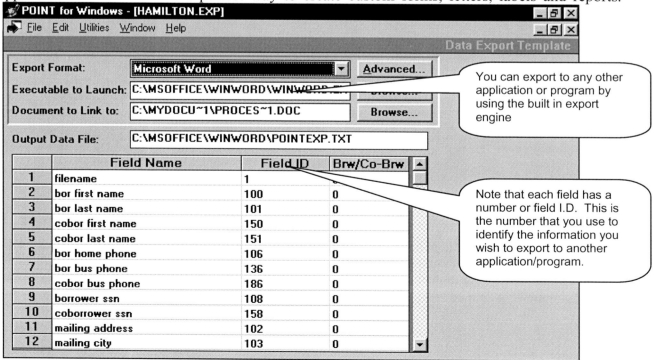

Depending on the software, all you have to know is what field number is assigned to the data you want to export. Some programs, like Point, Encompass and Byte, display the field numbers as you are browsing through the programs.

Building an Export "Template"

There are thousands of fields in the LOS processing program. Most export functions would never utilize all of these - so we need to tell the program which fields we will use. The fields you will use will be the borrower's contact information, the loan data, the property information and the information regarding conditions and service providers.

Using the Exported Data

The data that has been exported is most commonly exported to Word documents. There the data is "merged" into form letters which have been set up to recognize that certain fields go in certain places. It is wise to keep a separate file of these documents on your PC so that they can be called upon one at a time when needed. Also, once the document has been opened once, Word "remembers" that it used a Point export file, making future exports nearly automatic.

Suppose there is a letter you type over and over again - a welcome letter to a borrower. Wouldn't it be easier if you could simply capture the information in the loan processing program and give it to your word processing program so that all you had to do was print out the letter? This is what the export does. We focus on the use of this feature because from this point forward we expect that the documents you generate to communicate with borrowers, underwriters, investors, and others will come from the data in the processing program. You should insist on this. This gives you additional quality control checks - others see the data that is being output and can comment.

The number of forms you can generate is limited only by your imagination and the amount of time you are willing to invest in customization. At a minimum you should use these

- Appraisal Request
- Welcome Letter
- Individual Loan Status Letter
- Approval Letter
- Condominium Questionnaire
- Conditions Request
- Borrower's Authorization and Certification
- Closing Requirement Checklist
- Questions and Answers to Truth-in-Lending
- Lock In Agreement
- Certificate of Insurance for Condominiums
- Investor Assignment Letter

Status Reports

While it is the loan officer's responsibility to deliver and communicate status reports to the customers, it is the processor's responsibility to insure the integrity of the data in the system - whether computer based or a hard copy checklist. Learn to utilize the exhibit log in your LOS. As each piece of documentation comes in, the LOS should be immediately updated so that information can be delivered at the press of a button.

Sample LOS Provided Status/Tracking Report

```
                    L O A N    T R A C K I N G    R E P O R T  -  R E A L T O R
                    ================================================================
  Realtor     -




  File No     - APARICIO                              Date/Time       - 09/02/1999 12:33PM
  Borrower    - Juan Bautista Aparicio                Est Closing     - 09/30/1999
                202-362-3707 (H)                      Days in process - 1
                Rosa Perez de Aparicio
  Property    - 4620 Tilden Street, NW
                Washington, DC 20016
  Loan Agent  -
  Processor   - Jane White
  ------------------------------------------------------------------------------------
  Basic Documents:
                        Ordered    Received   Comments                  Days out  Days
  ------------------------------------------------------------------------------------
  Verification of Employment:
    B/C Employer                              Ordered   Re-order   Received Days out Days i
  ------------------------------------------------------------------------------------
  Verification of Deposit:
    Depository                                Ordered   Re-order   Received Days out Days i
  ------------------------------------------------------------------------------------
  Verification of Mortgage:
    Creditor / Landlord                       Ordered   Re-order   Received Days out Days i
  ------------------------------------------------------------------------------------
  Verification of Loan:
    Lender                                    Ordered   Re-order   Received Days out Days i
  ------------------------------------------------------------------------------------
  Miscellaneous:
    Item                                      Ordered   Re-order   Received Days out Days i
```

Sample Merge Letter - Additional Information Request to the Borrower

When a borrower provides additional information, it is important to respond that it has been received and whether it is sufficient. This is so the borrower knows that he or she has complied with all requirements.

Use the Loan Tracking, Conditions fields to update the borrower in this respect. Use the mail merge to create a request for additional information.

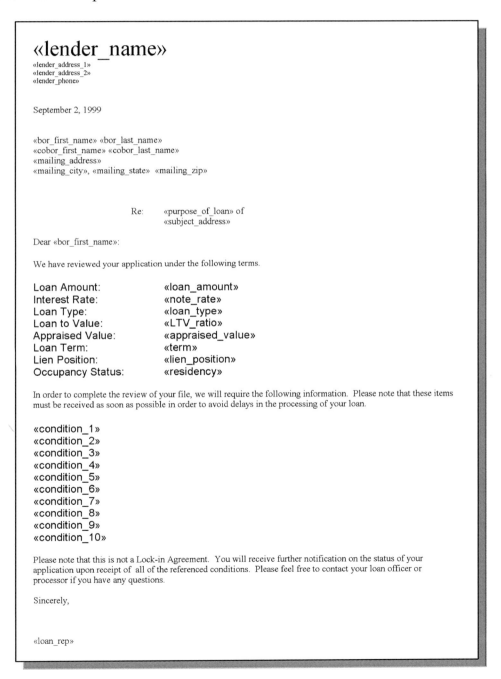

In Conclusion

The mortgage industry is, at times, turbulent. In your career as a processor you'll find that you are often challenged and placed under a great deal of stress by the conditions outside of your control. We hope that this book has given new tools to alleviate some of the stress by taking back some control over the process. The more you make the position your own, and add your creativity and analytical skills to the process, the more you will become an invaluable part of a team that helps to fill the American dream of homeownership day after day.